MIRACLES

ARE

REAL

C. M. STRICKER

Miracles are Real by C.M. Stricker

ISBN 978-1-955136-62-4 (Paperback)
ISBN 978-1-955136-63-1 (Hardback)

This book is written to provide information and motivation to readers. Its purpose is not to render any type of psychological, legal, or professional advice of any kind. The content is the sole opinion and expression of the author, and not necessarily that of the publisher.

Printed in the United States of America.

New Leaf Media, LLC
175 S. 3rd Street, Suite 200
Columbus, OH 43215
www.thenewleafmedia.com

TABLE OF CONTENTS

ACKNOWLEDGEMENT

To my friend, Rebecca, I appreciated your support and positive feedback with this project. You challenged me to be more honest about my life story and to do my best in this endeavor, so thank you. To Sherry, you have been a great encouragement to me throughout this lengthy writing endeavor as well. Thank you! Thank you, friend. I also wish to thank my friend, Debbie, for her continued prayer support each time I called her about this project. Thank you so much for believing in me and in this book!

DEDICATION

To my sons and daughters, you are my richness and my legacy. You've inspired me to be a better mother and person and you've brought so much joy and laughter into my life. Thank you, Robert, Jonathan, David, Sharon, Diane (Anna) Marie, Kristina Grace, and Catherine Denise. I am very proud of you all. May you all discover your true purpose and God-given destiny. My heart's desire is that you also achieve your dreams and experience a life well-lived.

CHAPTER ONE

Darkness has fallen around this sleepy, logging community situated in the Mays Harbor area. I had been asleep in my bed for some hours on that windy, cold evening. Suddenly, a dark, sinister nightmare imposed itself rudely upon my slumber. I tried to cry out for help, but no words came out of my mouth. What was the reason for my panic? In this nightmare, I was being chased by a man trying to grab me. I saw myself running away and it felt as if I was barely able to escape his grasp. Why couldn't I speak or cry out in this awful situation? What had managed to silence my plea for help? I needed someone to rescue me from this frightening dream which seemed so real. After laying my head back down on my pillow, I remembered hearing a tune on the radio which went like this, "*Only the good die young-Billy Joel.*" Next, I heard my own voice whispered this lyric softly as I lay there wondering if this could mean that I might die young. This thought shook me to the core of my being, and I wanted to stay awake rather than have another nightmare. I rubbed my sleepy eyes and buried my head in the goose feathered pillow to avoid any more frightening thoughts about this scary dream.

As I became more awake and alert, I sensed an eerie silence surrounding me. I sat up in the bed shivering from the cold night air. I felt apprehensive as I glanced around the room and towards the closet doors. A glimmer of moonlight shone through the torn, faded window shade which helped my eyes to adjust gradually to the darkness. As I scanned my bedroom with its high vaulted ceilings and the four-foot-high window, it took a moment for me to realize that there was no villain standing over me in this gloomy dark room, only shadows on the wall. What did this reoccurring dream mean? Would I ever feel safe at night in my own home? How could I get some relief from this strange dream which had such a hold on me as a youngster? I only knew one thing: I didn't want to keep having these nightmares. I felt very apprehensive and alone in the dark. As I'd snuggled beneath my thick blanket one more time that night, I wished I could go snuggle in my mother's bed. However, I didn't want to wake her and so I lay there feeling bewildered by this oppressive dream.

The next morning, I awoke with a feeling of sadness. I didn't want to climb out of my bed and step onto the freezing cold wood floor of my room, but I needed to get dressed for the day. I recalled again this sense of wanting to feel safe in my own home for some odd reason. As I grew into a young adult woman, I realized that I needed help to find an answer to this strange, unsettling feeling. Since our family didn't watch scary movies, I wondered where this nightmare came from. As a youngster, I remember thinking that there might be a monster hiding under my bed frame waiting to grab my leg at night. My natural inclination was to usually run into my room, leap through the air, and land with a bounce on my bed. Then I would wait quietly for a moment to see if I was safe. I eventually grew out of this silly notion. Thankfully, that nightmare seemed to fade with the passing years.

Later, when I was an adult, this same scary dream threatened to disturb my peaceful sleep one more time. I recall trying to cry out to stop this disturbing nightmare. After lying awake that night, I decided to solve the mystery behind this reoccurring dream. The fact that I couldn't cry out for help in the dream truly bothered me. Someone told me to look at the root issue behind this reoccurring dream. I started to wonder if this dream was tied into a bad experience in my youth. That day I didn't have an answer, but I began to pray for some insight about this problem.

Another troubling aspect from my childhood was the fact that I couldn't remember much about my life from six to eight years of age. This lack of memories really bothered me. As a young woman I was plagued with this question, why couldn't I recall that portion of my childhood? Having such a gap of missing memories just didn't seem normal to me. My journey to find the answers to this question had become a quest to uncover the missing puzzle pieces of my youth. I was determined to learn the truth about my family history. As a young woman, I decided to go to the public library in order to research this problem. There I stumbled onto a book that included women's stories about their childhood abuse. After reading the first three chapters of this book, I learned about an issue which happens when a child has suffered from abuse or trauma. I began to understand how a traumatic incident can cause a problem for a child and which therapists call 'repressed' memories. In one of the chapters, it described how these children of abuse tend to display certain symptoms. As I sat in that library room reading, I realized that I fit into a few of the descriptions. If I was suffering from repressed memories, then how could I recover from this psychological disorder I wondered? These next few chapters contain a few highlights in my journey to uncover the reason for the missing gap in my childhood memories.

I'd come into this world during the decade following World War II. America was settling down in the hopes of returning to a sense of peace and normalcy again. Many of the European countries had started the rebuilding process. In the Middle East, a small country called Israel had begun its endeavor to become a recognized nation. United Nations had created the World Health Organization.

Back before I was born in the United States, my mother (as a three-year-old) had been adopted by a wealthy family living in Canada in the early 1920s. She was adored by her new parents who could not have their own children. By the time my mother had reached the age of six, her adopted mother to everyone's surprise became pregnant with her own child and then two years later gave birth to a second child. Oddly enough, my mother at the age of nine was sent to live in the country with my Nana's relatives. She loved being on the farm where she spent some wonderful years with this family. She'd walk with her older cousins nearly two miles to attend a one-room schoolhouse and during the winter they walked through the snow and cold to attend classes. At the age of twelve, she was brought back to help with her demanding, active half-siblings. By the time my mother reached the age of fifteen, she had grown into a beautiful young woman. She was openly admired by the men in this large family and her beauty seemed to cause problems with the women folks.

During her teens, my mother was driven down to Washington State to live with some distant relatives. However, this next relocation did not improve her chances at having a happy family environment and sadly she had to move again. She found a job as a live-in nanny with a wealthy family in the next town. By the time she had turned seventeen, she had to leave this home as well. Later, after my mother graduated from high school, she met someone who was interested in her and they were soon married. I grew up in a type of family which was fast becoming a part of the growing middle class in America. My dad struggled for a few years finding a decent job. He lost a couple of jobs I was told which caused him to begin drinking alcohol more frequently. After he was given a citation for DUI, my father couldn't drive a car for a short time and so my mother decided to take care of other people's children in order to supplement their meager income. Eventually, he found a decent job working at a local foundry plant in the small logging community of Mays Harbor.

My parents' relationship had begun to deteriorate even more after the fourth child was born. My mother didn't know what to do with my father's sullenness and his drinking problem by the time I'd entered fifth grade. She finally turned to the church in the hopes of restoring this failing marriage. While attending the Presbyterian Church, my parents became good friends with the pastor and his family. For the next three years, our two families would go to the lake together and spend a day enjoying the beautiful scenery of the northwest. I can recall our two families driving for two hours to the Olympic Hot Springs Resort where we camped, hiked on trails, and spent the day swimming in a large outdoor pool. Shortly after becoming members of that church, my Dad got a terrific job in the school district working as a boiler maintenance person. Everyone knew him and he became friends with many of the teachers there. Our lives on the surface seemed to be better financially and yet, my father was gone from the home until late most nights. He spent many evenings at the local pub drinking with his buddies or playing poker with some of his work friends. For me, it became the norm to have an absentee father. Now, as an adult, I've come to realize that this was not the way the average families lived. I just knew as a youngster that our family was lacking in kindness and affection. I did my best to cope in those early years and stay out of trouble as I began to gradually withdraw into a protective shell. I can remember wishing that I'd felt loved by my own family.

I struggled socially in second through fourth grade of my elementary school experience. My mother didn't realize that I'd felt alone and awkward because I'd kept my unhappiness to myself. I knew what it felt like to be ignored by certain classmates. It's possible that one of the reasons for this problem may've stemmed from my horrid haircut. At the age of nine, my mother had decided to cut my long, luxurious brown hair. This new haircut called a Dutch-boy style consisted of straight bangs across my forehead and a blunt cut of the rest of my hair that stopped short of my jaw line. I recall my father coming home that night to see my short hair and then a loud argument ensued between my parents. I must admit I looked awful with this boyish haircut. I was horrified and I couldn't wait for my hair to grow longer. That same year, my grandmother, Nellie, and Aunt Avis were visiting our home. My aunt made a strange comment to my grandmother when she thought I wasn't around to hear her. "Poor girl, I feel sorry for her." To this day, I still wonder why they said this about my pitiful young life.

As a nine-year-old, I can recall feeling miserable and wishing that I lived with another family. I dreaded going to school where I didn't fit in. I had trouble finding a good friend since everyone had their own best friend since first grade. I felt like an outsider and a loner during my third year of school until in February, a new girl was placed in our classroom. This tall, blonde haired girl named Linda had just moved to town and didn't know anyone, so I invited her to sit with me at lunch. We became friends and I was happy for the remainder of that year. Then she moved away after fourth grade, and I felt rather despondent again.

There were no girls on our block to play with and so I joined in with whatever athletic activity my brother and his friends were doing every Saturday. My brother and I would ride our secondhand bikes around the block or tossed the pigskin football around most days after school ended. I was determined to learn the game of baseball and soon I could hit the ball better than anyone in our group. I wasn't afraid to challenge the annoying bully, Danny, who had tried to pick a fight with my younger brother one weekend. This neighborhood bully learned to stay away from us after that confrontation. I could keep up with any of the neighbor kids on our block and I was determined to excel in any sport they played. I remember one Christmas waking up to find a shiny, new red bicycle in my bedroom. I was elated to have a classy bike to race around town as an eleven-year-old tomboy with my younger brother, Roger, and our two neighbor friends.

It was during my pre-teen years that my life took a downward spiral emotionally. I had feelings of rejection and hopelessness that made me want to hide in my bedroom. I was unsure of why I felt so shut down and stifled as a kid. I became even more sullen and resentful. As I reflected on my youth, it seemed to me that there were too many blank years with no memories in my early childhood years; this problem nagged at me for a long time. When I was thirty-seven years old, my mom came to stay with us for a few months to work at my husband's carpet shop. To my surprise one day, she confessed her guilt about how she'd handled an incident when I was only six years old. She told me that I'd colored on my bedroom wall. She told me that she felt guilty for the horrible way she'd handled this incident. I was stunned by her confession. Thinking now about my mother's account of this awful incident, I can imagine that I'd been frightened by her hateful actions that day. How does one reconcile the fact that it was your own mother who caused you to struggle for your life breath? What if I had died in that terrible moment? She must've stopped choking me when I blacked out. I can almost imagine myself as a young girl dropping down in a pathetic heap on the hardwood floor in a faint and then seconds later, waking up feeling frightened and alone. After learning about her awful mistreatment to me, I can see why as a young child I never wanted to incur my mother's wrath. Along with this new understanding came the reminder of the same plaguing thought which surfaced while I was getting counsel from the therapist. I couldn't seem to get away from this strange phrase; *you would've died if you hadn't fainted.* Now, with this new information from my mother, I wondered if this strange phrase I'd heard in my thoughts pertained to her mistreatment of me or did it stem from an assault by a stranger when I was a girl. It was many years later that I realized I'd need to deal with the trauma which had happened to me during those two different, but frightening incidents.

I believe one of my coping mechanisms as a youngster was to be compliant and to stay out of my mother's way. I now can see that this was because I wanted to protect myself from her anger and mistreatment. One of the unpleasant memories I have of my mother was the times when she had to curl my thick hair around those pink sponge rollers. I recall how she'd been quite impatient with me, and she'd yank on my hair or slap my head to make me stop fidgeting. Sadly, as an adult it took a year of therapy with a professional counselor for me to put the puzzle pieces of my troubled youth back into a clearer perspective. During that year of counseling, it became evident to me that I needed more healing from the traumatic experiences I had endured from both of my parents. Back then our family had signs of being dysfunctional and yet, an outsider wouldn't suspect there was any mistreatment going on inside of our home. The only time the medical community suspects that a child may be suffering abuse is if they see signs of bruises or reoccurring broken bones. In my situation, the mistreatment from an angry mother and the misplaced affections coming from my father were hard to detect since it was more of an emotional or psychological bruising instead of a physical injury.

I had a flashback dream of being chased by a neighbor man named Mike and in that dream recall, I felt the terror of running away from him. I'd tried to share my feelings of fright towards this neighbor man and his wife who my mother had asked to watch me when she took my sick brother to the doctor. I have this vague remembrance that she didn't listen to me; instead, she managed to turn my words back on me and to shut me down that day. I have no clue as to why she chose to not believe me that day. I suppose it was because I was a young child and she maybe thought I had imagined what had transpired on those two occasions while I was in the care of these next -door neighbors. After that bad experience, I learned to keep my feelings to myself. By age seven, I became more confused as a child. I felt as if my mother had trampled on my feelings. It was as if I didn't really have a voice and eventually, I became sullen and withdrawn. She must've mentioned this to my father because one night he came into my room to say goodnight and a new kind of nightmare began for me. As a child I was helpless to stop this unwanted fatherly affection. Sadly, for me, the molestation, betrayal of trust, and the conflicting emotions continued until my baby sister was born; we are nine years apart. Keeping this devastating secret about my father's indiscretions firmly locked up inside of my soul was not healthy. However, since my mind had blocked out the worst parts of those bad memories, it was almost as if I felt nothing or remembered nothing of my life from the ages of six to eight and half years old. I still had the scary dream one more time as an adult to deal with though and flashbacks of the traumatic incidents of my youth which I didn't fully understand or know what to do with as well. I had no one to confide in and I became angry and confused as the years passed.

Much later as an adult, I gained some knowledge about a term which psychologists refer to as repression. According to my first professional therapist, this type of amnesia or repression can occur because of a traumatic experience. As an adult, I now know that I'd suffered from some trauma as a child. When I was nine years old the sexual advances had diminished, and my life returned to a more normal routine. I can recall my dad working late most nights; he'd become an absentee father in my eyes. So yes, I was somehow protected from further abuse from my father and yet, it had left a gaping wound in my soul and a scar that no one could see. As an adult now, I have this to say about my father, he failed to protect me as a young girl, and he betrayed my child like trust in him.

As I reflect on some of my family's drama and dysfunction, I can recall now that my younger brother was much more vocal and assertive than me. As a thirteen-year-old, he could yell and cuss angrily at our mom and get away with it somehow. Since I was the second-born child, I tended to be more of a people pleaser with a desire to keep the peace in our home. And yet, for me it became peace at any cost which is not true peace. Eventually my inner turmoil and anxiety began to surface on the outside of my body. At the age of ten, I began to develop a mild case of eczema on my hands which became dry, cracked, and painful. My only solution was to apply Vaseline ointment and bandages every night on my irritated skin. A few years later, this dry skin trouble eased up for me. I was thrilled to not have to keep applying the ointment to my hands. Things began to calm down at home and at my school that year and it's possible that I may've felt more secure. I've noticed that even now when I am worried about a problem, I will nervously bite my nails and pick at my dry skin. This is bad habit which needs to stop. I suppose this skin problem and the nail biting signifies a deeper root issue for me. I believe that I may've needed to confide in a trained therapist or a qualified physiologist by the time I'd reached the age of thirteen, however, this didn't happen for me!

CHAPTER TWO

The summer of my ninth birthday some things began to change for the better in my life. I was given a children's book titled, "Uncle Arthur's Bedtime Stories", from my Canadian grandfather. One of the stories in this interesting book really captured my attention. It showed a drawing of boy who had been hit by a speeding car and he'd suffered a severe head injury. A boy in the same ward of the hospital came into his room and told him to raise his hand so God would see his act of faith and take him to heaven. The next picture showed the kindhearted lad helping the dying boy prop up his arm with a few pillows for God to see and then he left the room. Sadly, this boy died during the night. This troubling story gripped my heart so much that I made sure my arm was also propped up with my bed pillows just like that young boy in the book. I went to sleep that night hoping God would notice my hand held up towards Him. This small act of surrender to a God I barely knew marked the beginning of my interest in going to a place called heaven.

When I was ten and a half, a neighbor who was director of the YMCA in town asked me if I wanted to earn money to go to summer camp. I replied that I would like to give it a try and so I went door to door asking folks if they would help me by purchasing a can of toffee flavored peanuts. After two months of concerted effort, along with a partial scholarship donation from the YMCA, I managed to have enough money to be able to go to camp in July. I was thrilled to be going there for the first time. My counselor's name was Ellen, and she was a bright light in my lonely world. She was a kind-hearted adult and it felt as if she cared about my feelings. I am grateful for those times I spent at camp, and it gave me something to look forward to each summer. I felt accepted by the leaders at this summer camp; it was an outlet for my energy and my love of sports as well. I gained an appreciation for the great outdoors and for an exciting game called 'capture the flag'. After a few years of being at camp with wholesome kids and caring leaders, I began to forget about the problems that were happening in my home.

As a young adult I still couldn't seem to get free of the fact that I had so few memories of my youth from age of six until I turned nine. I do recall one or two distant memories when I was four and five years old. One recollection I had was of the tall apartment building where we lived near a corner grocery store and a big German Shepherd dog jumping up and knocking me to the pavement. The other memory I have was of our move to a large two-story house that was empty of any furniture except for a large, old bed mattress leaning up against the front room wall. When I was nine and a half, I recalled sitting on the front steps of our two-story house and waiting nearly two hours for the clouds to finally dissipate and the sunshine to come out. Once the sun had appeared, I'd walk at least five blocks until I'd reached the city's park and could play for hours. This park, located next to the river, contained swing sets, one slide, an old tennis court, and a long, oval cement wading pool. This playground park area had become my safe place during the summer months. The following year my younger brother was old enough to come with me and together we'd walk for several city blocks in order to reach the park. We'd stay there for the entire afternoon splashing in the shallow pool waters until the park closed for the day.

I can recall plenty of my childhood memories after the age of ten. My younger brother and I would look forward to Saturday and the freedom it afforded us. In the morning we'd hurry to clean our rooms and put away our stack of freshly laundered clothes. Then we'd hur-riedly grab a wooden baseball bat, our leather gloves, and race outside to play with the neighbor boys. The two brothers living next door to us had a wide front yard where we could play corner baseball games. I remember a thick Oak tree on their property which was located right behind home plate area. Since the lower part of this tree had a strange bend in it, we could use the tree trunk as an excellent resting spot while waiting our turn to bat. Then when the game was over, we could take a run and make it halfway up the tree to grab onto a lower branch and climb up even further. From this vantage point we'd a better view of the neighborhood and the surrounding bigger world called our town. I had a growing desire to explore this new, exciting world which beckoned me to go discover places of interest beyond our street.

I loved playing any kind of sports activity with the boys, even if I was the only girl on the team. One day my brother got so frustrated when he'd struck out at bat that he turned around and stomped angrily back home taking the only baseball bat with him. This meant the game was over for the rest of us and I wanted to stomp on my kid brother for ruining our fun that day.

One sunny weekend we all rode our bikes to the railroad tracks just west of our neighborhood in a new adventure. Next, we ditched our bikes in the bushes and proceeded on foot to comb the tracks and surrounding area for something interesting to bring back home. We discovered an abandoned derelict shanty, and we went inside to rummage through the junk. We uncovered a few interesting items left in the old house which we carried back to our friend's house. After pedaling back to our neighborhood block, we all jumped off our bicycles, headed for our friend's woodshed, and tried to figure out why someone would leave their wallet, letters, and a two-dollar bill and coins behind.

Then the following Saturday we showed up to the same shack. By this time, the place was boarded up and so we threw rocks into the windows. Tired of this game, we decided to follow the railroad tracks for a mile until we discovered a better place to explore. In the distant was the old train station. We stayed on our bikes until we'd headed along the road next to the bay area where we found plenty of driftwood along with seagulls and sand piper birds. The bay water of the Harbor area stretched for nearly three miles along the old airport road and the setting beckoned us to go further as young explorers. We had a marvelous time climbing on the old, bleached driftwood and aged tree logs that had washed ashore from the water's high tide.

On one of our biking adventures the four of us friends rode west past the industrial section of the town's sawmills and lumber yards. Abandoning our bikes, we headed through a brushy terrain where the bay waters had flooded the marsh area and it was deep enough to splash around in. I proposed that we try to build a small, lightweight raft to navigate this narrow waterway. Thus began our exciting adventures like those of Huck Finn and Tom Sawyer, who'd spent their days floating on the swirling, muddy Mississippi River. My younger brother and his two buddies helped me scrounge the area until we found three short driftwood logs to tie together as the base of our raft. The next thing we had to do was sneak around the old sawmill to locate a few boards to attach to the top part of those logs. Finally, we grabbed two long wooden sticks to use as poles to navigate our makeshift raft and then we all hopped on to explore the water area. This grand adventure of rafting in the flooded area of town was one of the best memories I had as a youngster.

Another time we decide to use scraps of wood to build our own amateur go-carts. I ended up donating my doll's baby-buggy wheels to finish off the project. Since I'd become a tom-boy I no longer was interested in playing with girly things. This small vehicle which we built out of wooden boards, nails, and rope was sturdy and mobile. I could steer the front end of the go-cart by holding onto two short ropes tied to both ends of the short piece of wooden board called a (2 x 4 stud). I only needed to place my feet on this wooden 2 x 4 stud to also control the front action or direction of the moving go-cart. Once we'd haul the makeshift go-cart up the steep hill then it needed to be turned around to face downhill.

Next, my younger brother would stand right behind the wooden race cart and give it a big shove to help me gain more momentum. The other kids stood back at the top of the hill to cheer me on as they waited for their turn in the go-cart. After the cart stopped rolling, I'd climb out of the go-cart, grab hold of the rope attached to the front end and haul it up the hill for the next kid to have his turn at racing this wobbly go-cart down this steep incline. On my last trip down this hill a week later, our go-cart veered to the right side of the paved street and hit the solid curb. To my disappointment, the two front wheels had come loose during this impact and therefore, that was the end of our dare-devil rides down the steep hill in my hometown of Mays Harbor.

CHAPTER THREE

All in all, those years filled with extraordinary, youthful adventures, corner lot baseball games, and weekends spent exploring our town were some of my most memorial experiences before I entered junior high school. However, those cherished years of youthful adventures would soon be swallowed up in the drudgery of school life and the boring math homework.

By the age of thirteen, I had made another good friend, Terri, (not her real name) from school and we were inseparable that year. She started walking home with me and we always stopped at Bishop's Grocery to buy a bag of barbeque potato chips to eat. Near the end of that school year for some unknown reason, she stopped talking to me. I had felt dejected, bewildered, and slightly confused as to the reason we'd stopped being friends. Sadly, she never cared to share with me why she'd found another friend to hang out with. I grieved the unfortunate loss of her friendship for the next four years.

Years later, when I was married and had two young boys, I felt impressed to contact this same classmate, Terri, to reconnect with her. I'd learned from my mother that she'd moved back into her parent's old home in Mays Harbor. I asked my mother to give me her phone number and then I made the call. I asked her to forgive me for causing her any trouble and she explained why we'd stopped being friends. I had inadvertently embarrassed her by jokingly nudging her into a hedge right next to the sidewalk as my cute brother came down the same street behind us and he watched us that afternoon. I had no clue that she had a crush on my younger brother. I was thankful that she finally shared her true feelings with me and then we made plans to meet in two months in our hometown.

I will always cherish those few times I spent with Terri after our reconciliation. Since it was a long drive to visit her, we only met twice in the following year. A year later I learned from my mother who knew her family that she had been diagnosed with terminal cancer and didn't want anyone coming to the hospital to see her towards the end. My heart ached with this awful news. My friend died shortly after getting this bad news. I cried for weeks and continued to mourn her passing for a long time. I'd been so happy to have our friendship renewed and now I couldn't understand why she had to die so young. Life seemed cruel and unfair to me at this time since her two young boys were now without a mother.

***

After graduation, I got a job working for the city's parks and recreation center. I enjoyed teaching girls how to play softball as a part of my job. Those summer days I worked with two other guys at the city park where we helped young kids learn games like chess and kick ball or tennis. I really wanted to attend college and graduate with an Associate of Arts degree. The idea of moving away to attend Central Washington State college for my third year of school had kept me motivated and focused on my schoolwork. During those two years of college, there were no serious relationships with a guy to complicate my life and I breezed through my studies and graduated with honors.

Looking back on the few years after high school, I can recall wanting to find someone who'd truly love me. I was hoping to meet a guy who'd the same interests as me. And yet, without realizing that I was dealing with abuse and abandonment issues in my life, I was, as the song says, "looking for love in all the wrong places – Johnny Lee." After graduation, I dated a couple of guys, but didn't find the spark or attraction that I was looking for. Would I ever find the love of my life? How would I recognize him even if he showed up at my front door I wondered? As you may be able to tell from my story so far, I was struggling to find out who I was and what I really wanted in life. During this time of searching, I could've used a wise mentor person to give me the right advice and encouragement.

Towards the end of this summer job, I felt a strong inclination to move to Oregon to attend a different college. I made a weekend trip to my parents' summer place located on Hamersley Inlet at this time. While I was there for three days, I could relax, swim in the bay waters, and reflect upon my future. One day, I took a stroll down to the beach to look for shells and to enjoy the expansive view of the bay. Finding a large boulder to sit on, I rested there and soaked in the warm sunshine. I watched the outdoor water scene in front of me with delight. I loved spending my summers here. That day the water's surface seemed to glisten brightly as if it had been dusted with millions of sparkling, shimmering diamonds and multi-faceted light fairies.

I was enjoying my quiet time in my favorite summer spot when an eagle flew overhead. I shifted my attention to observe this majestic bird as I admired its beauty and strength. Then the eagle swooped downward towards the surface of the water. It appeared to be scanning the water's surface for food and then it flew up in the sky above. I could see its white head and tail feathers against the cobalt blue sky. Within minutes, this magnificent creature flew back down near the water's surface and snagged a fish in its strong talons. Flying triumphantly through the air, the eagle carried its prey off in the distance where it then perched on a towering evergreen tree branch. It was a grand sight to behold and since I love spending time in the outdoors, I wished I could've stayed at our summer retreat place for one more week. It was while resting there on that large boulder overlooking the inlet waters that I had the strange impression that my world was about to change dramatically.

That summer, as you might recall, I'd been struggling with the idea of returning to CWSC in September. Maybe I was avoiding my ex-fiancé by not going back to Ellensburg for another school year. Regardless of the real reason, I was also feeling a strong pull to move to a larger city located in Oregon too. I remember feeling slightly uneasy about living in a big city and I was worried about the fact that this was a private college. I would no longer qualify for FASA, and I only had enough money to pay for one year at this next school. However, I couldn't let the money issue prevent me from following my heart. The need to discover who I was and where I truly belonged was becoming a constant pull on me. What would my future in a big city look like I wondered? Was I doing the right thing by changing colleges? These were all questions I needed answers for and soon. I hiked back up the steep hill to our summer house to talk to my mom about this important decision. I wanted to hear what she had to say since she was now a praying woman and I felt like I could trust her counsel. I didn't want to make the wrong move back then; I needed validation for my decision that August.

I was planning to return to college soon and I had mixed emotions about going back there. That summer was a pivotal time for me as a young adult. I'd been trying to make good decisions for the last two years, but I felt like I was failing miserably. I'd turned twenty that summer and I was feeling discouraged about ever finding the right guy to date. I had serious doubts of ever finding someone I could trust my heart to completely. Amazingly, a month after my nineteenth birthday, I encountered someone who I felt like I could truly trust him with my heart's cry for a real and lasting kind of love. The following weekend I had a life-changing experience when a family friend named Eunice invited me to attend a Full Gospel Businessmen's dinner. Towards the end of the evening, I heard two women from our old church share their newfound faith in the Son of God. They did not talk about belonging to a certain church that evening. Instead, they talked about having a relationship with Jesus Christ, and I wanted this same joy and confident these two women were expressing that night. I decided to accept Jesus into my life. I knelt before the

Living God and asked him to forgive me of my wrong-doings and I felt His peace surround me. Then on my twenty-first birthday, I took another step towards my journey towards heaven by allowing God to direct my future completely. It was after this momentous decision that I began to seriously consider transferring my credits to a smaller college located in Oregon.

Another month went by, and I needed confirmation about leaving CWSU. I asked God to open the right door and close the wrong door for me. While I was spending one last weekend with my family at our summer place, my mom and I talked again about the idea of me changing colleges. She encouraged me to call Edie Iverson who was the pastor's wife in Oregon to ask her about coming to check out their small Bible college. We made the phone call to Edie, and she encouraged me to come spend a week at their Family Camp where I would be able to chat with the head of admissions of their college at the same time. I spent a week in Oregon where I met with a college professor, Robert L. Stricker, who was also the Dean of this college. I asked this leader for his opinion about transferring my college credits to this college. He encouraged me to consider the benefits of their unique study program and that as the Dean of this college, he assured me they'd accept most of my transfer credits from CWSC. I made the final decision to change colleges after asking him a few more questions. This move to attend Portland Bible College turned out to be the beginning of a journey of discovering who I was truly meant to be.

CHAPTER FOUR

I had relocated to attend this new private college by faith, and I was starting to worry about my tuition costs for each month. Trusting that God would provide for my finances was a new challenge for me. However, God kept opening doors of opportunity for me and by the end of that year, I'd procured a part-time job in the city. Fortunately, this income was enough to pay for my remaining school bill. One of my college roommates named, Shari, had invited me to stay at her parent's home in Lake Oswego for several weekends and this was a much-needed reprieve from college studies. I was very grateful for my new friend's kindness and for the chance to be a part of her wonderful family. Shari introduced me to her cousin, Randi, and before long the three of us were inseparable friends and college roommates. We created wonderful memories that first year and are still good friends even though we live in different states now.

After my second year of college, I was invited to fly to Canada to stay with my mom's relatives for two months. I really enjoyed my time on the farm with cousins. I spent a few more weeks in the city with my uncle and aunt who owned a fast-food restaurant. They had a young daughter who I played with every day. Towards the end of my stay in Canada, my uncle and aunt asked me to consider living with them and tutoring their daughter. I was faced with a huge decision: Should I stay in Canada, worked for them, and make some money or return to America and finish another year of college. I prayed and read my Bible hoping for an answer to this decision. After a few days of thinking about this opportunity, I read a scripture for the second time which spoke to my heart, and I knew for sure that I was supposed to go back to Oregon. As a young adult, once again I'd chosen to follow God's plan and not my own inclination which was to stay with these wonderful relatives. I often wonder if my life would have been different if I had stayed in Canada.

I was planning to graduate from this college with a degree (which I eventually accomplished in two years' time) and I was hoping to find a trustworthy marriage partner one day. Would I ever find this person I could entrust my fragile heart to? I was not aware of the fact that I needed more healing for my wounded soul before I could hope to have a healthy marriage relationship with another person. This kind of healing of my damaged emotions would come much later in my life. As a young adult searching for real love, I had just chosen to surrender my will to align with God's plans and this decision was slowly producing a change in me. In the past I'd known a little about God, but I hadn't encountered him in a real way until one early morning in November. I'd been on my knees seeking God in the college prayer room when I received these powerful life changing words in my heart: *young lady, I love you with an everlasting love.* This brief, but amazing encounter with the Lord produced a tangible love connection within my wounded soul that nothing else could have accomplished. That day I knew I was in the right place at the right time in my life.

During that year at this small college, my friend, Randi Whetzel, invited me to live off campus at her relative's home located on Wielder Street in the city. I'd found a part-time job at Lloyd Center shopping mall, and I'd usually walk home from work at night. One dark evening I was carrying my bag and some schoolbooks as I walked the four blocks to get home. I made the mistake of taking a shorter route and I noticed a man who was wearing camouflage clothing. Then he came back around the block walking towards me on my side of the darkened street. Even though I was one block away from my destination and safety, I quickly recognized that I was in real trouble. As I looked at the dark houses nearby, I knew I was on my own and defenseless. Then I recalled something my roommate, Shari, had mentioned about a young adult woman who had rebuked a man hassling her in an elevator by using the name of Jesus. In my situation, once the man drew closer, he reached over and forcibly placed his hand over my mouth to keep me from screaming, and then he shoved me to the sidewalk. The moment he moved his hand away from my mouth and grabbed my pants, I yelled these words twice. "I rebuke you in the name of Jesus Christ! "I rebuke you in the name of Jesus! Immediately he froze and stopped assaulting me. It was as if he'd seen something which frightened him. I watched in amazement as the man wearing the camouflage jacket stood up, turned around, and raced off down the street leaving me shaken, but relieved. I hurried home to tell my girlfriend and her suitor visiting her that night. After I had finished talking about my scary incident with the stranger, her boyfriend stated that I could've been killed by this guy. I felt like God had heard my cry for help and had spared me from a horrifying experience and possibly an early demise on the streets of Portland, Oregon.

A few months later, my friends introduced me to some cute guys and soon we were all hanging out together. One guy had caught my attention, but it seemed that most of the gals at this college were interested in him as well. However, he informed me one night that he wasn't interested in them. After we'd dated for a while, he began to talk with me about the idea of us having a long-term relationship. He was ready to get married it seemed and oddly enough, it seemed like I was also open to this idea as well. Had I finally met the one person who could love me and make me feel safe? We continued dating and then we had a six-month engagement. I began to feel as if I could possibly trust my heart to this young man.

***

We were married a year later and thus, began the journey of a lifetime. We had two boys born twenty months apart. They became almost inseparable growing up. It was like having twins since they played so well together, and they shared the same interest in sports. They even shared a bedroom until our first son went off to college in Oregon. My boys also played with the same neighbor kids where we lived on seventy-six street and Beaumont Ave. Most of the kids gravitated to play soccer in our backyard or shooting hoops in the front area of our ranch style home. Then sixteen months after our second boy was born, our first daughter arrived in our family. She was an auburn-haired child with an amazing personality. To my great surprise, this third baby needed to be delivered by my doctor ahead of schedule. He told me that there was a problem with bleeding in my placenta area. After consulting with another physician, my doctor decided to try to avoid a C-Section delivery and so he allowed me to try having a natural birth with the assistance of pretosin drug. Things went well during this delivery and God had answered our prayers. This sweet baby girl arrived safely that afternoon and we were relieved and thrilled with this auburn-haired sweet infant.

'Live and learn' was to become something I said often as I traverse through the trying years of raising children. It was not enough to simply feed, clothe, and keep your child in school. I had to learn how to be an umpire, a counselor, and a selfless and generous-hearted woman with the wisdom of King Solomon. Of course, there were times when I failed miserably as a mother, and it was only by the grace of God that I was able to impart love and kindness to these active young children. One of the reasons that I was struggling to keep my head above water with this lively brood was that my own childhood was fraught with episodes of angry, violent reactions from my own parents. These experiences had left invisible scars upon my child psyche. I did not have the proper training and experience to draw upon as I tried to discipline my children. My own anger and frustrations kept crowding in upon my life demanding to be dealt with during those trying times.

One time, a hair stylist gal had cut my hair and bangs way too short and suddenly, I found myself remembering the ghastly haircut of my youth. All the anger, hurt, and conflicting emotions from my past seemed to resurface and threaten to overwhelm me. I hated my new haircut, my exhausting challenges, and my inadequacies as a person. I couldn't seem to handle the daily stress and demands of having young children. I recalled the next day, after feeling so angry and upset with my haircut, my life, and the squabbling children that I picked up a toy and flung it across the living room and it hit the sheetrock wall. It became even more apparent to me after this emotional outburst that I had serious anger issues which if left unchecked might eventually cause us all a lot of grief.

Would I ever find an emotional stability which I needed in my life? I felt extremely helpless to change my world or to be in control of my own emotions. Since we'd moved away from Portland, Oregon and my two good friends, I no longer had someone to confide in or share my frustrations with. I needed a mentor woman to stand beside me and encourage me. This daunting task of being a parent and homemaker was threatening to drown me in a sea of exhaustion and resentment. During these trying years, I felt as if I was a single mom trying to raise our children by myself. In fact, I would finally get the children into bed and asleep by nine or so and then fall into bed exhausted. I was too tired most nights to even brush my teeth. I felt overwhelmed by my life and the daily responsibilities. I had graduated from a community college with a degree, but I couldn't manage my own household properly. I needed a long vacation break from the constant pressures of dealing with the ever demanding, crying children and the mountain of never-ending piles of dirty laundry. I recall many nights where I would spend the late evening time wishing my husband would come home early a few evenings and help me to get the children into bed.

During those dreary exhausting years, I felt distant from my husband, and it seemed to me as if I was still just surviving. I also felt a sense of guilt and condemnation since I couldn't seem to get a handle on my emotions. As a mother of little children, I was feeling alone and frazzled. As a child, I had been a survivor and here I was as an adult still in survivor mode and hating my dire situation. Ten years has passed and by this time we had five kids. Two years later, I had the opportunity to attend a woman's meeting in the neighboring city. On my way back home, I felt the urge to keep on driving north to Seattle to run away from the pressure of motherhood. I recall experiencing daily frustrations and moments of exhaustion in my life at this point. One dark thought kept plaguing me, and it was this: Had I made a mistake in getting married. I felt as if I was back in my youth and feeling hopeless about my life again. I was afraid I might come unglued and lose my temper with my children just like my mother had done with me if this stress continued.

One evening, while my husband and our firstborn son were sitting on a bean bag chair in the room off the kitchen, I made a feeble attempt to get his attention and failed. Of course, I didn't communicate my need for a break from the demands of the daily task of caring for four children. Feeling ignored and misunderstood at this time, I began to resent my husband even more. Why couldn't he understand that I needed his help? He seemed oblivious to the undercurrent of frustration that was mounting inside of me. For me, it felt as if my husband was staying late to work each night as a means of escaping from the pressures of our family life and demands from so many children. We were all vying for his attention and yet, he was too tired to meet our needs emotionally. I was starting to feel as if my husband had abandoned me, and I felt very alone and frustrated with my life.

Eventually, my husband's long hours of work became a catalyst which fueled my lingering anger to a boiling point. As a child I'd learned to stuff my true feelings. I'd been afraid to say what I really needed from my family members. Now I was continuing to squelch my feelings again to act the part of a dutiful wife. The children needed him around more and I needed some time away from the children and my never-ending workload. The result of having no help in the home day after day was that I began to exhibit signs of mental and emotional breakdown. My neighbor next door noticed that my eyes were starting to glaze over one day as we visited across the fence that separated our two homes. I wasn't quite into the conversation with her. She didn't say anything to me until much later and I probably would have not agreed with her anyway at that time. I finally became aware of my mental fatigue one afternoon when my daughter was two and half years old. I had lain down on her bed to help her take a nap when she climbed off and found the jar of Vaseline. She proceeded to thoroughly slather my head and hair with the petroleum jelly substance. It was at that moment of not caring what my child was doing to me that I realized that I was exhausted and on the verge of a mental breakdown from dealing with children twenty-four-seven.

I had heard about a friend who only had two kids nearly having a nervous breakdown and it made me determined to not fall into a similar dilemma. Since I had four youngsters at that time who demanded my attention daily, I needed to stay mentally healthy and on top of my game. So, I starting calling upon God to help me. I began singing a scripture worship song and this helped me. Eventually, I felt like I needed to work on my resentment towards my husband. In the past, I had felt justified in my anger. I suppose I was upset because I felt abandoned. I'd felt like my husband had failed me and I was not happy with him. I didn't want to let go of my resentment towards my parent or my husband. I was beginning to see that I'd struggled with these hurts and my feelings of disillusionment for too long by myself. I tried to talk to my husband and tell him that I was very upset with him for not being home enough to help me. I forgave him and we hugged that night. However, the sad part of this relationship was that I didn't know how to insist that he come home at least two nights a week to help me put the kids to bed or give me a break. I suppose I figured that he'd say he had too much paperwork and invoices to handle after the shop was closed. I felt stuck in my circumstances.

***

As a young adult, I had a troubling vision one day. In this quick vision, I saw my new husband standing there with two young girls who were crying and sad. I wasn't in that sad scene, so this remembrance really bothered me for years. Whenever I'd recall this sad scenario, I'd feel grieved and concerned for my future. Just what did this troubling vision mean and what could I do to prevent this disturbing scene from actually coming to pass?

This rather grievous reminder of two very sad young girls without a mother continued to plague me and it would leave me feeling apprehensive or worried. I would pray often for God to keep me safe from potential harm. My fear was that I might die young and leave my two youngest daughters without their mother. It would have helped a great deal if I'd shared this concern with some wise woman and yet, I kept it to myself for too many years. However, whenever the memory of this sad vision popped up in my thoughts, I would cry out to God for protection from an untimely death. A few more years passed by, and I'd gained a more mature outlook on this worrisome concern. I decided to stop being afraid of not being there for my two younger daughters; I chose to trust God to keep me alive. Strangely, there were a few times when my life was spared from grave danger for which I'm truly grateful.

One such scary incident did occur while I was driving my daughter to her high school early in the morning. I had decided to take a short cut along the back roads that morning in order to get her to school on time. As I drove down a sloping road into a slight dip, I'd entered a short section of the two-lane road where I was hemmed in by the opposite lane and a fence on the right side of this country road. Suddenly, out of the early morning shadows and down from a hill came a speeding car heading straight towards me in my lane. I literally had no place to swerve away from this young man's speeding vehicle. It would've been sudden death for us if we collided head on in the next moment. I knew even if, at the last second, if I'd chosen to swerve the steering wheel to the left to avoid him, his car would have still crashed into the front of my vehicle since there was not enough room to totally avoid his speeding vehicle. I didn't panic or swerve into the opposite lane, but instead I cried out to God to protect us. An angel must've intervened during those last few seconds because suddenly, the high school age driver managed to turn his steering wheel slightly and luckily for us, he'd managed to move back into his correct driving lane in time to miss my car by inches. I had stared into the face of death during that frightening moment and yet, mercifully, we'd been spared a deadly crash and lived to tell people about that scary incident.

***

As a young married woman, I still couldn't shake the feeling that something was missing in my life; later, I came to realize that it was the loss of memories during part of my childhood. I began to wonder what had caused me to withdraw and become so detached from my parents as a young girl. I started to question why I had such a bad relationship with my mother. Why did I feel as if I barely had any memories of my childhood years? Why did I struggle to feel accepted in my own family and with classmates during my grade school years? My life was shrouded in strange flashbacks, conflicting emotions, and feelings of resentment which I could no longer ignore. By the time I was twenty-two years old, I came face to face with the reality that I had some definite issues with my parents. After attending a Basic Youth Conflict seminar, I realized I was carrying some deep resentment towards my parents which needed to be resolved. It seemed that my anger towards them had been festering within my soul for years. I tried to change my attitude towards them and yet, my anger went much deeper than just acknowledging my bad attitude.

As I'd mentioned in a previous chapter, there was the time where my mother flew into a rage and choked me until I'd blacked out. I can imagine now how this dreadful experience must've made me feel insignificant and powerless as a child. I think that I may've felt a sense of rejection from my mother during those times when she was so angry. I can recall wanting to run away from home during those early years, I do remember wanting to go live with a young classmates' family a few times. I didn't seem to feel as if I belonged in my own family. Something was wrong with my life. As an adult, I couldn't seem to shake off those pressing reminders of being an unhappy, anxious young girl; I was just a hurting individual whose greatest desire was to feel accepted and loved by my own family.

There seemed to be too many empty holes in my memories of childhood that perplexed me and nagged at me through the years. Now as I reflect on my mother's confession of guilt about the time she choked me, I realized that this trauma had left a scar on my psyche and emotions. During my sessions with my professional therapist years later, I was able to connect the flashback memories to this specific incident. However, just knowing what had happened to me didn't seem to solve my life troubles. Since I suffered from a great deal of stress from that hurtful incident along with my obvious fear of my mother's anger, I feel that I was a prime candidate for mental health issues as a person. Can trauma from one's childhood hinder a person's capabilities to think properly or to respond normally like other people? How could I reconcile the fact that it was my own mother who caused me to struggle for enough breathe to stay alive? I now believe this to be true: since I grew up with an unhealthy fear of my mother's anger this could've contributed to the reason why I stifled my true feelings as a youngster. I'm sure I didn't want to incur her wrath and so I managed to stay out of trouble and out of her way.

Sadly, for me, it took a year of talking about my experiences with my professional therapist for me to put the puzzle pieces of my troubled youth into a clearer picture. Looking back on my sessions with the counselor I can see why I needed healing from these different traumatic episodes of molestation by my dad and the frightening incident of being choked by my mother. It was helpful to finally be able to remember something from my missing memories. I have a much better understanding of the unusual ways in which I still tend to respond to others. Looking back on my frightening experiences, I feel as if I can relate to the young lad in the Bible named Joseph. He was rejected by his siblings, abused, and then thrown into a deep pit where he languished for some time. He must've felt abandoned, angry, and hurt beyond belief! He'd been given a promise of success for his future and yet, now here he was in the dirt and feeling like he was in the pit of despair and loneliness. Just like Joseph, I felt as if I had a bright red glaring target painted on my back which contained the word, "Victim" written across the middle section of this bulls-eye diagram. Of course,

I wanted out of this horrible pit of despair which I was living in! The cry of my heart was to be free of this stigma of sexual and physical abuse.

As an adult, I had to accept the fact that I needed help and so I turned to a mentor friend named Marie. This woman could see that I really needed more counseling and healing to be able to adequately handle the stressful and upsetting situations that arose in my life. We began praying together on a weekly basis for me to be free of my emotional hang ups. I began to understand that I was suffering from certain issues which had caused me to feel anxious and intimidated by adults. I learned from Marie that the fear of continued abuse can leave a child feeling insecure as a person. Five years later and during times of counseling with my professional therapist, I would wonder if I'd experienced the same kind of post-war trauma syndrome that a soldier endures during his time in a war zone. Later, as an adult, I needed friends who could be supportive and who wouldn't judge me for my shortcomings. Once I began to share my story and be honest about my painful story with the right people, I began to experience a deeper healing for my wounded soul. However, I didn't want my life story to only be that of a wounded, hurting victim of childhood abuse so I continued to cry out to God. Yesterday, I came across a verse that expressed how I felt once the Lord had restored my soul and set me free from my pain and anguish. "I called upon the Lord in distress: the Lord answered me and set me in a large place." (Psalm 118: 5 KJV) The pain and shame of my childhood was slowly fading from my soul. Today, as I sit here typing at my computer, I am thankful that God didn't leave me where I was in my pain and grief, but instead he has been at work slowly, but surely restoring my broken, wounded heart and mind.

I believe that children need to feel safe in their early years at school and at home. I feel that children benefit greatly from verbal encouragement and affirmations from their parents as they grow up. Being a mother without a good role model in my youth, I've still tried to be more supportive and involved in my children's sports activities and schooling. I decided to treat my children with more kindness and love than I received. Many times, in my youth, I watched my parents fight in the home and I dreaded their next heated argument. I became aware of them starting to separate in their relationship. Eventually, my parents divorced. I was sad when it happened, but I understood that they needed to live separately in order to maintain a peaceful existence.

There were good times and trying times in my own marriage. My husband wasn't always able to handle my outbursts or my frustrations or show me adequate under-standing during those times of feeling hurt and sad. And yes, there were a few dreadful arguments and upsetting times for us as I believe there are in many marriages. I'd been taught in church that we were in a covenant relationship, and I wanted to believe that things would somehow change for the better one day. I suppose most marriages go through this kind of struggle. However, the Lord was apparently very involved in our relationship and by the grace of God we've stayed married. Forgiveness and prayer were the essential factors that kept us together while I continued to believe for healing of my damaged emotions and for things to change for the better in our relationship. Even though I wanted a healthy marriage and a stronger partnership with my husband, I didn't have the right tools or knowledge as to how to accomplish this goal.

CHAPTER FIVE

Looking back on my childhood struggles, I can recall my parents showing their animosity and anger towards each other. I dreaded these awful episodes possibly occurring again and again while I was in the same room. One time during their fighting, I remember hiding underneath a table hoping to be invisible and safe. Occasionally, my mother took her anger out on me as I grew older. I was caught up in the middle of what therapist call 'the cycle of abuse'. And yet, there was still something else that I believe may have attributed to my low self-esteem problems and deeply rooted resentments.

My hidden pain, lying just beneath the surface of my remembrances, was yet to be uncovered. As a young woman in my early thirties, I still wasn't aware of my abuse issues until the year I turned thirty-six. That same year, my friend shared with me her sister's story of being molested by a family member. As she was telling me about this situation, I reacted like I needed to throw up. Her story had really affected me that day and I wanted to understand the reason why I felt so troubled about her sister's situation. For the next two years this incident plagued me, and I started praying about my reaction. As I've already mentioned, I finally went to see a therapist in my early forties, and she informed me that I was dealing with repressed memories. I learned from this trained counselor that when a child suffers from abuse and trauma, they can have what she refers to as memory amnesia or repressed memories from those frightening situations. I told her I didn't want to live like this anymore and I was willing to do the work each week to discover the truth about my 'family secret'.

A few years before going to my therapist, a friend had mentioned this idea to me: Cathy, why don't you ask God to show you any root issue which could be causing you trouble. So, I heard her and made the effort to pray about this question. The more I sought God, the more I became convinced that I needed expert help in the area of memory recall. Then one day, as I looked over at my eight-year-old daughter who was standing there in our kitchen, it hit me that I had been abused at this same age and a sense of sadness and grief resonated within my soul. It was as if God was confirming what I'd already suspected about my own life. Of course, I didn't have all the pieces of this puzzle fitting together correctly yet. I just knew I needed help to resolve some troubling reminders that kept resurfacing in my mind. Looking back on my youth, I recalled struggling with feelings of inadequacy and doubts about myself that spoke volumes about a deep pain in my soul. As an adult now I began to ask myself this: Why did I feel rejected by my parents at times? Was my father really my biological father? Why did he abuse me? What was wrong with me that made my own parents mistreat me? These questions were like a dark, heavy cloud of despair hanging over my life. At times during my youth, I can recall feeling like maybe

I'd been adopted by my parents and yet, this was not the truth. I have my birth certificate to prove that I was their child and yet, there were times when I wished that I could have escaped from our unhappy home life. I needed an answer as to why I' felt so unloved and miserable as a child.

Eventually, I began to understand that I needed a great deal of help if I was ever to become whole as a person. You see, in my twenties and thirties, I wasn't aware that my own mother had choked me while in a fit of rage. I didn't discover this truth until my professional counselor recommended that I share with my mom what I remembered about my father's abuse. My father had already died of siroccos of the liver and clogged arteries by this time (1984) and so I couldn't confront him with my accusations of being molested by him. The therapist I was seeing at this time advised me to tell my husband and my mother about my memory recall efforts. I took her advice the next day and attempted to share these recovered memories with my husband. He was aware that I was seeing this counselor and he tried to be understanding. Then, a few months later, I met with my mother to talk with her about my counseling and memory recall. This turned out to be harder than I thought it would be.

My parents had been divorced for twenty years by this time. My mother had come to stay for six months with us in order to help my husband with his bookkeeping problems. I took her out to lunch one day and it was a pleasant meal of hot soup and sandwiches. When I told her about the mistreatment and sexual abuse from my father, her only response was: "You just need to forgive him because I had to for many things." Indeed, my mother had plenty of things to forgive him for during those years of marriage and yet, on this occasion it was about my painful issues which I was attempting to share with her. So, for me, it felt as if she wasn't showing me much compassion by her statement to simply forgive my own father for all his wrongdoings towards me (which I believe should be labeled as a 'criminal offenses, and punishable by law) I walked away from my mom with the realization that she probably didn't' have the ability to show me the kind of empathy and kindness I needed right then. Once again, I didn't feel like she really cared about my feelings. I had lost my childhood innocence and a sense of security and therefore, I wanted retribution however, sadly, this feeling of recompense never happened for me. Where was the justice in this matter, I wondered for a long time until finally, I made a choice to turn my pain and grief over the Lord and trust him to heal my soul and my damaged emotions completely.

It was at this same time that my mother made her startling confession of guilt to me. I was not only shocked by her statement, but I just wished she'd ask me to forgive her for that shocking mistreatment and the fear that it instilled in my young life. Of course, in the last twenty years since her honest confession of choking me, I've understood more about her own childhood grief and times of neglect from her adopted parents in Canada. Now as a grown woman, I've chosen to forgive her offenses towards me. Sadly, it seems that our painful childhood experiences can affect us more than we think. I'd wanted to run away from home many times as a girl and yet, in my heart, I only wanted to feel safe within my own family. The love I was so desperately searching for seemed to be like an elusive butterfly which kept flitting nearby and then eluding my grasp. Even as a young married woman, I found myself wondering if I'd ever find a real sense of belonging and as safe harbor for my soul.

As an adult I would shut down during an argument with assertive, strong people. An example of this is when my husband and I would argue there would be times where I needed to walk away from our heated arguments to have a moment alone. Once I was by myself, I could figure out what I wanted to communicate to him. Then after I'd calmed down, I could go back to discuss the problem. I hated the fact that I couldn't communicate as well as other people. I would feel intimidated by a family member's anger, and I would feel the need to distance myself from those upsetting arguments. I seemed to lack a definite sense of being safe with adults and I needed help to resolve my issues.

Self-preservation is a coping mechanism that most abused children use to keep from facing or dealing with an extremely painful or traumatic event. If we ignore a problem, then we don't have to deal with the painful reminders of our inadequacies or fears. I had managed to squelch my feelings and to pretend there was nothing wrong with me and yet, these feelings of fear, anger, and resentments were all screaming for my attention. Someday this fragile house of cards or self-protection might fall apart and then where would I be. I'd learned about a concept called 'arrested development' when I'd spent several afternoons with my mentor friend, Marie. She explained that this problem arises when a child had suffered a trauma or abuse. In fact, an abused child will remain stuck in that age where they were traumatized and not be able to progress emotionally or psychologically as they should. This had been my reality for many years. I had been afraid of the nighttime, afraid of my parents, and afraid to be honest with people. Through the years, I've reacted as if I was still locked into the emotions of a child of eight years of age. This term (arrested development) was an agonizing problem for me since I wanted to act like a mature woman in the times of disagreements or conflicts.

In the past, when my mother had used her anger or her verbal abilities to shut me down, she'd managed to strip me of a sense of self-worth. There was something that broke in my spirit when I was mistreated by both parents at different times. I felt like I couldn't trust my own parents to protect me or to understand what I needed. At times, as a child, I'd felt unsafe in my own home. Now, here I was once again, as an adult still unable to express myself sufficiently with another adult. This time I realized I truly needed more help. In fact, this conflict had made me feel so sad that I wept that following day more than I'd ever had for years. I didn't want to live like this anymore. I picked up my phone to call my good friend, Kim, to get her advice as to how to be free from the pain of this recent painful disagreement. I wanted to be secure enough as an adult to respond in an emotionally difficult conversation without feeling intimidated or afraid of someone's anger. During the following week of introspection, I began to understand my true feelings about that recent argument with the family member. It was as if I was still living back in my childhood and struggling to be truly heard again. I needed help!

Even though I had plenty of time to reflect on that upsetting conversation with this family member, I still couldn't grasp why I was so knocked off balance by her anger. During the initial confrontation, I'd chosen to take the low road and apologize for my mistake. After a few days of reflecting on this recent hurtful incident, I realized that I'd grown up trying to protect myself from people's anger or assertiveness. As an authority figure, my mother had been able to push me into a corner emotionally until I gave up and learned to keep my mouth shut around her. I recall spending countless hours alone reading a book in my quiet bedroom and it had become my hiding place for me. As a girl I would strive to avoid any conflict or trouble with my mother. I'd grown up with a deep desire to feel valued and affirmed and this essential element had been missing in my formative years. I recognized that a trigger point' of pain and helplessness had occurred for me during this last emotional conflict.

While praying with my friend, Kim, about my inability to handle that rather difficult confrontation the week before, she'd reminded me to bless that individual and to release forgiveness to them since God was working on changing the thing that was wrong in my heart. I had to choose to leave the matter in God's hands and believe for a better relationship with this person in the future. I felt frustrated with myself. Since I no longer want to be intimidated by people, I needed to figure out how to deal with my past issues and my trigger points. Apparently, I seem to respond better to people when I feel safe, and I can voice my opinions freely. One thing that has helped me immensely is that I made an appointment to attend a second Sozo healing time with two trained women from our church group. This was beneficial experience for me as God was slowly, but surely healing my wounded heart during the two sessions. I was learning that I could share my feelings and be honest without being worried about any serious repercussions.

Well, enough stories about my sad, disturbing childhood. This true story happened while my husband and I were on a snowshoe expedition with our daughters. Our daughter, Sharon, was celebrating her thirtieth birthday and she wanted to try a new experience up in the snow near Timberline Lodge. So that December, she convinced a few of us to join her in this new adventure. That wintry day, we walked along with our three young adult daughters all piled into the Toyota vehicle with our gloves, hats, and warm jackets to head to the mountain. First, we had to rent snowshoes at a quaint, rustic shop at Timberline located next to Mount Hood ski area. Next, we drove another twenty minutes to find a parking lot. Then we all climbed outside in the cold fresh air while my husband locked up the car. We were all excited to get started on this new adventure together.

Glancing around at this winter wonderland, I took a big breath of the fresh, cold air into my lungs. We all headed towards what looked like the start of a snowy trail which sloped downward. The sky was a powder blue hue overhead and I noticed a thin formation of white cirrus clouds spreading across the horizon. It was now one o'clock in the afternoon and I'd wished we brought inner tubes instead of these aluminum snow shoes which were awkward to use. We could hear the clamoring and shouting of these happy children as they zip down to land in a heap at the bottom of hill. I listened to their shouts of excitement as they sped merrily down the small hill and the idea of sliding down with them seemed more appealing to me right then. The six of us all began trudging down the steep, snowy slope and chatting about the weather and our lives. We soon learned that we had to stay to one side of the trail to avoid the cross-country skiers speeding pass us on their journey. An hour of walking through deep snow brought us to a beautiful sight called Trillium Lake. We were all happy to stop here by the water's edge and eat a light snack. I was enjoying the beautiful scenery around us and our rest time since it was strenuous walking for so long in these cumbersome snowshoes. As we sat there chatting, my husband came up with an idea that he wanted to continue around the lake and then finish back at the car. I vetoed the idea since snowshoeing in this terrain was difficult and had become an unrewarding activity for me.

The four girls also agreed with the idea of heading back to the car by going the same way we'd come so far. Our daughter said that I shouldn't leave my husband alone on the snow-covered trail that afternoon. I argue this point with the girls, but to no avail. They all managed to make me feel guilty for not continuing with their dad on this next hiking venture. I had a hunch that his plan to take the upper lake trail would take longer, but I finally gave in to their pleas. However, I did challenge my husband with a wager that went like this. Whoever made it back to the car first would get a free meal since the loser of the bet would have to pay for the cost of the other people's dinner meal. My husband was so confident he'd win this bet that he even refused to give the girls his car keys. I was not happy with him at that moment. Off we trudge until the path turned into a sloping incline which led on to a slightly higher elevation trail around the entire lake area. Now remember we were using snow shoes which are more difficult to use.

Halfway around Trillium Lake, I heard a strange, unsettling phrase come into my spirit which caused me some concern. *It will be alright; I will take care of your children.* This thought stayed with me for the next few minutes as I tried to comprehend its actual meaning. Why did that unusual thought come to me that afternoon? What could possibly happen to me out here in the cold, wintery climate of Mount Hood? I wondered if I might incur a problem with my heart from all this exertion and so I started to pray for my well-being as I plowed forward in this deep snowy path. I didn't share this worrisome thought with my husband since I wasn't sure what it meant totally, and I figured it would be difficult to explain this thought to him. Instead, I just kept trudging along wishing I hadn't decided to come with him on this much longer hike in the snow and cold. After walking deeper into the woods on this trail and passing a few hikers, we were faced with two different paths to choose. My husband decided to go to the left after we passed a signpost with three different options. I had noticed that one small sign had the words 'snow park' engraved into the wood while the others said something else. We continued for another forty-five minutes and that's when I became a little more wary of this trip ending well for us.

We passed a gurgling, small stream of water which flowed through the icy, snow-covered terrain near our trail. I stopped there to get a drink of water and I still had an uneasy feeling about the path we were taking. By now, I was beginning to wonder if this uneasy feeling was more of a premonition or a warning to pay attention to. I couldn't seem to shake off this sense of going in the wrong direction. I mentioned my concerns to my husband, and he assured me that he knew we were on the correct path. The next time we stopped, I told him about seeing the sign saying, 'Snow Park' and I wondered if this meant the place where we saw kids on sleds when we'd parked our car earlier in the day. Dusk was starting to fall on the winter wonderland scene around us and the clouds were turning into hazy, thin ribbons of white brush strokes against the pale blue skies. I felt like we were heading west which would bring us back towards where we had first rented our snowshoes earlier in the day at Timberline. I wanted to insist that we turn back and go read the signs one more time before going any further on this long hiking adventure.

I was starting to have images of the two of us being lost in this snowy wilderness during a long freezing cold night. Then I thought about the possibility of our girls huddled together to try to stay warm. What if they decided to walk for miles in order to reach Timberline Lodge. I certainly didn't want any of us to be on the nightly news as a missing person's report the following day. None of these ideas were appealing to me and so I was determined to head back in the other direction. By this time, I'd become convinced that if we kept going towards the west like my husband wanted, we'd travel further away from the girls and our vehicle. One more thing was making me nervous; we were no longer seeing people on this trail. To my mind, this was not a good sign. I was even more adamant this time as I told my husband that we needed to turn around and go back to read those marker signs to make sure of our directions.

My husband finally agreed with my request, and we worked our way back to the signpost. Once he'd read the third sign with the words, 'Snow Park,' imprinted in the wooden sign and a little arrow pointing east, he agreed that we should head in that direction. The skies were becoming darker, and we had no clue as to how much longer the trail went as we prodded along with our cumbersome aluminum snowshoes. An hour later, to my delight, I heard the familiar sounds of kids playing in the snow up on the same hill where we'd heard them earlier in the day. Once we'd reached the top of that snowy incline, we saw the four girls huddled together by our vehicle in the cold night air. They had been very concerned for our wellbeing as they waited and waited for us to show up. Since my husband had decided to keep the car keys, they'd been discussing the plan to walk out to the main road to catch a ride into Timberline to get help and buy some hot coffee. They were ecstatic to see us alive and safe. Of course, our daughters quickly grabbed the car keys to start the car to warm up their hands and feet inside the vehicle.

After this scary, wintery experience near Mt. Hood, I decided that I'd never again let anyone talk me into going on a long hike in snowy conditions. I was grateful we had not become a missing person's report on the nightly news that chilly December evening. Of course, now I have a funny story to tell at our family get-togethers. I firmly believe in paying attention to premonitions. Every time I have listened to these spirit-led promptings from the Lord, I've been protected from serious harm or danger.

CHAPTER SIX

I want to share another amazing testimony here. My friend, Vera, and I like to chat on the phone regularly and pray for our family members and our nation. She has one grown daughter who is married and lives in the same city as we do. One day, she called to ask if she could buy my first shorter book which was about our family and the miracles we'd experienced. I said of course and so we made plans for me to take this book to Walgreens where her adult daughter was working. I agreed and drove over to meet her daughter. While I was talking with her daughter about my book of miracle stories, she shared her miracle story with me right there in Walgreens. Her true story took place during the late 1990s. She was married to a nonbeliever at that time. Her first husband thought that he could go to heaven by relying upon any one of the many gods that were available to him. He believed that all paths in life led to heaven.

Meanwhile, behind the scenes, my friend, Vera, was praying for her daughter and this troublesome marriage. She mentioned to me that her daughter had been work-ing as a dental assistant for several years and suddenly one day her back muscle tightened up causing her some pain. She suffered from this trouble for some time and then her body started aching a lot from over-active nerves. Her overall body pain was diagnosed as fibromyalgia. The physician explained to her daughter that this affliction causes overall body pain, fatigue, and headaches, as well as sleep problems at night. She had problems standing or walking sometimes and would lose her balance occasionally. She also had problems with her eyesight and if she looked down at the floor, the vinyl designs would get closer, and this really bothered her too. She endured this pain for the next six months and had no actual relief from the prescribed medicine.

This woman shared with me that day in the store that she'd started praying and reading her Bible every day and searching for the healing promises in the New Testament. When a friend invited her mother to go hear a well-known preacher's meeting in Portland, Oregon, she decided to attend too. That day in 1997, things seemed to crowd her schedule and it looked as if she wouldn't be able to join her mother and attend the healing service that night. She kept pressing forward and believing that she would be healed if she went to this gathering to receive prayer from this man of God. It worked out that she was able to come in time to find a seat in the crowded auditorium. She had this absolute confidence that she would be delivered of this constant pain when this preacher prayed for her to be healed.

By the end of his preaching and declaring words of knowledge about God healing people in certain areas of their body, she went forward to get prayer for her own ailment. He anointed her with oil and when he prayed for her, she slid to the floor under the power of God. Although my friend was still feeling some pain in her muscles as she exited the building and headed to her mother's car, she noticed that her body functions were beginning to feel much better. She no longer had trouble with her balance or her eyesight. She hollered to her mother to toss her the car keys so she could drive them back across the Interstate Five Bridge to get home. She was able to drive home safely, and her mother was ecstatic about her healing. This woman has been free of this debilitating problem ever since that night of prayer for her healing.

The following day, her unbelieving husband stood there and mocked her as she made a bold statement of faith and declared that she was healed from the fibromyalgia symptoms. When he asked her if this evangelist had healed her body she replied, "No I wasn't healed at the moment this preacher laid his hands on me, but I was healed by God as I was leaving the auditorium to come home". Her doctor didn't believe that God had healed her either. He asked her how she was doing with her fibromyalgia pain one year later. She insisted that she was healed completely and asked him to record this statement in her medical files. Since this medical doctor refused to write down in her files that God had healed her of this affliction, she decided to go to a naturopathic doctor after that. Her new doctor was a believer, and he gave God the glory for healing her of this horrible infirmity. He also recommended that she take calcium and selenium supplements to boost her immune system and to change her eating habits. This doctor also suggests that some of his patients use selenium pills to keep their heart healthy and strong. I was excited for her good news and asked her if I could write about her story in my book. She responded with a yes, certainly. It is now 2018, and so for the last eleven years she has been free from the past body pains and fatigue. I was sure that folks who suffered from this disorder would want to hear about how God saw her dynamic faith and healed her of the fibromyalgia. She ignored her husband's negative remarks and continued reading her Bible that year. She now loves to share with people about her divine healing experience.

***

My one close friend with eight kids had moved to a different state some years ago and I missed spending time with her and her family. We still talked on the phone, but it wasn't the same as being there with them. Six months later, she'd invited me to fly there and spend ten days with her. I was looking forward to coming to California and she helped me to book a flight. While I was there one morning sipping on my hot coffee, she'd encouraged me to write in more detail about my childhood issues. She felt that I hadn't really got in touch with my emotional issues in connection with my past traumatic experiences. Hearing those words made me stop and think for a moment. I looked over at her sitting across from me in her beautiful home and I shook my head as if to say no thank you to her idea. I seriously did not want to have to think about my horrid past and the grief it had caused me, nor did I really want to share any more details with my adult children as she'd mentioned. What had started our conversation about my past was something that I'd told her about the last conversation I had with my daughter, Kris.

My daughter, Kristina, had been reading my life journaling and she made a few interesting comments to me during my visit with her. After reading about my personal history, my daughter looked over at me and said this: "Mom, I am glad that you wrote about your earlier years as a young mother because you are not much of a talker like dad. Before this, you really didn't share much about your childhood troubles with me. Mom, after reading about the abuse you'd suffered from your parents, I am getting a better understanding of who you really are as a person. Besides, I didn't even know about the difficulties and frustrations you had experienced while raising us kids." After hearing my adult daughter's comments about how important it was for me to share more about my life, I was glad that I had begun this new writing project.

Sharing more about my own grief has been a daunting challenge since I was not used to getting in touch with my feelings. I'd spent many years suppressing these feelings of pain and shame. For me, journaling was the best way for me to begin expressing what I had felt during those awful episodes with my parents. Once I sat down to write about my true feelings and emotions, I realized that my friend had been right. I am glad she is in my life to push me to be more real with myself, my family members and friends. However, I must admit it has been much harder this time to write my entire story as I sit at my computer to document my feelings and memories in greater detail.

It's true, for the most part; I do a better job expressing my thoughts on paper than I do in talking about them to people. In my defense, I just didn't think it'd be beneficial to share everything I'd suffered while growing up in a dysfunctional family. I suppose it's because I do not like thinking about the abuse. Plus, I wanted to see myself as an over comer and not just a victim of abuse. The other reason I hadn't shared my unpleasant life story in more detail is because it had been tainted by feelings of shame. I really didn't want to be so vulnerable and transparent about my own life. However, even though I'd chosen to self-protect and hide my shame along with the details of my abuse from people, it was still there to haunt my subconscious mind; I really wasn't living in true freedom.

Now here I was sitting in my friend's new home in California, and she was urging me to tell my readers even more truth about how I'd felt as a young girl. We continued our discussion about why I didn't want to write or talk about these kinds of details about my childhood pain. She knows how to be real and honest, and she was asking me to try to express my true self within my writing. I realized that my ego or self-esteem was fragile and that I simply wanted to protect myself from other people's scrutiny. She knew that I needed to face my concerns and fears head on. Finally, I agreed to write down a few things that I could recall from the times my father had molested me; however, I was not fully convinced about letting people or family members read this newest addition to my personal journal. In my journal writings, I'd alluded briefly to my childhood troubles, and I'd thought that was sufficient. She didn't seem to agree with me on this matter. My friend has this innate ability to call me out and push me to be more honest about my life issues. It has always been difficult for me to share my true feelings with people. I'd spent years suppressing this awful family secret' and so this kind of honesty was very unfamiliar territory for me. So, to comply with her request, I took her daughter's unused notebooks that morning and began writing about a few of the sickening times when my own father abused me at the age of eight.

As we sat at her kitchen table, I finished writing the last portion of my shameful memories and I made this comment to her. "I've decided that I want to burn this page and I don't want to share this portion with even my daughters. She once again confronted me about how I was still acting in a self-protective way. She expressed her belief that I needed to be honest with people and share my pain within my book because she felt strongly that there might be other hurting women who would be able to identify with this kind of pain. I tried to debate this idea one more time and then I realized that she was giving me good advice and yet, it was very difficult for me to admit to anyone the truth. My own father had made me endure some horrible acts against my will as a child. She understood my obvious discomfort and the reasons why I had not wanted to share any details of my abuse. It was too humiliating and degrading I said in response to her comments. Why should I share certain details of my awful childhood and the shame about my past with the world?

To be honest at that moment, I really didn't want to talk about the abuse at all. My friend just sat there across the table from me and waited for me to see the truth about this matter. The problem was that I needed to feel safe enough to continue writing down on paper about everything in my past. Within a few minutes, she went back upstairs to finish getting ready for the day. I suppose she prayed for me because I managed to keep writing about how the mistreatment and abuse had truly made me feel for the first time in my life. That day I remember wishing I could climb into someone else's skin and trade my life for theirs.

At one point, I'd decided to use my left hand to write about what happened to me in order to get the full effect of being seven and eight years of age. This worked for me, and I was able to write down the truth about my childhood memories and look at the pain my father had caused me. Of course, I took a purple marker pen later that morning and colored over the most embarrassing portions of my story. I must confess right here that facing the truth about one's own troubling life experiences can be daunting and overwhelming. However, for me writing the truth on paper about my childhood traumas has given me a new kind of freedom to be real. I am okay with sharing more of my story now with my family if they ask. Being more transparent with others has been valuable for me as a writer. I am truly grateful to have this caring friend in my life. She knows me better than anyone and has challenged me to be frank and forthright about my painful life experiences. At one point, my friend said this to me, "Cathy, who knows, maybe if you tell your true story of hurt and abuse, you might possibly help someone else who has suffered in the same way, and this would be a good thing!" I gave this idea some thought. Well, there was a hint of truth to what she was saying, and I had to agree with her statement.

Even now, I wish my childhood had been more carefree. I'd lost a sense of security and dignity when my father chose to become a perpetrator in our home. If I could have one thing change in our world, it wouldn't be to see world peace, truth be told, my hearts' desire is that no child would have to endure this type of emotional devastation associated with physical or verbal abuse. The saddest part for me to accept is that a pedophile can abuse their own daughter. When long term abuse occurs, it can cause great stress on a child's psyche and self-esteem to the degree that it hinders their emotional well-being for years. Some youngsters disassociate from reality in order to survive while others develop a split personality as a result of the physical or emotional abuse and trauma which they'd endured as a young child. It is very difficult for even a young adult to finally get up the courage to confront their own parent who abused them. When I finally learned the truth and accepted the part my own father had played in my painful youth after going to a year of counseling, he had already passed away and I couldn't confront him about the abuse. Some years later, I had the opportunity to spend quality time with my wise friend named Marie who knew how to pray effectively for me. She helped me to rebuild my sense of self-worth over the next three years as we met and prayed. I had to be willing to face the scary memories of my past. I was desperate to get help from the only one who can truly heal my broken heart!

Unfortunately for me, it would take a few years of being honest with myself in order to get free of the past shame. In the very beginning of dealing with the fact that I was a victim of childhood abuse, I'd kept asking this question. Why hadn't God protected me from all this pain and shame? Why was I born into this crazy, dysfunctional family? As I continued to ask these two questions and grapple with my personal hurt, I heard only silence for months. How could a God of love sit back and allow someone to hurt me so deeply? I struggled with this concept and finally, one day this unique phrase captured my thoughts, *you could've died during a bad incidence, but you were kept alive.* I clung to this thought, and it brought me some sense of comfort even though I didn't fully understand everything that I had been put through as a young girl.

What I did come to realize about myself was this: man had managed to destroy my self-worth and a sense of security, but it was not God's fault. I would be foolish to continue to demand that God make everything right for me. I had to finally let go of my bitterness, forgive my abusers, and allow God to restore my soul. I didn't want to be held captive forever by the chains of bitterness and judgments which had attended my soul for so many years. I made the decision to forgive my parents and one other person. And yet, there was still the other aspect which psychologist call 'childhood traumas' that I was learning about and needed to figure out a way to deal with this too. I would eventually come to recognize that this cycle of abuse and anger was hindering my mental or emotional health. I discovered that I needed to break this cycle of abuse in my family line and so I decided to renounce any partnering with anger and hatred with God's help.

Certainly, I started to realize that I had become a hot mess as an adult. Although I couldn't blame my mother for everything in my painful childhood, I still wanted to blame her for stifling my self-expression. It became more obvious to me that I had damaged emotions and self-esteem issues which needed to be resolved. Where was God in all this pain and emotional suffering? Since I had some wonderful experiences in my youth, I was able to present myself as a happy person for the most part. However, there was still this dark, worrisome secret lying deep within my subconscious mind.

Here I need to mention about the concept of family secrets. Often when a parent is the perpetrator usually no one knows about it. Since I had no advocate as a youngster and my own mother didn't support my accusations against my own father, he was free to continue abusing other young family members through the years. Where was the justice in all of this? I recall wishing he was still alive, so I could've confronted him. As an adult now I wish that my father had been held accountable for his wrongdoings against me and other girls. I had a judgment against my father who on the surface seemed like a nice guy and yet, subconsciously I knew differently. As I started to face my pain and shame as an adult, I experienced feelings of anger and hatred towards him, and I wanted him to feel my pain and suffering. However, any effort to confront a family member accused of being a perpetrator could've turned out to be fruitless. Plus, it would've been his word against mine back then and plus, I'm not sure I would have been strong enough to pursue this matter in the court system.

CHAPTER SEVEN

My childhood thinking consisted of words which exemplified my own feelings such as: distrust, abandonment, and fear of men in authority. I was affected by an absentee father and a mother who didn't know how to say the all-important words, 'I love you, sweetheart", to her own daughter. I recall even wondering if my family really wanted me. I needed to find a source of acceptance outside of my immediate family as I became a young adult woman.

The answer to finding happiness which I was seeking seemed to exist in having my own family one day to love. I needed God to meet my needs and heal my wounded soul first. Could I bring my hurts and disappointments to a God I couldn't see or touch? Little did I know that God was there all along waiting for my permission to allow him step into my life and rescue me?

One of the reasons for writing this book was to testify of how God has gradually restored my soul from pain and trauma and he healed my damaged emotions. The human mind is a fragile thing and I believed therefore the Lord chose to slowly peel away the painful layers of my heart in such a loving and cautious manner for me to avoid being overwhelmed. One of my greatest fears was that I would have a mental or emotional breakdown and be of no use to my family. I needed to face this fear and get answers. I now see that I'd been protected from a total recall of every aspect of my traumatic experiences as a young child. I don't think I could've handled remembering everything about my shameful past in the beginning of this process. In fact, to be honest, I needed to pause here briefly, get up from the computer, walk away, and go outside for a moment. I don't like feeling pain in my body as I recall the past abuse while writing it down now. I once read in a book about what therapists call a strong phenomenon where a persons' body members can still remember or still retain the same muscle pain memory. It's like the mind/ body has stored up muscle memories of the actual physical attack or the sexual abuse that happened even though it had occurred many years ago to the individual.

I believe that the heavenly Father's intention was to keep my mind and my emotions safe during this entire slower healing journey. I am very grateful for this blessing. As I've shared my hurting soul with all its pain, shame, and disappointments here, I can only hope that my true story of how God healed and restored my damaged emotions will help someone else and give them hope too. The truth of the matter is this: I cried out to God in desperation, and he heard my plea for a healing of my mind and my damaged emotions. and he delivered me from despair and extreme shame of my past. I made the choice to trust my heavenly Father to bring me his truth and his acceptance. I want to declare this to the world; God loves people, and he loves to heal those who come to him! Yes, I must admit one factor in the process here: The memory recall and healing process has been very hard on me and yet, it needed to happen so that I could be made whole and healthy.

Recently, I met someone who was struggling with a significant loss in his life. This young man came to our church and shared with the group about how God saved him. This is his true story. He'd lost his father when he was only four years old, and this lack of a father had a negative impact upon his formative years. During middle school, he began to drink, smoke cigarettes, and take drugs. Throughout high school, he used various kinds of street drugs until he became addicted to them. He told the audience that day that he'd become involved with bad people who sold drugs on the street. There were a few occasions where he had to hunt down people to make them pay what they owed him. Money came easy to get and he could buy fancy cars at the drop of a hat'. At times, he'd have about three thousand dollars in his pocket to spend on frivolous things; however, this easy money never brought him fulfillment or satisfaction. He confided to us that he was miserable and hated his existence despite his affluence.

This young man went on to inform the audience that he'd tried to commit suicide a few times. This individual was determined to end his life one day. In that very instance, he told us that he'd decided to call on the name of Jesus! He said these words aloud, "God show up in my life or I'll pull the trigger. I need you to prove to me that you are real!" He shared with the audience that if this didn't happen for him then he'd planned to end his life that day. A miracle occurred for this young man because God showed up at that very moment, touched him with a powerful, divine love, and delivered him from every addiction. He was literally set free and is now serving God and sharing his testimony wherever he goes. I was hearing the 'greatest story ever told' by a person who had been redeemed from death and destruction. This young adult had a profound encounter with the Living God who'd been waiting to show Himself as a true father to the fatherless. Just this week, I'd the opportunity to share this young man's true story with a young adult woman. Jenny (not her real name) listened and the following week she decided to stop taking unsafe, illegal drugs that were destroying her health.

There is nothing too difficult for God; no one too lost or too hopeless for Him to save. He loves to save, heal, and rescue people as it is clearly stated in the New Testament Bible, "That if thou shalt confess with your mouth the Lord Jesus, and shalt believe in thine heart that God hath raised him from the dead, thou shalt be saved. For with the heart man believeth unto righteousness; and with the mouth confession is made unto salvation." (Romans 10:9-10 KJV) To date, my young adult friend, Jenny, has called me to share that she has stopped taking drugs and wants help to stay clean! I was so thrilled to hear the excitement and happiness in her voice that Sunday afternoon. Her mother called me the following day to share about the recent phone call with her daughter. She shared that her daughter had asked her to facilitate the necessary steps for her to get connected with a local rehabilitation program. This news is amazing and has given me hope for this young adult friend. I believe that God hears the cry of a mother's heart; I have this conviction: prayer changes people. I have joined with my friend to believe for a victory for her daughter. This young adult must want to go talk with the counselor or the rehab center people on her own. It feels like there is a battle going on for her soul and all we can do is trust God to fully set her free from drugs. She recently moved to another state and has a good job now. I am happy to report that she is doing quite well, and we are all thrilled with her recovery.

CHAPTER EIGHT

My desire now is to have healthy relationships with people and to be a blessing to those I live with. I find myself even more dependent on God's help to accomplish this new goal. The good news is that God has been working in my life slowly but surely to restore my soul and heal my heart. Since reading certain scriptures in Proverbs, I have become more aware of my own problems and the need for more healing for my wounded soul. Over the last ten years, God has given me a sense of divine purpose and a new identity. When we understand God's purpose for our lives then we have a better understanding of how to live and flourish. I have chosen to go forward and put the past in His capable hands. I am a much healthier, happier individual now! This verse speaks clearly of the victory I now walk in, "He restoreth my soul: He leadeth me in the paths of righteousness for his name's sake." (Psalm 23:3 KJV)

I've also learned the value of making bold declarations of faith over my life. I now state these words aloud, 'I'm a virtuous, empowered woman of faith'. I am grateful that I've been set free from my past hurts, feelings of shame, and sadness that for too long had gripped my soul. I am rejoicing because the Lord has set me free from those crippling chains of fear, hatred, and anger. For too many years I'd believed a lie about myself, but now I am starting to recognize this problem. I'd felt like it had been my fault for the serious mistreatment from my parents. This was not the truth. I was a child in these situations, and I needed better parenting for sure. In the past, I'd felt trapped by bitterness and misjudgments which had been slowly suffocating my soul and causing me to react in an unhealthy manner. Thankfully, my times of reading the Word of God has helped me tremendously and I've been guided by his hand often. I am a woman who's been set free from those heavy chains of self-hatred, insecurities, and shame, and I've learned how to shake off the guilt that was attached to my past. Life is worth living now! It is a great joy for me to pray for others and to believe for God to heal them of their painful issues.

I was learning to trust God to restore my soul and to show me how to live with joy. I had to walked by faith and not in my own thoughts and feelings about this. I had to learn to put my hope in a few promises I'd found in the Bible. As I looked back to that eventful day when I'd stood on the frozen pond watching my children skating on the ice, I've come to realize that I'd only heard what I wanted to hear from the Holy Spirit. That day I'd concentrated on just the few good sounding words tucked within the phrase, *I am going to peel away the layers of your heart and heal you slowly, but surely My way.* To be honest, I'd focused mainly on the words "heal you" and this promise of healing had caused me to be excited and to rejoice. I went forward with the sessions that year with the professional therapist not realizing just how long this healing process would take thereafter and how transparent I would have to be to achieve the desired results. I just knew I wanted to be free of the past and to live a more productive life emotionally and psychologically. In other words, I was crying out for help to gain back that which had been stolen from my youth, my innocence. I didn't want to live as a victim of abuse and trauma any longer. However, since I'd not focused on the entire promise from God, it took much longer for me to be set free from the past pain and shame. My thoughts were not His thoughts in this matter. I'd assumed that God would heal my broken heart in a short amount of time, but this was not the case. In fact, the healing process took many years and a few tears on my part.

I'd like to share here about how to receive Sozo' healing for trauma, abuse, or wrong unhealthy soul ties with people and family members. First, let me explain that there can be four main inroads that might've occurred in a person's life which may cause them to struggle in this world. Therefore, it can be beneficial to ask God if you might fit into one of these four categories. These four areas include: 1) anger, 2) lack of forgiveness for offenses/ hurts, 3) rebellion, and 4) immorality issues. My past issues had caused me to fit into these negative situations and so I needed to deal with them. The first thing I had to do was identify the problem or exactly where I fit into these four categories and then I needed to acknowledge my pain and struggle. Secondly, I needed to repent and turn from my anger and bitterness which had become strongholds in my life. Thirdly, I had to renounce any inroad of anger and resentment for family members. Then I chose to forgive these same individuals and release them from my judgments. In my situation,

I had to ask the Father God to close the door to anger in my life along with the cycle of abuse and then ask the Holy Spirit these important questions: What am I feeling, why do I feel this frustration or hurt and finally, what does God want me to do about these emotions. Once I released my heartache and bitter root judgments to God, then in turn, the Lord showed me what He was saying or wanting me to receive as truth instead. I call this a God Exchange!

As a person who has suffered much pain and trauma from parental abuse, I can testify that only my heavenly Father can truly heal and mend a broken heart such as mine. For those who find themselves reading this book and you may possibly identify with my pain and suffering, I invite you to give your brokenness, your wounded heart, and loss over to God and allow Him to mend your heart and restore your soul. He loves you! God is powerful and waiting right there by your side to give you a hope and a good future! I am writing about my true-life story to encourage people to entrust their heart to the one who can turn their sadness and shame into something beautiful and meaningful for their life. If God can turn my sorrow into joy, mend my broken heart, and cause me to have such peace of mind, then I truly believe He can help anyone who has suffered a great deal in their life too. I encourage you to say this simple prayer today.

Lord God, I need you to heal my broken heart and restore my soul with your divine love. I welcome you Father God to come into my life and touch my mind, my heart, and my hurting life with your loving kindness and mercy. I chose to forgive my abuser and now I give you the right to deal with them. Show me how to release my pain and sorrows to you and give me a revelation about who you say I am in return. Thank you, heavenly Father for healing me in your way and your timeframe.

***

When our firstborn son was only twelve years old, I saw him in a quick vision, and it was as if he was trying to walk on a tightrope suspended in mid-air. I was not used to getting this type of vision or spiritual insight about anyone and it struck me as an odd thing to see. It was like having a daytime vision, but at the time, I didn't fully understand what to do about it. I recall praying for him to be safe and then I resumed washing the dishes. This was the second time in my adult life that I received this kind of brief spiritual vision or image. I didn't have a close friend or prayer partner back in those days to share this with and no one had taught me about the necessity of doing spiritual warfare for my son. Our son was struggling with some issues, and I didn't even know about them back then.

Years later, when our firstborn son was older and attending college, I experienced something much different. He'd come home from college to visit us on two different occasions. Two different times when he walked into our living room, I had a strange premonition or sense that his one arm was missing and so I began to fervently pray that nothing like that would happen to him. Then I forgot about this strange vision. Many months later while playing goalie for his collegiate team, he'd suffered an injury to his right knee and leg ligaments and was forced to quit playing on the soccer team. He was very disappointed and bored with nothing to do while waiting for his knee injury to heal. A month later when his two best friends asked him to get his hunting license and go with them, he gladly accepted. For some odd reason when he'd asked me to locate a necessary document so he could get ready to go with them, I had felt oddly reluctant to find the information, but the following day I searched in his bedroom and located it for him anyway.

The night before leaving on this exciting hunting trip our son, Robert, decided to call home. He wanted to chat with us however, we were out of town. In our absence we had left our sixteen-year-old daughter Sharon in charge of her younger siblings and that's why she answered his phone call that evening. After ending the phone conversation with her brother, she felt compelled to pray for his safety and that no hunter's bullet would kill him. The very next morning at six o'clock, Anthony's mother was awakened and impressed to intercede for her son's safety too. Neither one of these family members knew just how crucial their prayers for these two teenage boys would be.

So let me take you to the day before this fateful Sunday event to give you a picture of three excited teens getting ready for what they thought would be a fun campout/ hunting weekend. It was Saturday afternoon, and our family friend, Thomas Evans (not his real name) was driving his two teenage sons, Mac and Anthony, and my son, Robert, up to an area of about fifty acres of hills, grassland, and trees that was privately owned by a farmer he knew about. They'd parked their Ford SUV along an abandoned gravel road that had once been used to log the owner's available timber. Our friend, Mr. Evans climbed out to scout the sparsely populated woods for a clearing to park his camper for the night and soon he found a great spot. Meanwhile the two teens set up camp while our friend's oldest son unloaded gear from the camper. The idea was to spend the night to get an early start in the morning. After dinner, my son's younger friend, Anthony (not his real name) nudged Robert to follow him, and they began gathering sticks and branches to build a fire before darkness enveloped the campsite. After they made the campfire, the four guys sat around the hot campfire telling humorous stories and reminiscing about other fun trips. Then they all turned in so they could get up early enough to make breakfast before heading out in search for any signs of deer.

Morning arrived much too soon for the young hunters. As my son and his younger friend awoke grumbling, and finally stumbling out of their sleeping bags, they found Anthony's father and the older brother, Max, in this hunting party had already made breakfast. They couldn't wait to grab a cup of piping hot coffee as the rich, tantalizing aroma from the coffee pot drifted through the chilly air. After cleaning up a bit, the group headed off for a section of the countryside where Thomas figured there might be some sign of deer.

Splitting up, the father and his oldest son, Mac, walked down into a ravine near a slowly winding creek while our teenage son and his friend headed up the slope in a different direction. On either side of the trail the flowing knee-high grass brushed their legs as they continued up the winding slope. A nervous squirrel darted about on tree branches overhead. The next animal they saw was a flock of Canadian geese making their way westward across the skyline, heading towards a warmer climate. The sight and sounds of the noisy geese made both boys wish they were bird hunting instead.

Beads of sweat had begun breaking out on Robert's foreheads from the arduous task of climbing the sloping trail. The trail was still damp and slippery from morning dew. All around them, the air was filled with the heavy scent of cedar and pine trees. I know how much my son likes the outdoors and to hunt. Robert continued recounting the trek as he mentioned to me that his pulse had quickened as he scoured the hillside with the hope of seeing a deer or an elk grazing nearby. My son, Robert, continued to explain to me later that he pushed on with anticipation and joy at being in the forest area on this crisp, clear morning.

Next, my son described seeing a grouping of maple trees up ahead of them. There were tons of brightly colored red and yellow leaves which caught his attention as they rounded a curve in the forest trail. This explosion of autumn colors was astounding; he wished they'd brought a camera to capture the magnificent sight. I found myself scrambling to catch up with his story right here since I'd paused to reflect on the scene he was describing. My son smiled and then went on to say that it seemed to him as if the hillside was magically ablaze before his very eyes. He told me that it felt as if creation was showing off for them in that sublime moment in time.

At this point I was very interested in his account of the day in the woods. He recalled how he'd moved his rifle to his other hand and then he'd felt like stopping there to enjoy the quiet morning scene around him before continuing their search for deer.

"Hey, do you know something, Anthony?" My son asked his hunting partner that early November morning as they hiked up the sloping trail. "I can't wait until we make the ridge over there. Do you think we will see deer tracks soon?"

"No, and if we don't find any deer that's okay with me because then we can get back to our camp sooner and have dinner before it gets too dark." Anthony replied.

"Yeah, that sounds like a plan. I'm having a good time just being with my buddies here in the great outdoors. Before we left town, I'd called home to chat with my folks about this trip. They were out of town and so I talked briefly with my sixteen-year-old sister. I just wanted my family to remember about our hunting trip and pray for our success." Robert said.

As they continued walking up the slope, the younger teen, Anthony, was close behind his companion and deep in thought about his girlfriend. He enjoyed spending time with her, and yet he couldn't resist this golden opportunity to hang with his family and Robert. Anthony watched as his friend, Robert, shifted his weight uneasily and then reached up to pull on one of the straps of his pack to better secure the load.

Meanwhile, our son, Robert, was beginning to feel more relaxed as he watched a hawk circling above the towering trees next to their trail. Robert inhaled deeply, enjoying the pungent and woodsy odor of the pine trees. The many birch and alder trees gave the landscape a variety of unique colors to study and enjoy. As he glanced around at the forested terrain, he felt a new awareness and admiration for this spacious outdoor cathedral with its majestic natural beauty. Any time spent outside among the shelter of trees and blue skies above made him feel closer to God. At that very moment, he wished they were staying one more night in the woods.

CHAPTER NINE

Around our country home, as young teenagers, my three sons, Robert, Jon Scott, and David, could just walk down to the old barn with a friend and shoot at the pigeons sitting up on the roof of the old barn. It became a sport to see how many birds they could hit back then. However, as it turned out on this fall day, Robert's hunting trip would not be as fun or as successful of a venture.

Suddenly, an explosive gunshot shattered the stillness and subtle beauty of their morning trek. Somewhere in the distant on a nearby ridge, a hunter had taken aim through his rifle scope on the two boy's movements. The man's rifles' powerful bullet ripped straight through our son's right arm with an impact like that of a mule's kick. The deadly bullet continued, plunging into Anthony's lower abdomen, ricocheting and slicing through his colon, and then exiting out his backside. The two dazed youth found themselves crashing to the earth, their lives drastically changed in a split second by a careless hunter's gunshot. The next thing my son remembered was hearing the recoil of the rifle after the bullet had left the rifle's chamber.

As both Robert and Anthony lay in a crumpled heap on that wooded trail, the world around them seemed canvassed in an eerie fogginess and a shadowy, foreboding atmosphere. Not realizing yet what had just happened Robert decided to get back up on his feet. He made a concerted effort to push upward with his two arms, but the right arm collapsed with no ounce of strength left in it. Our son, Robert, then shoved himself up with his one good arm and he noticed a man on the upper slope lying prone with his gun and scope aimed towards their position. When a second bullet whizzed past his head, he realized that they were under fire from some crazed hunter.

He screamed, "I've been shot!" Robert hollered.

Pinned down with his face in the muddy trail, our son couldn't hear any response from his fallen friend. Needing to get up from his prone position to check on his injured buddy, he yelled at the shooter on the ridge in order to bluff the man.

"Quit your shooting or we'll shoot back at you, mister!" He cried out.

My son's head was beginning to drift into a fog, and yet he was vaguely aware of someone tromping through the underbrush some fifty yards below them and getting closer. The next thing he recalled was being aware that his other friend, Mac, (not his real name) had finally reached their location with his rifle drawn as if ready to shoot in the vicinity of the lone hunter.

"Stop shooting or I'll fire back!!" This last emphatic demand came from Anthony's older brother, who was standing there with his rifle ready to return fire towards the other hunter. The man must've been shocked at discovering that there were more than two people in this hunting party, because he stopped firing his 45-70' rifle. (This type of weapon is usually used to kill elephants) The teenager could hear the man beating a hasty retreat through the brush a few seconds later. The man left the scene without any offer of help to remedy what he had just done to the two teens. Anthony's older brother, Mac, stood his ground waiting to make sure the man did not return to the scene or attempt to shoot his gun again.

After waiting momentarily, the injured teen's father began climbing the incline to get a better view of the situation. Once he was confident the hunter had departed and was no longer a threat to his family, he then proceeded rather hastily up the sloping incline where he found the two teens lying face down in the dirt and rocks. Approaching the injured boy, he realized teen's arm didn't look good. Visibly shaken, Thomas wrapped a shirt around Robert's bleeding forearm. Apparently, the bullet had sliced through his arm muscle and somehow it had managed to pass right between the two thin bones in his arm. If it had hit the bones, then the bullet would have shattered the bone and at the same time it would have taken away his upper arm section as well. After realizing that my son's wound was not fatal, he then attended to his own injured son. As this distraught father looked over his son's body, he soon discovered his sixteen-year-old son had been shot in the abdomen. The bullet had exited out his backside. This father groaned as he cradled his son in his arms while thinking to himself, *this looks bad. My son may not make it to the hospital alive.*

Gathering his wits, our friend picked his wounded son up, and with Mac's help they began moving the two injured teens back down the hill to SUV, several hundred yards away. Mac supported his friend, Robert, with one arm as they started walking, and held his younger brother's legs with his other hand when his dad asked him to do so. A short way down the hill, our son began to black-out, unable to see anything in front of him. It was then as he was recounting the incident that our son told us how he'd heard these words resounding clearly within his heart, "I am not finished with you yet, Robert." Later, as he shared this part of the experience with us, he believed that this phrase had come from God. In the next few seconds, the trees and green foliage reappeared in front of him, and our son took two huge breaths into his lungs and tried to ignore the throbbing pain in his arm. The shock of being attacked was beginning to wear off, and he could feel the burning pain in his arm with each awkward, pressing step. When the group finally reached the car, Thomas told his oldest son to drive the vehicle and to head straight for a fire station he remembered passing on the drive up. Thomas shared with me that he sat in the back seat holding his wounded son.

When they reached the fire station, the older brother leaped out of the vehicle and raced over to pound on the front door of the brick building. After a fireman opened the door and listened to the frantic young man's description of the gunshot wounds, he rushed inside to gather the paramedics. Because of a prior trip to an accident, an EMT vehicle was still next to the fire station. The firemen helped carry the two injured boys into the back of this vehicle, and the paramedics rushed the two injured boys to the closest hospital which was nearly forty miles away. Anthony's father and his brother followed behind the ambulance still in disbelief over what had just transpired. Hoping to get his dad's mind off his brother's desperate situation the oldest son, Mac, told his father to make sure to call home as soon as they reached the hospital to let the family know about the boy's injuries. Then he focused all his attention on following close behind the emergency vehicle with its flashing lights. By the time they came to a halt in front of the ER entrance to the hospital, nearly an hour had passed from the time of the initial shooting.

Meanwhile back in our hometown, one of the family members called our church pastor and informed them of the emergency involving the two teenagers. Then the pastor took the initiative to call our home phone number to get in touch with us. Since we were out of town for a much-needed retreat, one of our relatives had to keep calling the entire group of Motel 6's phone numbers in the Columbia River Gorge area until they were able to locate my husband and give him the startling news. While driving the hour and a half trip to the hospital, my husband and I tried to comprehend this unreal situation.

"Gosh, I don't understand what happened to the boys. Did our pastor friend tell you anymore details?" I asked my husband. "From the phone call information, it sounded as if there had been a small war waged against our son and his friend."

This entire morning after receiving the horrible phone call, I'd been in complete disbelief that this bizarre attack had happened. I finally found my voice and asked a question to my husband. "Why would anyone want to shoot two innocent teenagers who were wearing their hunter safety clothing while hiking in the forest? It just doesn't make any sense to me. I can't believe this has happened to them." He didn't have an answer at this moment and so we just began to pray for the healing and safety of these two teenagers. With very little information to go on we knew we needed to pray for our son's recovery from the gunshot wound and that his friend wouldn't die from his serious wounds. We also prayed for the authorities to be able to discover the name of the hunter so they could apprehend him. Eventually, the police learned the name of the hunter who had wounded our son and his teenage friend.

Upon arriving at the hospital, we rushed inside to locate our son. We learned more of the details about this awful incident from others who were already up at the hospital and waiting for more news from the medical staff. We were so relieved to see our two pastor friends waiting for us there as we walked into the hospital foyer. Knowing that they had alerted the prayer teams from our church to begin interceding for the teens was a tremendous support to me. I was anxious to locate the emergency room where our son was located. In my numbness, I only noticed the expanse of white colors all around us. There were stark white walls, white medical coats on people, and ivory tinted faces of nurses. I can still remember our concern as the medical staff worked on our son's arm to get him ready for the surgery procedure. Our son, Robert, told us they could not give him pain pills yet and he was writhing and thrashing about in agony while they inspected his wound. Aunt Cindy was standing next to our son trying to comfort him by rubbing his chest. Uncle Don was standing nearby this scene. When he looked up to see us coming into the hospital room, I saw a look of relief spread across his face.

The most difficult part for me as I saw my teenage son being tended to by the medical team was listening to him attempt to talk with us. It was very emotional for us as parents to see him breakdown crying as he said these words, "Mom, I thought I was going to die. I didn't think I would see my girlfriend again and the doctors said I could've lost my arm if it had hit the radius bone." Our son exclaimed.

He also shared with me this gruesome detail which he'd seen while in the pre-op time. "Mom, I saw my open wound that day in the hospital and it was a terrifying sight. Parts of my shredded muscle was hanging loosely from my wounded arm. It shocked me and I wondered if I'd be able to fully regain the use of my arm muscle again." He said with emotion.

It was at this moment that I recalled the strong premonition about my son possibly losing his arm. I felt so very grateful to the Lord for answering my continued prayers for his safety and to protect his arm from serious harm long before he'd ever thought about going hunting that year.

Later, that same week, we heard from our son's physician that this large 40 caliber bullet must have had eyes because it missed hitting either of the two arm bones and the main portion of Robert's arm muscle, thus preventing his right arm from being shattered and torn completely off. A week later, Robert's surgeon told him that if his arm has been ripped off from the impact of the bullet, it would have come off near the shoulder area. The doctor went on to inform our son that this could've been much worse. When a person loses a limb in this manner there is nothing left to be able to apply a tourniquet to in order to staunch the blood flow and therefore, the injured person will die before they can get to the hospital. This was a shocking piece of information for us to hear about this type of gunshot injury.

The doctor also told the other parents that the same bullet was slowed down considerably after hitting our son's arm muscle. As this one bullet travelled on into the sixteen-year-olds abdomen, it didn't hit him with the normal mushrooming affect. The doctor also informed Anthony Evan's parents that somehow this large caliber bullet had been redirected just enough to miss their teenage son's spine by an eighth of an inch. This prevented Anthony from being paralyzed that day. We were amazed to learn about these medical facts. Both teenagers were spared a worst injury or possible death blow from that oversized bullet. It was becoming more and more apparent that God had intervened on their behalf. These two teenagers had been struck down, but not killed by a crazed hunter that day in the woods.

The next four days passed by us in what seemed to me like an almost unreal blur of hospital activities and untold hours of waiting and praying for the boys to recover from their surgeries and the frightening ordeal. The second day, a female reporter from Channel Two news in Portland came to interview our son and his friend's father concerning the shooting. After hearing about the incident on the nightly news some kindhearted folks offered my husband and I a place to stay for the next four days. It was located just a few blocks from the hospital, so we were able to be close by the hospital. This was a real blessing and we told them just how thankful and appreciative we were for their kindness and hospitality. Another family offered their spare room for the other injured teen's parents. We were able to be supportive to this teenage friend and his parents during that exhausting and emotional week as our son's friend went through the first of his two surgeries to begin the process of repairing his colon.

During this weeklong stay at the out-of-town hospital, we talked with our sixteen-year-old daughter, Sharon, who had been taking care of our three youngest girls. She told us that she had talked with her brother, Robert, the night before this happened. She recalled feeling strongly impressed to pray for his safety and I was truly grateful for her immediate response to this distinct prompting. I also want to acknowledge at this time just how thankful I was that she took care of her younger sisters that week while we had to stay close by the hospital. Thank you, for caring for your brother enough to pray for him on this hunting trip. Our son was allowed to go home after that first week since we promised the doctor that we would tend to his dressings properly. Unfortunately for my son, he had to return to the hospital for a second surgery so the doctor could cauterize the wound to promote proper healing. A college classmate was kind enough to drive him the hour and half to the next city for this surgery because he couldn't drive properly now that his right arm was in a sling.

That following month we were very happy to have our son home with us during his few weeks of recovery time. However, as glad as I was to have him nearby, when it came to cleaning out the infected wound in our kitchen, I found myself unable to look at the spot or clean out the pus in his wound. It was dreadful looking and caused me to back away quickly. Therefore, my son had the unfortunate job of cleaning out his own wound. I have to admit, I do not do well at the sight of blood or seeing someone in great pain; I guess I am the squeamish type. I admit I would not do well in a job in the medical field.

Eventually, he was able to return to college and his studies with the help of a good friend. She helped our son take his exams by writing down his answers for him since he couldn't use his right arm at this time. The recovery was slow and painful in more ways than just the physical. These two teens had to deal with nightmares, anger issues, and a sense of resentment which slowly took its toll on their emotional well-being that year and for many years thereafter. I wished our son had taken the advice of a wise person who suggested that he spend some time with a grief counselor in order to better process the anger he experienced towards the man who had shot him. Just recently, my son and I were discussing this incident so I could get a clearer picture of how he felt after being shot.

"Well, mom, I was so angry with this man for shooting me and my good friend that I wanted to take my good left hand and choke him." Robert remarked vehemently.

I understood that my son was experiencing some conflicting emotions at that time. During the first week while he was recovering in the hospital, the police investigator was able to talk with the landowner who informed him of the shooter's name and his location on the Oregon seacoast. The one boy's father and my husband then contacted a proficient lawyer who began to quickly freeze the hunter's bank accounts. He informed us that this man had homeowners' insurance which would cover the ensuing lawsuit brought against him. During that time, I received a phone call from this hunter who tried to apologize to me for hurting my son. He offered to give me his elephant rifle as some type of penance act as if this would console me or placate us. I suppose this man was trying to make some amends for his act of violence towards my son, however whatever the reason, his offer was so unreal to me at the time that I didn't know quite how to respond; so, I just said, "Mister, I don't want your rifle". Who in their right mind offers an upset, grieving mother the very same hunting rifle that almost tore her son's right arm off and came close to killing her son's best friend? If I had taken his elephant rifle, which is almost illegal to hunt with, I might have thrown it into the river since I was so upset with him. However, this act wouldn't have been smart since the police needed this rifle as evidence in the ongoing court case against this hunter.

Once the detective, who was hired from the St. Helens prosecutor's team, had talked with my son, he was able to gain a much clearer idea of the incident which occurred in the woods that day. To help in his investigation, this same detective requested that the older teen drive back to the exact spot to re-enact the incident for him. The man took notes as he listened to our son's friend's give detailed descriptions of the colorful clothing they'd worn, the type of rifle and its powerful scope that the shooter had used, the clear day with perfect visibility, and the fact that the hunter had fired at them twice. The detective became convinced that they should begin prosecuting this man to the full extent of the law. Nearly a year later in 1994, the case went to trial; the hunter did not show up for this hearing. He was indicted on fourteen counts of negligent wounding and lost the right to ever hunt again. This hunter was forced to pay for both boys' hospital costs and to give them a substantial amount of money for personal injuries, which by the way was barely enough to compensate for their traumatic experiences.

The doctor had told our son right before doing the surgery on his injured arm that he wouldn't have full use of his arm and hand. However, we give God all the credit and glory for strengthening his arm since this doctor's report did not come to pass. Our son only lost twenty percent of the strength of his arm muscle, and he still has a functioning left arm today even though he bears the ugly scar from the bullet and surgery. Most definitely, our son was spared a lifetime of devastation and sorrow because he did not lose his entire arm from the hunter's bullet. Even though he'd experienced God's divine intervention that day, he realized almost two years later that he was still very angry with this man for what had happened to him and his younger friend.

Our son eventually worked through his bitterness towards this hunter, thank heavens! Robert started to telling folks that he won't ever go deer hunting with a gun now. Instead, the two buddies have decided that they will only venture out in the woods to hunt with a bows and arrows. Whenever I listen to their discussions about future hunting expeditions, I usually hear them refer to this scenario: they feel that it would be safer to go during the season of bow hunting since they think most bow hunters are more intelligent and less prone to drink alcohol while sitting in the woods for days at a time and far less likely to shoot someone in haste as well.

A few years after this event, I spoke with Anthony's father, Thomas Evans, (not his actual name) more about his initial reaction and thoughts about his son's brush with death. This is what he shared with me.

These were the heart -rending words which his injured son had spoken aloud as he was being carried to the vehicle. The father told me that his son said this to him while being held in his father's arms, "Dad, if die, I love you."

As I listened to this father right then, I felt as if I was there in the woods walking with them and I tried to imagine how he must've felt that dreadful morning as he looked upon his seriously wounded teen. Thomas mentioned to me about how worried he'd been that his injured son might die before they reached the hospital which was miles away from the woods. As I listened to him tell this part of his story, I thought to myself, this must have been a gut-wrenching time for our friend.

Then I asked him what he remembered about the first meeting with the doctor in the hospital that morning. He shared with me how the attending surgeon was telling him that to his amazement, this teen's life had been spared. Even though this doctor did not believe in God or miracles, what this doctor had described to the parents sounded very much like a miracle and certainly a divine intervention.

The doctor had explained to Thomas another fact which was this: He mentioned that since his sixteen-year-old son had been bleeding from his mouth, it was not a good sign. The doctor had told the parents that after working on their son's stomach, he could tell that the bullet had sliced through the spleen and then ripped off the colon wall. Since there was only a non-structural liner holding his colon together it seemed almost impossible for this thin membrane to still hold up given the fact that an entire hour had transpired before they'd brought him into the ER. If the colon had burst (which it should have since there was only the fragile liner holding his colon in position) then peritonitis would have set in within thirty seconds. And they were told by the doctor that this type of complication can cause death for the injured patient.

The next significant miracle about this shooting incident was that the hunter's bullet didn't mushroom like a bullet usually did. Then there was the other fact that it missed this teen's spine by an eighth of an inch and this was amazing too. If the bullet had hit Anthony's vertebrae, then it would have severed his spine in half. This all seemed slightly impossible to the medical doctor and yet, he couldn't deny the absolute fact that this teenager had been kept alive by some unseen force at work. Besides these two details, there was one more aspect of this story to share; the doctor also informed the parents that the shattered shrapnel had managed to seal off the bleeding areas to help prevent serious loss of blood during the long trip to the Emergency Room that day. I believe God heard the prayers of our daughter along with the other mother's prayer for her son's protection during that hunting trip.

Being a good friend of the Evans family, I was shaken up by how close they'd come to experiencing a potential tragedy. It was almost unbearable for me to fathom. This couple had almost lost their teenage son. After hearing everything the doctor had shared with our friend, I was truly grateful that their teenage son had not died that day in the woods. We are so thankful that our son still has the use of both of his arms. A few years after this awful ordeal happened, our son married a beautiful young woman whom we all love, and they now have three beautiful children. He had always wanted to be a policeman and so he went through the academy and passed all of his tests to become an officer of the law. Our son eventually became a gift of hope for one of his siblings as you will discover later in our family story. I believe that when I received that strange premonition about my son possibly losing his arm it caused me to persevere in constant prayer for his well-being. To this day, I am very thankful to my heavenly Father for giving me that specific warning premonition about my son when he was a young adult.

Our eldest son, Robert, had been married for two months and it seemed that he'd been suffering from a pain in his abdomen. He called me while I was out at Yale Lake with my youngest daughter and her four friends celebrating her eighth birthday. My son sounded awful as he talked to me on the phone. He mentioned that his wife was taking him to the ER because he was very ill and throwing up. Call it intuition or a mother's instincts, but I believed Robert was suffering from appendicitis. With this strong impression in my mind, I decided to quickly gather my two young daughters and their four friends into our small Mazda car and drove the hour back home to drop all these youngsters at my good friend's house. I asked her to watch my two daughters while I drove 205 Bridge to be with my son. It turned out to be two days of waiting for the doctors to know what to do for him.

While being there in this hospital, I'd kept trying to get information from his nurse and I felt the strong urge to become Robert's advocate. I was persistent and finally, I went to the nurse's station to ask if we could get a different doctor to come and reexamine him. This finally happened and after twenty minutes of examining my son, this diligent physician decided to cancel the ultrasound and have the staff prep him for exploratory surgery. I was elated upon hearing the physician's answer after waiting for nearly two days with my son. I went to call my friend to pray an agreement prayer for my son's safety. When the doctor returned to give me his medical report of the surgery, he informed me that as he was removing the appendices, it literally burst in his hand. We were astounded and very grateful to God for preserving our son's life again. The doctor told me that usually when an appendix bursts inside of a person' body it can cause the patient to die from the toxins spreading throughout the abdomen. I knew that God had spared my son that day.

When our teenage son, Robert, was driving a van full of his teenage friends one evening a drunken motorist going eighty-five mph crashed into the van and injured our son. He had to have knee surgery to repair a torn ligament. One teenage girl was knocked unconscious for a short time. The other teenagers' injuries were minor lacerations and whiplash. Months before this accident, I had a vision of three EMT vehicles arriving at the scene of an accident with their lights flashing. This scene caused me to be very concerned since we had three teenagers driving that year. I prayed often for their safety after getting that vision; I believe God protected our son and his friends from life threatening injuries that night. The claims adjuster informed our son and the other front seat passenger that when these kinds of car crashes occurred, they've seen how the impact can cause the front seat to flip backward and cause a fatal neck injury for the person driving the car. Miraculously, Robert only received a serious injury to his knee ligament during this crash. The truth is that three different emergency vehicles with lights flashing had indeed arrived at the accident and the paramedics transported the group of teenagers to the hospital that evening just like what I'd seen in my vision many months before this awful accident occurred.

About four years later, our son was working as a security guard for the Bonneville Power Company. It was a decent job and would look good on any future job resumes. He eventually applied for and was accepted to police academy based in Shelton, Washington. Being an officer has been his lifelong aspiration and our adult son had passed the six months training and was a determined officer ready to apprehend anyone who decided to break the law. During his first four years in law enforcement, his superior asked him, as a sergeant, to go under cover for a few months in order to observe and eventually apprehend a couple of corrupt officers who were taking money unlawfully. Of course, he had to keep his name out of any emails or written reports in order to keep his family safe from any kind of retaliation after that incident. We all understand that being a police officer can be a dangerous job and yet, for the most part it is very rewarding occupation. For instance, a few years later, he was attacked by three convicted felons and survived this onslaught. One time our son's wife had a dream of some criminal trying to stab him in the back with a knife. When she shared her concern with me, I told her it was time to pray more earnestly for his safety as a police officer.

Our son was also attacked by a "Murder Two" assailant who had been hyped up on drugs. It took four officers to assist in arresting this enraged individual that day. The result of this confrontation was that he had to have major knee surgery and hand surgery and he was off work for one year to get physical therapy. He's glad to be alive after all these vicious attacks on his life. As to this date, our firstborn son is a part-time pastor of a Latino Church, and he is on a special police unit that goes on deployment assignments to locate and apprehend escaped fugitives as well as on calls for search and rescue missions in the state of Washington. We were very grateful that God had delivered our son from these life-threatening situations and a few years later he'd be there for his younger sibling as she'd been there for him when he was a teenager. In August of 1998, Robert's sister would need a perfect match donor in order to survive a horrible disease which would threaten her very existence. In my estimations, our son, Robert, is a true hero and we are very proud of this young man.

CHAPTER TEN

Our first daughter, Sharon, was very active and competitive girl growing up. She was an excellent student, avid reader of books, and an intensely serious athlete. She played soccer from the age of ten until entering college. During high school she played on the varsity team all four years for the public high school even though she was enrolled at a private high school in Portland, Oregon. During her senior year of playing with her teammates, she injured her ACL and needed surgery. This prevented her from finishing the soccer season. This was very disappointing for our daughter. After graduation, she still played indoor soccer where she again injured the other knee and tore her other ACL requiring a second surgery and painful recovery and physical therapy. It was during these early adult years that our oldest daughter became sick with something much worse than the flu. When she was only twenty-one years of age, she was admitted to the hospital to keep her from dying from a serious blood disease called leukemia. This diagnosis turned into a major battle for our daughter's life, and it captured the attention of our family, friends, and people we didn't even know.

Let me share with you the side stories that involved our daughter's siblings who went through this gut-wrenching time with their sister in 1998. Some years later, I had been writing in my journal book about our daughter's battle with cancer and I felt impressed to ask our young adult children how they had felt as they visited her in the hospital that first month. I could imagine they were wondering if their sister would survive this horrendous battle against leukemia. The first to share was my son and his wife. This is how they felt when they first heard the news of their sister's unexpected trip to the hospital that Sunday in August.

"As soon as I got this awful news from my mom, I changed clothes and drove my wife up to the hospital in Oregon to be with my sister. When she showed me the purplish bruises on her body, it looked as if someone had hit her with a baseball bat to create these huge, dark bruises." Our son shared these next words and he started to get emotional. "Since we learned that the doctors would not be able to give a sufficient diagnosis for two more days, I decided to take my pregnant wife home to rest and wait to hear more news."

"Son, what were some of your immediate thoughts about everything the doctors finally shared with us two days later concerning your ill sister?" I asked.

"Well, Mom, I didn't like learning from the doctors that she was dealing with the worst-case scenario called Acute Myalogenos Leukemia and that it was the most aggressive form of this type of disease and that she had a compromised immune system now. Plus, on top of this bad news the doctors also told us that she probably had only three months to live! This was the ultimate shocker for me."

"Wow, son I never heard this last dreadful piece of information the first week while we were at the hospital. I wonder why I wasn't informed of this." I replied.

"Maybe you didn't hear about it because she was twenty-one years old, an adult woman now, and they weren't required to share everything about her condition to her parents."

"Oh, I see, you're probably right about this." I responded sadly.

"Then I came to visit my daughter every night after work to sit by her bedside and pray for her. I found myself heading for the small hospital chapel to pray and petition God on her behalf." He stated.

"That was the same thing I would do each day and night while I slept at the hospital that first week as well. I would like to hear what your wife thought about this difficult ordeal as well." I had tried to switch the conversation over to her to give my son some time to collect his thoughts and to gain control of his emotions. Our daughter-in-law came on the phone to chat with me, and I asked her how she had felt back when my daughter was admitted to the hospital for treatment for this very serious disease.

"Since I didn't know anything about leukemia, at first, I didn't think this was a very serious problem for her. When my husband took me to the hospital to see his sister and I saw the huge number of bruises or (discolorations) on her body; I was shocked. After learning more from the Oncology doctors about her serious illness I felt worried and a mixture of unbelief and more shock with this horrible news. I was pregnant with our son and my emotions were like a rollercoaster ride that week. I called my parents who lived down in Mexico at this time and asked them to please pray for her since she was fighting for her life. I also realized how important it was to join him in going to the hospital to be with her every night for a while." She replied.

I thanked her for sharing her thoughts and got off the phone to reflect on that emotionally packed first week when we'd almost lost our daughter to this dreaded disease. I was thankful that they had both shared with me and given me their perspective on our family ordeal. I was quite grateful that we could talk so easily about this dreadful experience twelve years later. Have you heard the old saying, time heals all wounds? Well, in this situation time didn't necessarily heal or take away the bad memories or the grief that each of our children experienced while they watched her fighting to live against all odds. Some of our family members may still need to have counseling for their grief. I've come to realize just how much this crisis event in her life affected our entire family. My continued prayer for all of us is that God's love will heal our souls and heal our daughter's memories of the horror she suffered during that year of fighting for her life and undergoing extreme radiation.

The difficulty I experienced during the first week of her hospitalization was feeling like a displaced mother and had turned to another person to stay with her that week and my son wasn't happy about this situation. Being the oldest of our children, our son felt the responsibility of maintaining our family unit and to him this meant having only one mother in the hospital for his very ill sister. Even though I was feeling left out and sad about this new development, I didn't care to force the issue. I was more concerned about my daughter staying alive! I think my daughter didn't feel like she could trust my responses to her health crisis. She was twenty-one years old at this time and had the right to not tell her parents everything as she fought for her life. While our daughter was so ill and lying there in the hospital my only concern had been for her well-being and recovery. Honestly, the only way our family would be able to get through this ordeal would be with God's help and the support of everyone connected to Sharon and thus, I was thankful for this other woman's involvement in the hospital that first week. Eventually, this difficult situation with Sharon's advocate friend worked its way around to our family becoming more unified and she had to go back home and take care of her own three kids and husband. Another troublesome problem for me was the challenge of finding a place to stay after the first week in the hospital. For the first four nights I'd managed to sleep somewhat comfortably on sofa in the hospital chapel, until one of the medical staff learned that I was there and requested that I find a more suitable place to sleep.

Because I didn't want to leave my daughter during her battle with cancer, I drove six miles from the hospital to ask my friends if I could stay with them for a while. They graciously invited me to stay if I needed in order to be close to my sick daughter. During my time of great need, they were a marvelous, generous caring couple. I was extremely grateful for their hospitality, meals, kindness and prayers during that time. While I was staying with these dear friends, I had a vision about Sharon.

During this inspired vision, I saw my daughter being held in her Savior's strong arms. I noticed that her arms were wrapped around his neck, and I was following them both by placing my feet into the Lord's footprints as he walked ahead of me. It was almost as if Jesus wanted me to stay close to him in this terrible journey and follow his leading every day. So that is exactly what I tried to do throughout this frightening ordeal.

It was also during this time as I would take walks around a quiet neighborhood that I proclaimed this declaration from scripture each day: "(Sharon) shall not die, but live, and declare the works of the Lord." (Psalm 118: 17 KJV) I also began to ask God for a specific request. I wanted to see this happen that the doctor would put in writing and add his signature to his professional estimation on paper stating this fact: Our daughter, Sharon, was in remission and then she could hold the official paperwork up to the world as documented proof of God's healing, delivering power! God must've grown weary of me making this request so much because He chose to answer all our prayers by the fourth week, and she now has that specific paperwork signed by her physician and enclosed inside her hospital photo album. She can pull out that physician's signed paper today and show it to anyone who is interested in hearing her miracle story.

One other problem faced our daughter during her first month stay in the hospital. Some of the prayer support people who brought in food for our family also thought it would be a great idea to stick up papers on her bedroom wall in the hospital. On each page they had written scripture verses to encourage her to believe for her healing miracle. Having faced death twice in one month, our daughter had decided she didn't want to allow anyone to control her environment. She insisted that the hanging pages of words be taken down. I agreed with my daughter in this matter since I could easily declare these scriptures as I walked up the flight of stairs to her hospital room each day. She needed to have control in her world where she felt it was out of control. She needed people to have faith and to encourage her from a distance. I was glad that she could voice her feelings, and no one needed to be offended by her decision.

At the beginning of this challenging week in the hospital, she had been facing a daunting giant called cancer and I wondered if she'd lose this battle. During this time, I'd wanted desperately to believe for my daughter's health and recovery. The medical team began an aggressive round of chemo drugs to save her life. One day, my daughter's good friend shared with me some important and powerful words which I later chose to incorporate into my daily prayers. She said these words to me: "God hears the sincere cry of a mother's heart! So pour your heart out to Him and watch what God will do in this situation for your daughter". I went into the hospital's small chapel that night and wrote my prayer request in the chaplain's book lying open there on the pedestal stand. I began to cry out to the living God to rescue my precious daughter from this evil disease. As I waited there in the stillness of the night, wondering what would happen to my girl, I heard the Spirit of the Lord share this insight within my spirit: *If you will fast for six days on the seventh day, I will give you a victory.* I took this divine promise to heart and began to fast for seven days in faith. Eventually, a family member learned of my commitment to fast from food, and they passed this information on to another friend in our church and soon the youth pastor was encouraging his staff and youth group to join with our family in fasting for Sharon's recovery. Her red blood cells were low and so she had to have a blood transfusion to replace the blood that the chemo had destroyed. On the seventh day of my fasting, we received encouraging news from the doctors. Our daughter was beginning to respond to the strong doses of chemo. We were told that she was not in immediate danger of dying because her body was responding to the intense chemotherapy measures and the doctors were much more hopeful at this point.

During that first week in the hospital, a dear, older friend named Harry informed us that his wife, Liz', had a vision while she had been sitting in church worshipping the Lord and it was about our ill daughter being visited by angels in the hospital. She described her vision from God to her husband and then he typed this beautiful vision onto paper to give it to my husband. His wife had shared about seeing angels and she stated that they were bringing gifts of healing and love to our daughter while she was there in the hospital.

I started to envision an army of angels walking through the halls of this hospital to minister to my daughter. Even though her dynamic healing didn't occur like some of the amazing miracles in the Bible did in just one day, nevertheless, God's intervention on her behalf was just as powerful and exciting. That month of praying every day for our daughter had been very stressful and overwhelming for our family. We finally had something to celebrate on the day she was wheeled out of the hospital a month later in September. I recognize that it took many relatives along with a host of faithful people interceding for this sick daughter to bring about this powerful life-giving miracle and we are truly grateful for everyone's faith and prayer support.

After that first week in the hospital and the evidence of a breakthrough in our daughter's battle, my oldest son arrived at the hospital to visit his sister again. I'd felt strongly impressed to have him lay his two hands on her head and begin to intercede for her health. Next, I felt that we were also to praise God for his goodness and mercy for the next seven days and expect another miracle from God's hand on behalf of our daughter. We proceeded to walk in this new and unusual type of spiritual warfare and saw even more progress in our daughter's situation. The following week our youth pastor suggested the youth group might want to shave their heads in support of my daughter's fight for her life. Surprisingly, some of the teens did shave their hair off completely for Sharon. They also made up a new slogan about this medical challenge by coining the phrase 'Saving Private Sharon' which had been used originally in the war movie about finding a soldier during WWII. From that point on, the youth in our church began to intercede for our daughter with greater intensity and fervor. Thankfully, things began to turn around for our very sick daughter in the next two weeks. The God of miracles was doing a mighty work on our daughter's behalf. She was still alive and there was a renewed hope for her to get well and leave the hospital soon.

During this first month in the hospital, I was struggling with the strict guidelines that some relatives wanted to establish in order to keep our very ill daughter from encountering germs and viruses which could be carried into the hospital by unsuspecting visitors or friends. I didn't appreciate being told to not visit my own daughter one day by a well-meaning relative and so to avoid any opposition, I took a different longer route in order to reach her hospital room the following day. At the end of that week, I finally mentioned this problem to my daughter, and she decided to contact our pastor's secretary about this brand-new problem. This friend from our church stepped in to help communicate our daughter's new wishes to the family members who were monitoring her constant stream of well-wishers and friends. At one point during those first two weeks, there must've been a hundred visitors wanting to see her and bring gifts. Our ill daughter needed to make a stipulation to the relatives who were monitoring things in the waiting room by presenting them with a list of all the people she'd allowed to come visit her in the hospital that month. This list of names included her parents, her siblings, her closest friends, and her pastor. I was thrilled to see how she'd managed to solve this stressful situation by involving a mediator/friend who was willing come to the hospital and be her advocate.

There were several other incidents that threatened our daughter's well-being during this first horrific month in the hospital. Each time I learned about her next health issue; I would make another phone call to my wonderful friends to request more prayer support. At one point, I beseeched God to take my life in place of my ill child; I would have willingly allowed God to stop my life here on earth if I could have given her back her health and well-being. Somewhere in the middle of this challenging month of hospitalization, I made the choice to surrender my daughter to the Lord. I made this statement to the heavens, "not my will be done, but your will be accomplished with her life, Father God".

I was driving home from the hospital one afternoon after spending a few hours with my ill daughter when a song came on the radio. This song made me cry because of what the musician was saying in the lyrics. I hear the words of this song that day and they made me get in touch with my true feelings of pain and deep sorrow about my daughter. The music and its words spoke powerfully to my own grief, my helplessness and my inner soulful cry for our precious daughter's healing. Even though there were hundreds of people coming in and out of her hospital bedroom that first month to love, encourage, and pray for her, our weakened daughter told me that she had to finally cry out to God on her own to make it through this horrible ordeal.

Our daughter was finished with the large doses of chemo eventually and she was sleeping for longer stretches of time each day. During the following week, she was inundated with numerous friends and well-wishers coming up to see her at the hospital. This continual flow of visitors began to take its toll on her. I looked in on my weak daughter one morning and realized that she was trying too hard to be her usual pleasant, gracious, humorous self with everyone who entered her room. I sensed in my heart that something was not right with this situation. My concerns were that she was afraid to be herself or be real with these friends. I began to wonder if she was falling into the trap of being a people pleaser.

How could I communicate this new concern I had with my daughter? I wanted to somehow express to my daughter that it was okay for her to get upset with God and her parents. I hoped that she would understand that God knew what she was feeling inside her heart. It was important that my daughter take the time to be honest with Him.

One day when I walked into her hospital room where she was resting and trying to appear pleasant and hospitable to the visitors, I knew I needed to speak to her about this. She was trying to make it okay for these well-wishers and kindhearted friends even though she was struggling with grief and despair in her own life. I noticed that she'd put on her happy face with all the friends who came to visit her. It seemed apparent to me that she was responding to their expectations in an unreal manner even though she was suffering great pain and loss.

As a mother, this was hurting my heart. I was watching her put on a happy face for people. She needed to let her friends know how difficult this ordeal was for her. I felt the need to find a way to help her be real and honest with people. It wasn't her job to make people feel comfortable as they visited her in the hospital. I waited until she was all alone and choose my words carefully. "Young lady, you do not have to entertain all these visitors and friends. You do not have to be so strong and caring right now. It is all right to get real and honest with God about how you are really feeling during this devastating time. This has been the worst experience of your life. You need to share your honest thoughts with someone who is a good friend to you. Since God already knows how you feel and what's going on inside of your broken heart, it's okay to express your feelings to Him. God can handle your emotions and feelings of anger or disappointments." I expressed to my daughter.

After speaking into her life, I could only pray that she would get honest with her heavenly Father and become free to be herself in the process. I learned later during her year of recovery that my daughter had indeed taken my words to heart. That afternoon she'd called a friend to make an announcement at church asking that all the visitors stop coming for a while. My good friend, Janice, the week before this episode, had encouraged me to be totally real with God about my own feelings and grief. As I drove home from her school office that hot day in August, I knew Janice had been correct in her advice to me. Once I'd arrived at our house in the country, I walked towards the old barn and stopped to take a moment to express my fears and true feelings of anguish and frustrations. After that heartfelt, truthful explosion of feelings and angry words towards heaven, I felt much better. I had to believe that this same kind of honest communication would also help my struggling daughter. We were all grateful that people cared enough for her well-being to give her space and time to heal after expressing her true feelings. She was now free to invite the few close friends she needed to sit with her and share her world of pain and deep disappointment.

It is difficult to put into mere words all the trauma and devastation that our young twenty-one-year-old daughter went through during that first month in a hospital and the ensuing month at a larger hospital facility and yet, I will attempt to share her story from her limited memory of this time. One time I recalled how my daughter spoke honestly with me about how she hated lying in bed for so many hours with nothing to do for days and weeks at a time. When friends and well-wishers would come into the room, she would pretend to be asleep, but she could hear them talking about her health issues and tentative condition. This frustrated and bothered her for days; she couldn't handle the number of visitors who wanted to visit and console her or tell her they were praying for her. The few gracious relatives who brought in food to our waiting area the first two weeks tried to help monitor the visitation times for the hundreds of friends and well-wishers trying to see our daughter. Eventually, the medical staff had to limit the number of friends coming to see our sick daughter. At one point in her hospitalization, she had to talk with her friends and ask them to take turns spending the night with her in the room so she could feel safe and get some much-needed rest.

One afternoon I offered to take the night shift to give our daughter's caregiver friend a break. During the long night, I went to find a different bathroom to avoid bringing germs into her personal bathroom. When I returned, I saw that she'd fallen in her small bathroom and needed my help to get back up again. At that time in her recovery, I regretted leaving her even for the short amount of time because I didn't realize that she was so weak and needed someone to be always there for constant supervision. As a mother and a new caregiver, I felt horrible that I hadn't stayed close to her the entire time. As time went by, I learned that there would be other times of regret. She chose to speak her mind to us about situations that had caused her grief. We had to listen and not try to defend ourselves as she confronted both of us about our inadequacies and failures as parents. Even though our daughter was brutally honest in her confrontations with us, I am thankful that she did talk with us; we have a better relationship now with her. She taught us so much during those two long years of her recovery and we are thrilled to be a part of her life today.

CHAPTER ELEVEN

One time during her second week in the hospital, our daughter's entire body was covered with blue and purplish spots, and she itched constantly from this horrible rash as a result of the chemo burn in her body. One morning in the hospital, my daughter voiced her feelings to me one day by saying these words: "Mom I feel as if all my throat, esophagus, and stomach linings have been burnt and I can barely swallow food." It seemed to me as if she was enduring more horrible pain than anyone should have to for those unbearable two weeks of suffering. The doctors discovered that she was allergic to Benadryl and so they had to find another form of medication to alleviate her awful itching and rash problem. This situation was extremely hard physically and emotionally for her. It was quite difficult for me to watch her suffer so much. I felt convinced that she must've wished every day that she could escape this confining hospital room, the needles, and the terrible chemotherapy treatments. I was wishing to have our lives return to normal. She needed another miracle by this time. As the days wore on it seemed to me that nothing short of a powerful encounter with the living God would guarantee this becoming a reality for our young adult daughter. She was a fighter by nature and yet, she was desperately hanging onto God by a slender thread of hope at this point during her second month in a different hospital.

Back when I, as her mother, first received the news of her frightening diagnosis of (AML) or Acute Myeloid Leukemia from her doctors, the news was unbelievable! I was in shock at first and then I broke down and wept that day. As the week progressed for me, it was as if God had begun to wrap me up in a blanket of his love and peace. Yes, there were scary times that first month when I had to turn to my faithful friends and ask them to pray for our daughter. I believe that all the prayers and the kind support we received that entire year made all the difference in the world for me. I wasn't anxious or frightened of this horrible disease anymore. This type of cancer develops quickly and begins in the soft tissue of the bone marrow. The cancer grows from cells that would normally turn into white blood cells. For me, as a mother, the most difficult situation to deal with eventually would turn out to be the comprehension that my firstborn daughter had turned to another mother figure for comfort and help during her crisis. Yes, this new knowledge had become an extra painful emotional issue for me to deal with along with dealing with the fact that she was fighting for her life now.

To be honest, I was not prepared to deal with this extra feelings and conflict. It was only by the capable help of a trusted friend that I was able to handle this new dilemma. I first needed to face my own lack as a mother regarding my relationship with this first daughter before I could forgive her for looking to someone else for comfort and encouragement. Accountability for our own actions and mistakes is often very difficult to accept especially when it concerns our relationship with our offspring. However, I wanted a better, healthier relationship with her and therefore, I was willing to acknowledge my shortcomings and apologize to this daughter. Today, because of her honesty in expressing her frustrations with me and a fair degree of humility on my part, we have a much better relationship. I am grateful for this second chance to be a better person and a more caring friend to my daughter. I enjoy being involved in her life now and make every attempt to be the kind of parent and friend who listens and support her choices in life now that she is free of that horrible leukemia disease.

Just recently, I sat down with our youngest daughter and asked her how she felt back during the horrendous first month of her sister's chemotherapy and hospitalization. This is her story:

Catherine Denise recalled a rather painful experience which related to her sister's battle against cancer. She was in the fourth grade during this crisis in our family. I had returned home after one month of staying in Portland to take care of my young children again. By this time, I was feeling more hopeful about Sharon's future and health issues. She was staying with her capable friend and therefore, I could relax and know that it was okay to have fun again. I wanted to do something with my younger girls and their friends, so I took them to a movie called "A Walk to Remember". I was hoping to treat the girls to a good Nickolas Spark's movie. However, as it turned out my youngest daughter, Catherine Denise did not like the storyline very much. She confided in me much later that she had a dreadful time sitting in this movie because the main character became very ill from leukemia and had died at the end. She was very upset with me for taking her to this troubling movie about such a real-life drama which was very similar to our family situation. I didn't have a clue how she truly felt that day because she kept silent about her grief.

I also had a similar experience when I went to see a movie called "Step Mom" with my friends. I started crying towards the end of the movie because the mother was dying of cancer. After enduring the entire sad movie and seeing this family suffer such heartache, I realized I needed to talk with my third daughter, Kristina, to find out how she'd felt during her sister's illness. This is what my daughter said to me:

"Well, Mom, I remember having to go stay with our friend's family because you needed to stay up at the hospital in Oregon. We were all playing outside and jumping on the trampoline, and I was twelve years old at the time. I felt scared and I wondered just how sick my older sister was since she had to get more tests from the doctors. A friend of the family was staying with our sister in the hospital that day and this woman called the home where I was staying and asked to speak with me; she told me that my sister had cancer and needed to undergo chemotherapy as soon as possible. I asked her if my sister would lose her hair because of this treatment process and her reply to this was this, yes, your sister will eventually lose her hair"

"How did you react to this awful prognosis that evening?" I asked my daughter.

"Oh Mom, I was so sad because I didn't want my sister to lose her beautiful, long hair. Her gorgeous thick auburn hair was such a part of her very personhood. I didn't like the fact that my younger sister and I were barely allowed to visit our sister that first month at the hospital in Oregon; it was as if she had been taken out of our lives and I wanted so much to go see my sister and be a part of her life regardless of the scariness of the prognosis or the apprehensions I may have felt walking into her hospital room then. After spending a week with the first family, we were moved to stay at Patti's home for another week. They had three girls all who were the same ages as us and so it made the time go smoothly.

Then the next place I was taken to stay was another friend's house where I spent fun times playing with their twelve-year-old daughter. The last week of this long month I was invited to stay with my best friend. I was very happy to be staying with her during this ordeal. She had lost her father to cancer just after she was born, and her mom was very kind and understanding of my feelings and emotional turmoil. I was very grateful to be with this family who helped me the most during this time. The third week of her stay in the hospital she lost her hair completely; it was a traumatic change for us all. She still looked beautiful, but fragile and thin, even though her long flowing rich-looking hair was missing. Countless friends and well-wishers brought her cute hats of various sizes, shapes, and colors to help her get through this horrendous loss. She was in a time of grieving and loneliness, and I couldn't imagine how desperately sad she must've felt with this new devastating loss. I could also sense that my sister was trying to pretend everything was fine for my sake the first time I visited her in the hospital and sat by her bedside. I recalled coming the following week with my older brother and his wife to see my sister again and I cried that time." She confided to me.

Yesterday I phoned my son, David, who lives in Wisconsin to get his thoughts and honest reaction to his sister being in the hospital when he was only nineteen years old. I asked him to share his thoughts with me.

"Son, how did you handle the month when your sister was undergoing chemo treatment in the hospital, and we were hardly home for you?" I asked with trepidation.

"I was living in the basement of my high school friend at that time and working a lot too. I spent a good deal of time with my high school girlfriend, and so it was doable for me. As far as the visits to see our sister in the hospital, that was very difficult for me to see my sister suffering physically from the chemo burn throughout her body system. During the middle of this pain-filled month I visited her one more time to support her in her struggle to live. Fortunately, the nurse had left the room, so we were alone and then she made a startling comment to me.

"I can't do this anymore!! I don't want to live like this. It's too hard, the pain and the terrible nights and the drilling into my hip bone to retrieve the bone marrow results is so excruciatingly painful and agonizing. It's too much for me to bear any longer.' She responded.

"She broke down crying right there and I held her hand in a feeble attempt to comfort my sister." The next thing I did was to look her straight in the eye and firmly speak to her very soul essence these words of strength …. "Sis', you can't give up. You're a fighter and you are going to make it. We are all going to be here to support you and to fight alongside of you, sis." Hearing my son's heartfelt comments and the depth of his feelings for his sister made me glad I had asked him to share his thoughts with me that day.

If someone would've asked me back in August of 1998, how I'd felt about seeing my daughter's first month in the first hospital while she was fighting to live, I'm not sure what I would've said. I now have had a few years to consider what I was thinking and feeling during that very painful, trying experience. I can honestly say that during that first six month of her illness, I was literally hanging on to God with both hands hoping and believing for a miracle for our beautiful, gracious daughter.

CHAPTER TWELVE

My faith in God's intervention in people's desperate situations comes from the undeniable promises and true stories I've read in the Holy Scriptures. One example of divine intervention is seen in the Book of Mark where it tells how the Lord healed a man instantly. "…, blind Bartimaeus, the son of Timaeus, sat by the highway side begging. And when he heard that it was Jesus of Nazareth, he began to cry out, and say, Jesus, thou son of David, have mercy on me." I found this next sentence quite interesting as the Lord asked the man this question.

"…,wilt thou that I should do unto thee?"

The blind man said unto him, Lord, that I might receive my sight!" And Jesus said unto him, Go thy way; thy faith hath made thee whole. And immediately he received his sight,…"

The Son of God had compassion on this blind man and healed his eyes. (Mark 10: 46–47 & 49–52)

I believed that our Father God could do the same thing for our beloved daughter. He could touch her life and give her a much-needed miracle. I kept calling upon God and declaring certain healing scriptures from the Bible over our seriously ill daughter. I truly believed that these scripture promises were for all who called upon His name. My faith remained unshaken during the fourth week of her hospitalization as we waited for a miracle of deliverance to happen for our daughter. I was relying upon the Lord's heart of compassion to be extended from heaven towards our beloved girl.

That last week of my daughter's stay in the hospital, a man I didn't know came to visit us in the oncology ward. He mentioned to me that he knew one of our acquaintances who lived in Portland. He asked me if we could pray together for my ill daughter, and I was delighted to have his support that day. We chatted briefly and then he told me he was looking for a specific word to speak over my daughter. I responded by sharing one of my favorite scriptures from the New Testament which states this: "But if the spirit of him that raised up Jesus from the dead dwell in you, he that raised up Christ from the dead will also quicken your mortal bodies by his spirit who dwelleth in you". (Romans 8: 11) This visitor got excited and said that this was the word he was looking for, the 'quickening or life' word to declare over her. So, I invited him into her hospital room to join me in an agreement prayer for her healing. As we both laid hands on her weakened body, I declared that same scripture of life over my weak daughter and he prayed something as well. Then as we continued to pray for my daughter, I heard these powerful words come into my mind, *"The cancer is gone; the cancer is leaving her body"*. I knew that I knew that this thought had come straight from God's heart to my mind and so I accepted it as fact.

Isn't this true, faith is an intangible concept which we believe will produce a living reality of healing for a person who needs a divine intervention in their physical body. Our part in the challenge to expect a miracle for someone is to not allow unbelief to produce any kind of doubt about God's goodness and His ability to heal. A few years later, when I mentioned about this man visiting us in the hospital to my two friends from Portland, they didn't recognize his name. This seemed strange to me and yet, I wasn't that concerned about tracking him down, I was just thankful for his two timely, ordained visits to the hospital. Now as I reflect on this eventful day in the hospital, I wonder if this man had been one of God's messengers sent to bring God's divine healing and wholeness to our ill daughter's weakened body. Then I remembered the vision our friend, Elizabeth, had where she visualized in her spiritual eyesight angels coming into the hospital bringing gifts of healing for our daughter. I rejoiced as I thought back on our friend's beautiful vision from the Lord where he was sending His powerful angel messengers to assist the doctors and to bring healing touches to our daughter during this battle against cancer; these types of supernatural events did happen too. Whoever this man was or wherever he'd come from might still be a mystery to our family, but to this day, I believe this was a part of the divine intervention and miracle provision from God which we'd been asking for that first month of her hospitalization experience in 1998.

Our daughter, Sharon, had been told by the doctors the day before her release that her cancer was in remission, and she could leave the hospital to begin her long-term recovery. However, even though our daughter was now living in a clean-air house with her mentor-friend, she was still having some other difficulties. She asked me to pray for her to stop having horrible nightmares and so I did. It seemed we were engaged in a new kind of battle for our daughters' well-being those next few months. The frightening night terrors were robbing her of valuable sleep and so I asked my daughter's good friend who was a prayer warrior to come over and join me in making strong declarations against this attack. As this young adult and I took authority over this distressing nighttime trouble, our daughter experienced more relief from the nightmares.

A week later she had to go back into the doctor's office for help with her meds. The latest problem facing our daughter was that her protein drink was not flowing correctly through IV tubing to provide her with sufficient nourishment. During this visit, our daughter's oncologist handed her the medical paperwork declaring that she was free of the disease that had threatened to destroy her existence. I rejoiced because this was what I had cried out for to happen for her. Now she is able to show the medical release paper which documents her healing to anyone who asks about her battle with cancer. That first month in the hospital while she was battling to survive, seemed to me to be more like a trial by fire' and yet, the Lord had been right there with her in the fiery furnace of affliction.

During her long time of recovery and rest, she had to be quarantined and stay in a safe, clean environment. All she could do was stay in bed watching movies. She was advised to stay away from the public places and gatherings of people like going to church, the stores, or to theaters. It was a difficult dreary time for our beloved and sociable daughter who had so many caring friends who wanted to visit her. During those few interim months, she had to meet with her oncologist who counseled her to do a precautionary procedure called a bone marrow transplant. The specialist believed that this extra radiation treatment and the transplant procedure would give her the chance to live a much longer life because it had the potential to eradicate any hidden cancer cells in her body. Sharon opted for this procedure.

At first, I was hesitant to trust that an experimental BMT procedure was the best and safest way for someone to go, but as the medical team explained the purpose and the benefits of going this route I started to relax and trust in their medical expertise. Plus, I'd talked with my good friend who was with us during the consultation, and she gave me good counsel and encouragement about what she saw for a future hope for Sharon. This transplant would take another difficult month up at a larger facility in Oregon and then a year of recovery if she didn't get complications from the graft vs. host disease. The doctors told her that because she had the perfect match from her older brother's bone marrow donation that she had a much better chance of avoiding this dangerous grafting disease which can occur in a recovering patient.

We were extremely grateful that our son's life had been spared during that awful shooting incident and it turned out that he was our daughter's perfect bone marrow match. He was happy to give his sister a portion of his bone marrow and the hope for a new, healthier immune system. She had felt death's evil breathe upon her face that year, and yet, she had survived. The following year, as our brave daughter became stronger and more confident of making it to her five-year mark, a youth pastor from our original church fellowship named

Steve had encouraged our daughter to share her story with his youth group. After she finished telling the teenagers about her battle with cancer, Sharon's youth pastor mentioned to her that he believed that each time she testified of how the power of God had healed her body, he believed that God would in turn restore more strength to her body. Our daughter is alive today and she has become an inspiration to all who hear her amazing story of God's mercy towards her. We stood in faith beside our daughter in her battle to win over cancer and with God's divine touch she received her miracle healing. There is no other reason for her being alive today; it was God's mercy and love that reached down that day to deliver her from a possible death sentence and bring healing to her physical body. we are extremely grateful to our heavenly father God for this divine miracle. Every Christmas season as we gather with family to celebrate her life, we are thankful that we can keep making memories together with all seven of our adult children.

****

I'd like to take this time to share how God rescued our daughter a second time that same year. She'd been released from the first hospital at the end of September 1998. As you recall I'd referred to the second hospital time for her, and it involved our daughter deciding to undergo a bone marrow transplant which was an experimental and rigorous treatment. As we listened to the specialists, I learned she'd be required to have more chemo and five days of radiation on her entire body to prepare for the bone marrow transplant. Sharon would need even more prayer for protection as she went through this frightening, dangerous procedure. The percentage of successful bone marrow transplants was quite low. Remember, this was back in 1998. Therefore, I was nervous and a bit apprehensive upon hearing the statistics surrounding this kind of intense treatment plan. Her six siblings were tested to see if any of them might have the perfect match. Her little sister, Kristina, was a perfect match and so was her older brother, Robert. We were all delighted to hear this encouraging news.

Her physicians in the second medical facility had decided that her oldest brother was the best sibling to be able to handle this painful extraction process. Since the second candidate from our children was only thirteen years old at the time, the doctor didn't want to drill into her hip to extract the bone marrow for fear of cracking her hipbone. They'd decided instead to drill into her older brother's hip bone to extract a portion of his bone marrow. Next, the medical team would infuse Robert's bone marrow substance into Sharon's body through an IV tube setup. The week prior to this procedure they'd radiated her body to get rid of the old bone marrow. In other words, she would be without any protective immune system until the transfer had begun and for at least a few months thereafter the procedure.

Once her brother's bone marrow had been infused into her body by an IV method, then her body would hopefully rebuild its own new healthy baby bone marrow. She would then require drugs to help her body recovery and to safely assimilate the new transplant donation from her brother. Her brother was a perfect donor match and therefore, his gift of new bone marrow had all the signs of promised health for her. The only drawback they warned us about was the 'graft versus host disease' which had afflicted many of the patients in this hospital ward. Also, when someone receives daily radiation treatment to rid the body of any hidden cancer cells then this means they could easily become susceptible to germs, viruses, and pneumonia which could in turn possibly kill them. She was blessed to not get pneumonia either time in the two hospital stays and for that we were all extremely grateful to the Lord for answered prayers in this regard. Despite all the dangers and possible threats to her well-being, she survived. It was during this second experience in the other hospital that our faith was tested again.

After nearly a month at this well-known hospital, our daughter was again released by this team of specialists and allowed to go back to the safe, clean home to recover. She had to stay away from the public for long periods of time to be totally safe. Then later she needed to rely on me to drive her back to the infusion room in Oregon for many months of medical care. I have encouraged my daughter to someday write a book about her battle with leukemia and how God delivered her from certain death that year. I believe in miracles. I pray for people I hear about who are battling any type of disease and who need a miracle. A couple of our relatives need healing from cancer and so I asked my prayer partners to join me in agreement prayer for their healing. To date, our nephew has been in remission for two years and he is active and enjoying life with his family. We thank God for this marvelous answer to everyone's prayers for him.

My part in this unfolding battle for our daughter's life was to intercede and believe for her continued safety and for the healing/recovery to be complete. Some days it was very hard for me to stand by and watch all the challenges, heartaches, and extreme sorrows that she'd endured while suffering so much loss at a young age. It was hard to watch my daughter struggle to regain her total well-being and to believe she'd be safe from any more attacks on her health that following year. It was not fun to hear doctors tell her that her immune system had been compromised or that she had to keep taking certain drugs long-term. I continue to petition God daily to infuse her with His mighty strength and courage as she battles to recover completely from the effects of radiation and chemo on her body. She was told by the specialist that if she made it to the ten-year mark, she would be able to celebrate a new lease on life. When that day arrived, we all celebrated. We'd purchased a nice pair of diamond earrings to give to her as a gift. It was December and so our daughter went downtown to shop for a special Christmas ornament for her home. She wanted to find the perfect item to remind her of her victory over cancer. After browsing in the store for a while, she finally decided on a silver star-shaped ornament. She purchased this item, returned to her place, and then hung the ornament on a high bough of her evergreen tree for all to see. She mentioned to us all that she simply stood there admiring the gift and then she paused briefly in reflection to give thanks to God again.

One memory I had of our daughter's time in the second hospital for another month was how enormous this place was as we entered the main lobby, made our way up in the elevator to the fifth floor, and then took the long walk to her infusion room. Sometimes I'd walk the halls where I could see the doctors and staff members walking about and I marveled at their dedication as they cared or their many patients. At one point, I recalled a word of prophecy by a leader in our church which had been given to our daughter about traveling to different countries and it was almost like she was wearing roller skates as she moved easily from one foreign country to the next. I decided by faith to purchase a pair of roller blades for my daughter and give them to her while she was still in the hospital. My encouraging words to Sharon were of this nature, "These roller blades are for you to wear when you're released from the hospital. I believe that you will roll right out of here with God's mighty power quickening your physical body and legs to live a life of serving God and going wherever He sends you!" And that was exactly what transpired; she left that hospital to go and attempt to be active again. Two years later, we both put on roller blades and skated on the paved sidewalks down by the waterfront area in Portland, Oregon. Of course, I managed to hit a water fountain towards the end of our skating experience, but fortunately, I was able to remain upright barely without any serious injuries to my body.

My most unforgettable memory was the day I wheeled my daughter out of the facility, across the street, and through a long walkway which led to an elevator and then down to my car. The reason this stuck out in my mind was because she seemed so frail, and she had to wear a small blue mask over her nose and mouth in order to protect her respiratory system while she breathed in the air. The act of breathing in oxygen was such a normal everyday occurrence for most people. I was not used to seeing my daughter so weak and susceptible to germs and viruses swirling around her and so I was very relieved when we finally arrived at her safe place where she could take off the blue hospital mask.

Our family is very thankful to God for sparing her life and giving her a renewed sense of hope. She eventually decided to go back to college, and she is now a registered nurse. Sharon got her first nursing job at a wonderful hospital in Oregon. We are very grateful for all the doctors and nurses who took such good care of our daughter. Shortly after being released from yearlong visits to the hospital's infusion room; her doctor invited our daughter to come speak to the new interns about how they could provide better care for cancer patients. When she was finished sharing her story, Sharon ended her talk by giving praise to God for healing her fully. One day, I recalled God giving me a vision of Jesus holding my daughter in his arms and footprints in the ground right behind him. I prayed about this beautiful vision and the Lord told me to follow in his footsteps and trust him for her well-being. I also heard something powerful for Sharon during this time of praying and waiting on the Lord where he shared that our daughter would be a messenger of hope to a hurting world. I have continually made this declaration over her for the last fifteen years. I had managed to walk through the fire with my firstborn daughter that difficult year and I clung to the hope in God's promise for Sharon. Looking back on this ordeal, I can see now how I was greatly sustained by the Lord as I learned that there were hundreds of people along with our many friends who continued to pray and believe for a miracle to happen for her that year.

On the other hand, I cannot begin to comprehend what others who've lost a child must be suffering as they constantly deal with a deep ache and loss in their heart. I can only weep with them and extend a hand of comfort as I say a prayer for their hearts to heal. For me, I have found that journaling my thoughts have been a great healing tool to bring me consolation and restored peace. My prayer for those who read this book is that they receive God's help during a trial or whatever challenge they might be facing in life. When someone mentions that God is sovereign and we must trust him in all things in our life, I find this of no comfort or solace. Quite the opposite, this term, 'Sovereign' God, scares me a bit. I feel like it could mean that I have no chance to change God's mind or to entreat the mighty God of the universe to deliver someone I care about from a dreadful situation. I am determined to call upon God in every situation and ask the Lord to give me a better understanding as to how to pray effectively for people. I no longer worry about the sovereignty of God and how it might affect everyone, but instead I know this to be true: Our heavenly Father really loves people, and he hears our desperate cries for help. He has provided promises of healing for all diseases and troubles. These wonderful promises can be found in the first seven verses of Psalm 103. Miracles can happen when we believe in God's amazing promises.

CHAPTER THIRTEEN

As I was thinking about the word, miracles, I wondered if there were any scriptures to back up this concept and so I searched out this word to see if it was mentioned in the Bible. Sure enough, the New Testament recorded about nine times where a miracle occurred. On one occasion, a centurion official asked Jesus to heal his servant even though this person lay in his sick bed miles away in the city of Capernaum. Later, the centurion received news that his servant friend had recovered completely. (Matthew 8: 5-13) Jesus also raised his friend, Lazarus from the town of Bethany, from the dead which was an absolute miracle and there were first-hand witnesses to this great event. In another passage, Jesus was approached by a synagogue leader named Jairus who then asked him to come to his house and lay hands on his daughter to heal her. This is what the internet site stated about this miracle done by the Son of God. "The raising of Jairus' daughter is a reported miracle of Jesus that occurs in the synoptic Gospels, where it is interwoven with the account of the healing of a bleeding woman. The narratives can be found in Mark 5:21-43, Matthew 9: 18-26 and Luke 8: 40-56." I love reading about these divine miracles which happened while the Son of God lived and spent time ministering to the Jewish people in Israel. I tend to say this declaration expression when I need a divine intervention from heaven, "Do it Again, God!" "Do another miracle for the people of America!"

Recently, we needed a similar kind of miraculous type of assistance since our daughter, Sharon, had set her wedding ceremony for July 30, 2022. The weather that week was in the nineties and the forecast for her Saturday wedding had been predicted to be 101 degrees. I asked the Lord to bring a cloud cover for that afternoon since we were scheduled to have family photos from two-thirty to four o'clock and then the wedding ceremony and celebration was to start at five pm. The words that came from my mouth were these, "Oh Lord God, do it again like you did in the days of Moses leading the Hebrew people through the hot wilderness region. Bring a cloud covering to protect Sharon and Mark's wedding party and each family member and the grandparents from the heat! To my delight and relief, clouds began to appear over this exact spot where we were gathered for wedding pictures in Troutdale, Oregon Then two hours later, the cloud coverage disappeared and the heat became almost unbearable and yet, we still had the tree shade for the guests who were being seated for the actual ceremony. God answered my cry of "Do it Again, Almighty God in heaven! Do a miracle of cloud covering for Sharon and Mark!" "Sustain us Lord during this extreme heat wave and protect the senior visitors and grandparents from any kind of heat exhaustion and misery!" This wonderful natural blessing occurred that afternoon. In my mind, this was a wonderful, divine intervention since several large clouds came over us just when we needed them to block the sun and to reduce the tremendous heat problem for us. Of course, we all kept hydrated and fortunately, I was blessed to be able to join my four daughters as they relaxed in the small room on the property which provided our family with enough air conditioning relief. One of my sayings is this: *"Expect a miracle and God will find a way to provide a miracle for you!" Amen*

***

I believe God loves me and my family. I am confident that he is close by waiting to comfort me and teach me how to live in this world. I am learning to listen more closely for his important counsel during times of adversities. I will usually turn to the passage written by King David to rediscover the true heart of the Father for his people. He loves us more than we can comprehend and is willing to help us when we turn towards Him with a broken and contrite heart. One thing I must do in the face of these kinds of tenuous battles is to place my family member back into God's hands and say not my will, but His will be done in our lives. I cannot determine the length of their years here on earth and so I must surrender them to God and trust Him fully as I intercede for my children.

When I made the Son of God my Lord at the age of twenty-one, I was in a sense allowing Him to redirect my future life plans. I became more accountable to the Lord for major decisions after that time. For me, learning to submit to God's plans for my life, meant trusting him more and realizing that He only wanted the very best for my life. There was a time later in my life when I'd struggled to see God's goodness after losing our nice three-bedroom home. At that time, I had no warning from my husband that the bank was in the process of a foreclosure on our home. Once he told me about this problem, it hit me hard as we boxed up our belongings that following week; I experienced shock and grief with this disturbing news. I felt uprooted and blind sighted as we boxed up everything but our beds and sheets. I also wondered where we would find a house since we had a lot of children and only one income. Feeling overwhelmed and slightly distraught, I finally packed an overnight bag, bundled up my three-month-old baby, her diaper bag, and drove in the car for an hour to stay at a Renewal Center near the town of Silverton. Their only request was for visitors to donate what they could afford to stay at the retreat center. I donated forty dollars and enjoyed three glorious days as I rested and put my future and our house problem into God's hands. I had to choose to give my loss to God and find some peace for my hurting heart which I managed to do by the end of my stay there.

Some weeks later, a friend suggested we rent an old farmhouse from someone she knew. This house was vacant and less than two blocks away from her place in the country. We were happy to learn that the landlord would allow us to move into this large house the following week. Plus, this landowner was willing to let my husband remodel the unsightly, old kitchen and put down new carpet and vinyl flooring in exchange for two months free rent. I still had to learn how to work though my loss and my feelings of resentment towards my husband during that year, but we recovered and grew to appreciate being out in the country surroundings. The setting is peaceful, and it has a beautiful view to enjoy. Since there were no annoying neighbors to deal with at this location, we've had less problems to deal with here.

Even though we'd lost that nice home, that year of loss had become a teachable time for me. You may be asking a question here—So what did I learn from this discouraging time with its unexpected move? I realized that life could present us with challenges and there will be times when we face disappointments. It's not if we will face trouble in our lives, but rather what will we do with the disappointments and heartaches that come our way. Yes, it's true, a woman has a basic need to feel like her husband is providing for her and having a nice home can contribute to this security factor. Besides not wanting to ever lose a home again, I've learned how to trust God to provide for us. And yes, I learned a valuable lesson about viewing this older house as a gift instead of a daily embarrassment. Once I changed my attitude about this place and started thanking the Lord for a decent place to live, the landlord decided to fix up and repaint the outside of our house in time for our daughter, Catherine, to have her wedding celebration on that land.

***

I love hearing stories about how God heals people even today! I'm looking forward to seeing a mighty revival with signs, wonders, and miracles happen more and more in our region of the Pacific Northwest. I want to share this man's testimony here: One of my heroes in the faith is a man named Demos whose parents had immigrated to the United States. As a pre-teen, he'd suffered from hearing loss, and he cried out to the Lord to heal his ears. God touched him and restored his ability to hear. Eventually, after years of being a successful dairy farmer and businessman, Demos was guided to start the Full Gospel Businessmen's gatherings which eventually spread across America and over to many other countries. In his lifetime he was instrumental in bringing countless businessmen together to pray and fellowship in many cities. A friend invited my mother and my younger sister to one of these fellowship dinners in a large hotel in our small town. I was curious about why my mother was going to these meetings and so one evening I climbed into the family car with her friend, Eunice, and we all went to listen to the quest speaker. After attending a few of these meetings, I chose to become a true believer. I am thankful that this man obeyed the Lord and started this grass roots movement which made its way to my hometown in the small logging community located in Washington.

Just last week at church I met a lovely couple, and I prayed blessings over them as they were leaving the building. As we chatted there in the foyer, I asked them their names and discovered that they were immigrants from the Ukraine country. I was intrigued by his enthusiasm and friendliness and so I asked a couple more questions. That's when the husband informed me of their family miracle. I asked him if I could take notes about their miracle, and he agreed with this idea. Eventually, he needed to go get a woman friend who could interpret for us. This is his wonderful testimony.

"My name is Marc (not his real name) and this woman is my wife. We had an eight-month-old son. When we were living in Kiev, Ukraine our young son fell and hit his head and this injury made a crack in his skull area. The impact caused a severe injury to his brain functions. The left side of his body was affected by this problem. My son's arm went limp, and he couldn't move it or use his hand. We had to take him to the hospital to be examined by the doctors." At this point, I was writing fast to keep up with his words and yet, struggling to understand his broken English. I needed to ask him to repeat his sentences in order to be able to record his story correctly. He realized that I needed someone to help him with his English and so Marc motioned to a friend to come assist him in explaining the medical stuff better for me. Then he continued speaking as she interpreted for me.

"The medical staff had placed our son into an enclosed capsule-like tube so they could get an MRI picture of the inside his head and neck area. The doctors informed us that this injury had affected our young son's brain ability to send normal signals to the left side of his body. In other words, the fall had caused a short circuit in his brain capabilities and there was no signal flowing from the brain to his arm muscles and nerves. Some friends who had joined them at the hospital made a call to their church members with a request for much prayer for our precious child. The group of intercessors prayed all night for this child to be normal again. The following day, he had an improvement in his body.

The doctors were amazed at his quick recovery. In fact, they couldn't believe that he was now acting and functioning as a normal healthy boy with the full use of his left arm. My wife and I realized that God had intervened on our young son's behalf and made him well again. I must tell you that our son's healing was a divine miracle from God. We saw our son acting perfectly normal! He was able to use his arm and hand as if nothing was ever wrong with him." The father finished talking with a big smile on his handsome face. I agreed with my new friends and couldn't wait to meet their young son. He continued sharing his story with the help of an interpreter woman as I wrote it all down in the note section of my Apple phone.

"The doctors insisted that we keep our son in the hospital for two weeks so they could monitor him and make sure he continued to progress and not digress in his brain functions. They were being cautious since they didn't understand about divine healing and miracles. They had to do the right thing by making sure he was completely well before releasing him from their care." He stated happily.

I watched as their now seven-year-old son approached his father to talk about his time in the Sunday school class. He appeared to be a normal active youngster with all his limbs working excellently that day. I was delighted to get to meet this youngster. I watched this boy interact with his parents and then I introduced myself to the father's boy. The lad said hello back to me and then went over by his mother. It was wonderful to see the actual evidence of a miracle in the flesh standing right before my very eyes. They have been living here in America for the past three years and are very grateful to be in a country that provides so much opportunity and freedom of worship for their family. He and his wife give God all the glory and credit for healing and restoring their son to full health and mobility. I was thrilled to hear about this marvelous testimony that Sunday morning and so

I asked the father if I could include their true story in my book. He looked at me and smiled and replied with this answer, "Yes, of course! We are happy to have you tell others through your book writings, Momma Cathy, about how God answered people's prayers and healed our son completely."

CHAPTER FOURTEEN

I have a testimony concerning my third daughter, Kristina, and her husband which I would like to share with you. One day, my son in-law, Paul, was standing in our kitchen conversing with me about my first short nonfiction book and the reason I'd written it. He asked me if I would consider writing a second book about the more recent victories and miracles which have happened for our family. I responded by saying I would give this some thought. As the days passed, his words kept coming back to me and I couldn't seem to shake this notion that I had another book to write. As I pondered this next writing project about our family's more recent events, I recalled the time I was out of town and my daughter was going through a miscarriage. I knew this was an important story which needed to be included in a second book. However, I was concerned about my attempt to write an actual book based on only one event from our lives and so I started asking God what else I should put in this manuscript. I was then reminded of the ten days I'd spent with my friend in California and her children. I recalled that her eighteen-year-old daughter had asked me questions about my daughter's difficult experience in the hospital in 1998. My friend's daughter mentioned how she loved the part of my first shorter book where I shared about how our dear friend, Elizabeth, had received a powerful vision of messenger angels coming into the hospital to bring healing gifts to my daughter Sharon. I appreciated what she was reminding me about this powerful healing miracle and so I decided to include it in this next book about our family and the healings which happened.

Then my friend's daughter turned to me and said something profound that I shall never forget. This young adult told me that she thought I should write more about my own my life struggles along with my true feelings and emotional responses and to include this in my next book. I kept this encouragement and insight close to my heart until one day I realized that I was being encouraged by at least three people to write about my life in greater detail than ever before. This same young adult's mother had also tried to point out to me the value of sharing with my readers in a much more transparent and vulnerable way concerning my abuse issues. And so this book is a product of my son-in-law's challenge to write a second book and my friend's request for me to share more of my own life. It turned out that during my year of working on this book, I would end up adding more chapters and include other people's amazing stories which they happily shared with me. Apparently, those closest to me knew in their heart that there was a deeper story to be told besides our first miracle. And so that was how this book came about. My hope is that these true-life stories will be a blessing to all who read about them.

Here is one of the miracles which happened recently for our daughter, Kristina. In September of this last year, 2016, I had flown to Raleigh, North Carolina to help my second daughter with the new baby and her three-year-old daughter. After being there in Raleigh for one week, I learned that Paul's mother had made plans to drive the two hours to stay with my daughter, Kris, while he was out of town hunting for deer meat for the family. Upon hearing about my daughter's grievous loss of her recent pregnancy, I was relieved to learn that our daughter's mother-in-law was there with her. I still wanted to be with my daughter during this stressful time as well.

The next morning, I received a short text from our family member informing me that our daughter had been taken to the hospital because she was bleeding after having the miscarriage just two days before. I learned some more details about this problem when I was able to connect with my nurse daughter back home the following day. My daughter informed me that the mother-in-law had been caring for her two children while a friend was there at the hospital with our daughter. At one point, this young friend called our relative to tell her she'd watch the children back at the house so the mother-in-law could come to the hospital to spend time with my daughter. When Paul's mother showed up in the hospital room things became quite chaotic for my daughter. The medical team wasn't sure what was causing the trouble for our daughter.

I had awakened the night before this all had happened to Kristina and had found myself praying for all my children and then I'd gone back to sleep. After seeing our family's text message on my phone, I understood why I'd been impressed to intercede the night before. After learning about this emergency, I tried to call my son-in-law, Paul. He finally texted me back saying he was still driving back home to be with his wife. I felt a sense of relief and peace knowing he'd be there by nightfall to stay with my daughter. As I often do in a crisis time, I called my friend, Sara, (not her real name) and asked her to pray for this situation. We agreed together and then she asked God to give me peace to be able to trust that my daughter would recover completely. She understood how I was feeling since I was thousands of miles away and couldn't be there to comfort my daughter during this frightening experience. When I did get another phone call from my daughter who is a registered nurse, she gave me more information concerning the incident. She told me that her sister's miscarriage had developed a bleeding spot which had been missed by the doctor. This resulted in my daughter being taken to the emergency room. While she was in the hospital the medical team didn't know what was causing the problem.

I later learned that Paul's mother, Staci, had been suffering from a migraine headache that Friday morning, but she'd still decided to drive up to be a support to my daughter, Kris. I believe this was the mercy of our heavenly Father watching over her. It was obvious to me that her life might have been in jeopardy if no adult had been with her that day. Once again, I am joyfully recounting the victory and mighty deeds of our God on behalf of our family. In this book I've shared about God's divine intervention in our lives, and I am truly thankful for this protection for our daughter, Kris.

Throughout my adult life I've experienced getting warning dreams, visions, and definite premonitions. After getting one of these warning-type of dream for someone, I'd felt impressed to pray even more fervently for that person I saw in the dream. God answered my many prayers for this family member and their life was spared in a horrific motorcycle accident. I am thankful that God has taught me the importance of paying attention to the various ways He can speak to us through what I call warning dreams and visions. I rejoice in the fact that our heavenly Father has given us great promises in the Bible, and he is a trustworthy promise keeper. I can certainly trust Him with the safety and well-being of my loved ones.

My daughter and her husband are pastors of a church plant endeavor in Oregon. They need plenty of prayer and love support as they tackle this assignment from the Lord. I am excited to see what God will accomplish in that city through their obedience and faithfulness. So, to my wonderful pastor son, here is the book you asked me to write which includes our family's most recent testimonies of God's protection, healings, and his divine intervention; I have to say this, "To God be the Glory, great things He has done for our entire family!" Here is a scripture verse which is one of the reasons I've chosen to write this book, "...; I have put my trust in the Lord God, that I may declare all Your works." (Psalm 73:28) I've worked to finish this book in order to leave it as a legacy to my grandchildren. My hope is that those who come after me will read about these true stories and believe in a God of miracles for themselves. My desire is that the next generation will remember how we chose to believe God for miracles. Yes, God still performs miracles and divine healings today just as He did in the ancient days with the Israelite people! I know that God honors the faith of his people. Do it again, Oh Mighty Yahweh, the Great I AM, Lord of heaven and earth.

Recently, while recording my daughters' story onto paper, I decided to call my daughter's mother-in-law to ask about her part in this scary situation. Staci was happy to share her part in this dramatic story. She'd heard from her son that my daughter Kristina, had been feeling very sad with the loss of her third pregnancy. Paul had shared with his mother that Kristina was missing her own mother who was unavailable to stay with her that weekend. Since Staci knew how important it was for someone to come there and stay with Kristina and her kids, she offered to take off work from her school job and drive up the two hours to help the family. That morning she'd been suffering from a bad headache and yet, she was determined to help care for her two young grandchildren.

Staci continued relating her story with me as I grabbed an ink pen to jot down my notes.

"I had arrived at my daughter-in-law's home around ten a.m. Friday and I offered to take them all to breakfast. After eating their meal, we needed to stop by Fred Meyers store and grab some groceries, but we could only grab a few items since my daughter-in-law began to feel sick and weak. Then I drove back to the house and put the two children to bed for their naps. During this rest time, she had to go into the bathroom two times because she was still bleeding. I soon realized that my daughter-in-law, who was a petite, lightweight woman couldn't afford to have more blood loss so I decided she should go to the hospital. I was asked to call her good friend to take her instead so that the kids wouldn't be upset after their naps to discover their mother had gone to the hospital.

Once her friend had arrived at the house, I put Kristina into the car and the friend drove her to ER. Later this same gal called me to come up to the hospital too." She paused briefly and then continued sharing her part in this dramatic event.

"After I'd entered the emergency room to stay with your daughter, I learned that the doctor was not use to this kind of complication and so things got crazy for a while. The doctor made the statement that there was a major problem for this female patient, and she didn't know exactly what to do for our daughter. When I heard this comment, I made the statement that the ER staff should get someone in the room who knew what to do. At this moment, my daughter-in-law seemed to crash physically and then she had a mild seizure. The next thing that happened was that one of the team members called up to maternity ward and got the same doctor who had delivered Anne's second baby the year before. This doctor came down to ER and assessed the problem and took control of the situation properly. This other doctor was able to slow down the bleeding and finally get an IV into her vein to inject the necessary fluids into her body. She managed to scrape away the attached remainder of the placenta which had been causing the problem. I'd been allowed to stay in the room with Kris for the entire procedure. Even though I was fighting a bad headache I didn't leave her side the entire time." Staci mentioned.

I am very grateful that Staci had come that Friday and that she insisted on them getting another doctor for my daughter. When I asked Paul's mother how she'd managed to stay up on her feet that frightful day while dealing with a migraine headache, she replied, "I didn't recall feeling my headache during this stress-filled time at the hospital, I just did what needed to be done for her and I didn't recall having any pain during the entire time until I'd left the hospital for the long drive home. I made it safely back to my own home and was glad to have been there for your daughter." As her mother, I am very grateful that Staci had pushed through the headache pain and made the long trip to stay with my daughter and make sure she went to ER. She was a great blessing and instrumental in preventing a worst tragedy from happening. I believe that God intervened that day to watch over this potentially dangerous situation and to protect my daughter, Kristina, from serious complications. I am so thankful that our daughter's life was spared back then, and she is now expecting her fourth child this coming December.

CHAPTER FIFTEEN

Now almost a year later after her miscarriage, my daughter has shared her feelings with me about this disappointing loss. She had recently been on a weekend trip with her husband, and they had enjoyed the quality time together. Kristina mentioned how suddenly on the last day of their trip she broke down crying again about her miscarriage. Then after talking some more with her husband, Paul, she felt like she was ready to finally give this unborn child a name. Two months before this, I'd read a book about a four-year-old boy who'd died briefly and went to heaven. In this excellent book about heaven, the father describes how his young son saw his other sister in heaven. When the young child mentioned about seeing his other sister to his mother, he told her that his sister wanted to be given a name. I shared this part of the book with my daughter and encouraged her to find a name for her baby now up in heaven as well. She said she would think about it.

Six months later, she started thinking seriously about a good name to give the baby she'd lost during her first trimester. My daughter told me that she had found a name she liked enough to give it to her unborn child while reading a book and this name was Tirzah. She'd

·also heard this same name mentioned in a recent movie about Hebrew people and she decided to call her baby living up in heaven by this name. This name Tirzah in Hebrew means "My Beloved". I was thankful that she is feeling stronger now. Recently, we learned that our daughter is once again pregnant, and we are thrilled for her. She called me on the phone last night and shared her excitement at seeing the ultrasound pictures of the tiny infant developing inside of her womb. I am so thankful to see my daughter walking in more joy as she begins to heal and can see this loss from a different perspective. Kristina is a great mother, and she really cares about her children and their learning progress. They are getting their home ready as they are look for their new bundle of joy to arrive in June of 2018.

This is how my daughter, Kristina, shared her story with me:

"Mom, as you may recall, I had the miscarriage during my third pregnancy on August 24th, 2017, and I grieved for two days along with my husband and then he left to go on a hunting trip. My mother-in-law was spending time with me and my kids that Friday. We were all at the grocery store getting a few items to add to the tomatoes from my garden in order to make home-made salsa. My abdominal pain and cramping started to increase. We hurried home and I tried to rest, but my body began to show signs of trouble. After some blood loss, I texted my husband to let him know I was going to the ER. I also called a few good friends to see if anyone could take me there. Fortunately, the hospital was close by. I kept feeling like I might pass out and so at the ER, they put me into a wheelchair. The nurses quickly triaged me, but then the nurse was skeptical as to just how much blood I had lost." Kris exclaimed.

"My good friend told them that I'd lost at least two quarts already, but the ER doctor came in and began questioning me if I was even having a miscarriage. After talking with me for some length, she finally examined me and said, "I can't see anything and so I'm going to call our on-call OBGYN." My mother-in-law, Staci, was now up at the hospital room with me, and she said that the doctor was shocked, and her face was white. This doctor left the room and the nurse tried to get an IV going in my arm. I was praying out loud asking God to help the nurse find a good vein for the IV. Then I told them I needed to throw up and they placed a throw-up bag over my shoulder. My daughter mentioned that she'd recalled thinking this, "Why didn't they give it to me because I can't move my arms because I'd started to lose feeling in them." My daughter, Kristina, continued relating her experience to me and she included her one thought. She had wondered this concern; *would I get to say goodbye to my beloved husband?* She paused momentarily and then she continued sharing with me. "I remember feeling very scared and wondering where God was during this awful ordeal. I mean why couldn't I feel peace or His presence with me? Then I awoke and realized that I couldn't move my arms or legs and so I told the nurse about my concerns." She stated.

"The OBGYN staff member was there with me, and she told me, "You are okay now, your body is a little excited because of the adrenaline and you had a seizure after passing out." They called in more medical staff when I had the seizure, and someone was able to finally find a vein. This doctor said that she needed to go in and remove the tissue that remained and was causing the bleeding problem. I asked her for the morphine drug and her response was that since I needed fluids first, the morphine would have to wait. The pain was excruciating as she scraped my uterus. I asked my family member to talk to me during this awful procedure to keep my mind from feeling the pain. She reminded me of the time when my son had been delivered by this same OBGYN doctor and her conversation served as a distraction for me. At last, the scraping was done, and the doctor asked me if I wanted a shot to help my uterus close. She told me that I'd get this shot in my thigh and I was relieved to know exactly where I'd get this shot and so I said yes. Then they were able to give me the morphine shot too. By this time, I was feeling very exhausted." Kristina said.

"After the medical staff cleaned things up, they wheeled me to another clean room, and I felt like throwing up again and passing out. At this point, my husband joined me. My new nurse was a great comfort to me. She also gave me some meds to stop the nausea problem. I told her that I hadn't had food for the last four hours and my stomach felt queasy. The doctor mentioned they could release me from the hospital soon and my nurse said, "If you don't mind, I'd like to monitor this young lady overnight." The contractions started and they were very painful. I asked my nurse if this was normal occurrence and she said yes and so I asked for stronger pain meds." These contractions lasted until nine o'clock that evening. Then my husband and I shared some of our different experiences over the past fourteen hours and he mentioned how he hadn't received some of my texts about what was happening with me. He realized that he was needed at the hospital and so he ditched his hunting gear, came down off the mountain, and then proceeded to swim against the strong current in a river in order to reach the other side and race back to the hospital. He'd been feeling very emotional as he drove back to town. My husband prayed for me for the two-hour trip home. He'd felt afraid that he might lose me, and it bothered him not knowing what was happening while he was so far away." Kristina said.

"As I reflected on this dreadful experience surrounding the loss of my recent pregnancy, I have come to understand that even though it was very upsetting, sorrowful, and traumatic event, God had provided me with everything I needed by bringing the right people to be with me during that hospital (ER) experience. With the help of the Lifespan Integrative Therapy method, my counselor was able to help me take this traumatic event and move it from the trauma center part of my brain to the front lobe of my brain. Thus, I could hold the trauma as just another memory rather than a bad event which would continue to trigger more feelings of fear and sadness. The past awful event had made me feel very unsafe and sad and I needed to be free from this trauma. God's hand of protection was all over me that day and I'm very grateful for how God has brought a healing to my life after losing this child. Mom, I feel that the Lord has used this experience and sorrow as a catalyst for a deeper healing in my soul and in my marriage." Kristina added.

This book about recent healings and victories has developed into much more than a short memorial to the goodness of God for our immediate family members. I am thankful that the doctors managed to keep our third daughter safe and prevent a serious tragedy this last year. Our daughter, Kris, had lost nearly four pints of blood that weekend and our entire family realized how close we came to losing her. Since I've chosen to include this true-life incident involving our daughter and her hasty trip to the hospital, my writing project has grown to include many other people's amazing testimonies as well. I'd like to add this comment here: I believe that when God heals someone it is beneficial for them to consider asking this question. *Now that I have been healed Lord, what is the work you have for me to do while I'm still here on this earth?* My prayer for all our family members and for anyone who decides to read this book is this; if you've been healed or experienced a miracle then consider sharing your exciting experience with others and see what God will do with your encouraging testimony. When we fully commit our lives to learning what God's next plan for our life is then we will truly honor the Lord. I've chosen to ask God what He wants me to do daily. I am no longer striving to be used by my heavenly Father, but instead I'm learning to listen, to enter into his rest, and be guided by His love.

***

During my travels abroad, I learned of a powerful testimony from my Brazilian friend, Adielene. She showed me a video of a man who had trouble walking and he needed someone to help him walk as he went to the hospital in Serra, a city located in Victoria, Brazil. Then my friend pointed out a pastor named, Antonio Marcos who was also in this video. I was intrigued and so I listened and saw how this pastor goes to the hospital with his church friends to bring the sick people back to his church building by bus. He has the women cooked a hot meal for the visitors while he prays for them. As the video continued playing, I watched this pastor talk with a man who was using crutches and in obvious pain. After receiving prayer for his bad leg, the Holy Spirit of God touched this man. He felt the pain leave his leg and he also experienced the spirit of God upon his heart and his mind at that moment. He decided to invite Jesus of Nazareth to come into his heart and to become a believer in God's only son. I watched this man begin to weep as he began to slowly walk a little at first and then he began to walk more freely and without pain. The most exciting part for me was how he'd chosen to receive God's salvation message and truth.

The next portion of this video showed another person being interviewed. He had been coming to this same church for food and friendship from the Christian believers. The person doing the interview asked him a question. "Sir, have you seen any miracles from God since you've been here these six months?"

"Yes, I have seen God heal people. I have also become a true believer of God myself."

This church provides a shelter house for the sick people to be able to have a shower and a bed to sleep on while they wait for the doctors in hospital to eventually see them. One time this pastor took a Brazilian man to his shelter to help him get cleaned up and receive prayer. This pastor believes in the scripture verse that states, "…; they shall lay hands on the sick, and they shall recover." (Mark 16: 18) Then this man asked the pastor a question— "You healed these poor, sick people, you are a good man." This pastor responded with this answer, "It was God the Lord Jehovah who does the healing and miracles! He has shown me to care for others and to feed the hungry and sick people of my land of Brazil." The pastor replied.

I loved learning about this actual true-life story of a man who is an example of how God wants people to minister to the poor and sick of this world. This Brazilian leader is a good example of a true shepherd who cares for people even those he finds on the street or in a hospital waiting room. I was grateful my friend, Adeline from Brazil took the time to locate this video of the Brazilian pastor for me to watch.

CHAPTER SIXTEEN

In 1982, our fifth child another girl was born. While she was growing up, I remember feeling so amazed by the fact that she rarely needed any correction as a youngster. In fact, she seemed to be more like a little angel since she was very sweet and cooperative as a youngster. In 1985, our next daughter was born and a few years later our fourth daughter arrived in November of 1987. A few years later, I was feeling overwhelmed and frustrated with the daily demands on my life and of course, with the many active children running around in our three-bedroom house. There was plenty of laundry to clean, loads of dishes to wash, and exhaustible demands upon my body and mind during these early years of child rearing.

I also recalled a time when I'd felt a slight judgment towards my husband's mother for leaving huge piles of unfinished laundry in her basement laundry room. She had eight children (nine including my husband) to care for and feed and therefore, finishing all the laundry was not an easy task for my mother-in-law to accomplish. I'd left her home that day thinking that I would never let big piles of dirty clothes lying in a heap on the floor for days like she had done. Of course, after having a few of my own children myself now, I was faced with this same laundry problem in my own home. I recalled some wise advice my mother-in-law had given me as a newlywed. She'd mentioned to me that when I realized that I was judging another person that I should stop being negative and instead consider praying for that person. Her insightful advice has stayed with me all these years and now I am passing it onto my sons and daughters.

During those difficult years of child rearing, I needed daily strength to handle the workload. In my desperation, I cried out to the Lord to show me how to have an impartation of his abundant life into my own body and soul. I had read about this abundant life' scriptural truth in the Bible and believed this promise was for me and yet, I wasn't sure how to receive this promised provision of abundant life. I was a candidate for getting more strength, more joy, and more help in my life as a homemaker and mother. Since I had no one to mentor me in this concept, I started declaring that I had an infusion of God's abundant life strength. On my own, I decided to appropriate God's life force and I also started thanking Him for this extra infusion of strength and vitality each day. Within six months, I was sensing a new ability to take care of my duties and play with the children without feeling so physically depleted. I no longer had to plow through my day hoping to make it to evening before falling exhausted on the sofa after the children were asleep. I am now a woman who truly understands the meaning of a breakthrough and victory. I am an over-comer today because of this infusion of abundant life. God has unlimited resources at his fingertips. I believe the Lord is waiting for us to call out for help and to learn how to appropriate this promise of his 'abundant life' by making faith statements over our selves.

When the Bible instructs people to seek the Lord, I believe this means for as long as it takes to get a specific answer to their problem or questions. Sometimes we must continue to wait, trust, and believe that God cares about the details of our lives. When we seek the Lord and his wisdom with an open heart then He will show us how to make a good decision or how to solve a problem properly. Whenever I search the scriptures, I see that the scriptures contain many wonderful promises for believers to avail themselves of. It is our part to reach out and to receive the Lord's perfect love and strength as a result of reading the truths which we see in certain verses. I am a person who believes this idea to be true: It is our responsibility to believe that we can receive God's impartation for a powerful infusion of His life into our own weak or tired bodies or minds. I believe that we must be willing to acknowledge these truths and to walk in these scriptural promises for our life. In reading the Book of Ephesians, I've learned that God had a good plan for me and that I needed to ask what this plan entailed for my life. I began to understand that as believers we are to walk in good works as well as the instructions found in the Bible. In other words, we cannot simply wait for God to perform His plan in our lives if we don't take steps to incorporate the Bible truths into our thinking.

One day as I was reading the Bible, I came across another important verse that mentioned how God was preparing something good for our future lives. I decided to start thanking God from that point on for whatever He had planned for my life even though I had no actual insight as to what those plans might entail. I continued to walk in this new kind of grateful heart and expectation of good things for my future. The years went by, and I was spending my days working at schools and encouraging students to be the best they could be in life. Then I began to see how God was using me to touch lives more and more. It was as if I was walking in God's will for my life, and I became more excited about my time with students at the school. I've learned that God has a written scroll in heaven that contains a beautifully designed blueprint for my life. As a supreme architect, God knows exactly how to rebuild and restore our lives to enable us to become more successful and in tune with his creative purposes. I have determined to fit into His master plan for my life. God loves you and He has a marvelous plan for your life as well. There is nothing better than discovering what God's destiny is for you and learning how to walk in His wonderful, perfect plan as we trust him to make us into his beautiful masterpiece.

Now, fast-forward with me to twelve years later and our children have become grown adults so now I have more free time to pursue my dreams. I am no longer working as a reading group teacher for a local school district. I've travelled to different states to spend time with my grandchildren. Life is good. I've also come to understand that part of my destiny is to travel to other countries to share my faith and to pray for people who live overseas. During my visit in Israel and later in Uganda, I watched as God blessed people supernaturally as I prayed for them. I had some amazing, memorable experiences because I'd chosen to take that step of obedience and to follow His plan for my life. I believe God is waiting for us to ask how we can fit into His excellent plan and to rely on His help to accomplish the Father's divine purpose.

***

Today, I am sitting in my friend's mountain home looking out over the vast wilderness at Mt. St. Helens and its snow-capped majesty. Below her front yard is the panoramic view of Yale Lake in the distance. I paused to take a short break from jotting down notes of her life that I'd intended to include in this book. I never thought I'd publish a nonfiction book about my own life journey, but here I am doing just that! God is working in and through me to accomplish his plan for my life.

That afternoon while my friend was cleaning up her kitchen, I decided to head outside and enjoy the sunshine for a moment. As I strolled around her mountainside property, I was happy to be out in nature enjoying the sublime beauty of her flowers, the raspberry bushes, and the vegetable garden tucked into the bank of a sloping hillside which borders her front yard. Then moments later, I sat down on the porch to admire God's magnificent creation around me. I was pleasantly surprised by two butterflies flitting about among the hydrangeas bush, a few smaller flowers, and the tall, green grass in her front yard area. This wonderful mountain-top property is like a mini–retreat getaway place for me. I can relax there as I enjoy the wonderful peacefulness and quiet beauty of their secluded mountain-top home. It is like no other place on earth. Sometimes I wish we could move closer to my friend's mountain place. Maybe then we wouldn't have to listen to the constant noise of busy traffic, or the daily siren sounds of the police cars or the noise of the EMT vehicles which pass by our home residence.

My husband and I live in a two-story house that sits on two acres in Washington. During the month of August of 2017, things started transpiring which caused me to feel apprehensive and uneasy about our living situation. The landlord had sent over an excavation team to dig up a few sections of the field next to our front yard. There had been talk of the owner selling off most of the property around our place. This idea was making me nervous and unsettled about our hopes of staying long-term on this property.

Finally, I asked my husband to talk with the landowner to see what his new plans might entail. During this time, a friend had suggested that I ask God a different question about the property. She said this to me: "You should ask God what He desires for you and your husband during this time of concern and change." I realized she was right and then she stated something else important. "I believe God wants you and your husband to have a conversation about this problem. You might consider forgiving your husband for not preparing you in advance for drastic changes in your living situations in the past. You need to let go of any resentments and hurts from the time you lost your lovely ranch-style home in 1978. I realized that her assessment of my attitude towards my husband was correct and so I choose to forgive my husband for that loss of our nice home and the fact that he didn't give me any warning before the bank repossessed our house.

A week after that discussion with my friend and after the landlord had met at my husband's business location to discuss another matter; I learned that the owner was getting ready to eventually sell off ten acres lots of his fifty acres behind our house. He discussed with my husband about scheduling some repairs and replacement of the duct work underneath this old home to keep the rats and mice from entering our place so easily. Nothing was said about our family having to move out of this rental house. I was greatly relieved. Some twenty-five years ago when we first moved into this older house, I had been walking around the two acres when I heard in my spirit these words, *everywhere your feet tread on this land, I will give it you. I* recalled how this thought reminded me of the verse located in the Book of Joshua where it states*:* "Every place that the sole of your foot shall tread upon, that have I given unto you, as I said unto Moses." (Joshua 1: 3 KJV)

Back then, I had felt like God was telling me to claim this land for our family. Now as I think upon this same promise, I want to once again believe that God will help us either purchase the title deed for this property or be able to live here for as long as we need to since the rent is very reasonable, and it has a beautiful view of a rich pastureland and evergreen trees. There is a quality of peacefulness here as we look over the scenery to the west of our home. I am very grateful we live here especially since the owner has finally repaired, painted, and fixed many problems on this aged house this last year. All my friends who come here to visit me all tell me that they love our country view. When I take them back outside on a sunny day, we will go out front and sit down on a lawn chair to marvel at the quiet beauty of the pasturelands and the tall Evergreen trees off in the distance. It brings a renewed sense of tranquility that can't be found for folks living on busy, noisy streets in the city.

As my friend and I were talking one afternoon as I lay relaxing in my hammock, I recalled something she'd taught me a few years back. She'd told me that whenever I was angry, hurt or upset with someone that I should make a concerted effort to take this problem to the Lord and ask what to do about the trouble. She told me there were three things necessary to maintaining a healthy soul and to have a free flow between my heart and God's spirit. The first question I was to ask went like this: What am I feeling when someone offends or hurts me? The second question was: Why am I feeling this way after someone attacks my character or my actions? And thirdly, what does God want me to do about these hurtful words or with my angry feelings? I've learned to walk in more grace and forgiveness by using this new method of taking my hurts to God. In other words, I've started seeing things from the Bible's perspective which instructs us to desire a better kind of resolution. I am convinced that nothing good comes from hanging onto negative thoughts towards people who've hurt or offended us. At one point in my adult life, I had to give up my right to be angry or hold a certain offense against someone and it was worth the effort to release that person from my judgment or resentment.

The medical field has even mentioned that these negative thoughts can produce trouble for our health. I firmly believe that forgiveness withheld from others can contribute to diseases like cancer. I think that when a person harbors bad feelings of hatred, bitterness, and anger for a long time then, if left unchecked, these negative or angry thoughts could become a contributing factor for diseases. Is it possible that a person should take spiritual inventory of their heart issues? I don't believe we should ignore the potential danger of holding onto bitterness. I can imagine that when someone hates another person this anger can cause inflammation and destruction to one's physical being. I think we need to guard our hearts from bitterness and resentments. I've found if I don't follow this idea then my negative attitudes may eventually cause the enemy to have a foothold in my life. The devil is a wicked instigator and his main objective throughout the centuries has been to bring lies, sickness, weakness, and all kinds of diseases into people's lives. I've counseled my children to guard their hearts and make it a practice to forgive those who cause them hurt or offenses.

***

Here's a little side humor about our family. One Mother's Day, my daughters surprised me by bringing over to our house three cans of whipping cream as a gift and this made me very happy. Like most people, I enjoy a good dessert and good food and yet, I believe in eating certain foods in moderation. I am slight of build and so I refrain from overindulging in sweets and too much heavy meats at each meal. Most folks marvel at my capacity to keep up with the young children who beg me to play outside with them, plus there is the other factor that I can run circles around even my adult friends who are much younger than me except for my one friend who lives in Glendale, Arizona. I give God the credit that I've had such good health, abundant energy, and the blessing of a joyful heart all these years.

Speaking of whipping cream, my friend and I had stopped in at a local restaurant to get some hot coffee after taking a long walk in the wildlife preserve yesterday. We'd enjoyed a delightful hike that day. We saw many Canadian geese resting on a water pond area along with three white swans in one of the waters spots before heading back to the place where she'd parked her vehicle. We had finished our exercise and she wanted to treat me to coffee and dessert. We went in search of a good restaurant. She knew of a nice place, and we only needed to walk a block to locate it. Once inside and seated at a small table, my friend ordered us two hot coffees and a sumptuous carrot cake. The young waitress took our order and as she was leaving our table, I asked her for some whipped cream to go with my hot coffee. She said of course you may and then she returned with two glass cups of coffee with a topping of delicious, whipped cream. It was a grand sight to behold. Then I reminded the waitress about my request for additional whipping cream for our cake. She brought the can to our table and applied the foamy, rich topping to our cakes as well. Then I asked her a question and found out that she had moved from Alaska to live here with her biological father. After she left us to wait on another customer, my friend mentioned to me that she'd seen pain in this young adult woman's eyes. I thought we should whisper a quick prayer for this young woman and so we did and then we devoured our moist carrot cake dessert.

When this same waitress came back to check on us, my friend mentioned that God loved her, and I added that I thought she had great auburn colored hair and a wonderful smile. Next my friend proceeded to share with her the one thing she'd sensed about this young gal's life and the waitress responded by sharing her sad story with us. Two years before this her boyfriend had committed suicide and she was very sad about this sudden death and loss of his friendship. We told her we would keep her in our prayers after this meeting. Then we paid for our coffee and dessert and left after I gave this young waitress a warm hug. As we were walking down the street towards the car, my friend said she thought we should go into the small antique shop across the street and buy the waitress a gift. It was the month of December already and the season for giving to others, so we prayed for just the right gift as we walked around in the quaint little shop. Within a few minutes of searching the premises, we found a brass-colored chain with an old-fashioned key attached to the chain along with a circular, metal piece that contained an inscribed word, LOVE, on the front portion. It was the perfect gift for this young woman and so we purchased the necklace item. Then we walked back down the street and went inside to give this waitress our gift which we hoped would be a blessing for her during the holiday season. My hope is that this waitress will recall our visit and our words about how God loves her and wants the best for her life.

CHAPTER SEVENTEEN

T his October I made an important trip to visit the land of Israel. I had been thinking and praying about travelling on this overseas trip for several years. For me this was a journey of great importance. It was a unique experience being in the Holy Land with its ancient cities and the biblical history of the Hebrew people. I marveled at the unusual landscape of this small country. In the southern region around the city of Jerusalem, I saw plenty of crème-colored boulders and stones everywhere I travelled. I started calling this place the land of stones, creamy-colored boulders, and many larger boulders. For the most part, the climate was very warm and dry, but I missed seeing rivers and lakes, green grass and Evergreen trees like we have back home. As an American woman, I felt out of place in the region called Bethlehem where only Muslims lived. During my walks about the city, I would see an unfamiliar sight. There were tall mosque buildings that housed a large megaphone contraption which they used to shout out a strange prayer for all to hear and which I could not understand. I felt like they were infringing upon my peace and quiet as I wandered about exploring shops and searching for a museum to visit. I could hear the loud chants and prayers very early in the morning and again late at night if the hotel window was open.

Back at my hotel in Israel, I became acquainted with a young adult man who worked as a clerk behind the front counter of the hotel. His name was Mosefth and I began to pray for him to truly understand God's truths. As we talked one night, I made a reference to the well-known man called Moses and the miracle stories found in the Old Testament. He knew of this Moses and so I felt free to share about my first book. He was interested in this book and so he asked me how to order it online. I wrote down all the information and informed him to go first under my name and then type in BarnesNoble. Com. He was looking forward to getting my book and so I prayed for him and his family to prosper and be safe. For the next ten days we greeted each other, and I enjoyed talking with him in the hotel lobby.

Two days later I met a young woman who worked in the same hotel during the day shift, and she informed me that my new friend, Mosefth, had told her that I was a writer. We chatted for a few minutes and then I asked if I could pray for her. She responded to my question by saying yes. So, I prayed a blessing over her. I felt prompted to ask if I could pray for her and her co-worker friend to find a kind, godly man to marry. She smiled at me and again said yes to my question. I finished praying for her and her friend and then went upstairs to my room on the ninth floor to relax for an hour. Each morning after that encounter, I decided to pray for divine appointments and an opportunity to meet new people while I was staying in Jerusalem. I hope that these new acquaintances living in the town of Bethlehem will one day come to know the Prince of Peace as their Savior.

While staying in Israel that week, I listened to a female speaker share what had happened when she spoke at a Harvard University gathering of students. As I listened to her recounting some true events, I was amazed to learn that this Christian leader, Heidi Baker, had been invited to speak to well-educated college students in the east coast of America. Heidi Baker and her husband, Roland, have spent many years in Mozambique helping rescue young children living on the streets. She went on to share with this group of students about her journey with God and how she has prayed for years against the Aids disease which has plagued so many Africans and their young children.

While she was under the direction of the Spirit of God as to what to share next to the large group of college students, she waited for a moment in silence and then she proceeded to end her talk with an invitation for anyone who wanted to know God and to receive prayer to come forward. In response to her invitation, a group of students came to the front of the auditorium. Then she heard an Asian female student crying loudly somewhere in the crowd of students. During Heidi Baker's time of sharing to this group of intellects, this college student had been getting a download from God's spirit about how to deal with and produce a cure for the Aids disease. This young lady was in her fourth year of obtaining her PhD in medical research and she was obviously astounded with the divine revelations that were coming to her during this meeting. Heidi Baker approached this young woman and as she got closer, she saw God's Fire' upon this female student. Right then and there, this guest speaker felt strongly that God was doing something significant in this young adult's life. I was intrigued by our speaker's words right then and so I prayed for this young woman to be successful in her research and to be able to discover a cure for the Aids disease.

It seemed to me as I sat there in the conference listening to Heidi Baker's story that God might want to use this student to bring a major medical breakthrough to stop this epidemic-size plague on behalf of the African people. I shall keep praying for this young lady to continue her college education and provide the world with a profound discovery and advancement to medical science in the fight against Aids. Let's all join in this prayer for the medical world to find a cure and to see innocent children of Africa freed from this awful, deadly disease.

I had really enjoyed the prayer conference that week in Jerusalem. That first week my hotel roommate, Esther, had introduced me to her friend, Dr. Praveen, a pastor and psychologist from India. She'd invited him to join us for the next day of sightseeing fun. We had a remarkable time exploring King Hezekiah's tunnel which is located deep underneath the old city of Jerusalem. My friend had to park her car at the lower end of the tunnel which was near the pool of Siloam. This pool was fed by the waters of Gihon Spring and carried to the next pool by two aqueducts. Next, we hiked up a steep paved street for some ways in order to get to the entrance where we could purchase tickets. After giving the attendant our tickets, we then walked carefully downward for about thirty-five minutes by using wooden steps until we reached the tunnel. This famous site had been skillfully chiseled out of stone by the Hebrew soldiers many centuries ago. Hezekiah's tunnel still has clean, clear water flowing through its channel many miles beneath the ancient, beautiful structure they call the old city of Jerusalem. While we were walking down the steps which led to a deeper portion of the famous tunnel, I'd felt a twinge of concern knowing I was deep within the bowels of the earth. For a few scary moments I had the awful thought of what if suddenly one of the wooden beams would come loose causing the overhead support structures, the above ground buildings, and the heavy rocks above us to come crashing down upon us.

If ever there was a time to experience fear and insecurity, it was during this downward journey leading us into the dark bowels of the earth below ground. We had one tiny flashlight to help us see and I was wishing that I hadn't come on this adventure. At one point in this experience, I decided to push away these scary thoughts and to instead focus on the beauty of the stone walls and the smooth flooring of the narrow, water-fed tunnel. While I was traveling through this water path dug many miles below the solid ground, I suddenly felt like singing. I began to sing my heartfelt praises to God in a loud voice. I didn't care if any other tourist could hear my songs of praise to the Lord. It was a beautiful, amazing experience as I worshipped the God of Abraham, Isaac, and Jacob while trudging through Hezekiah's Tunnel many miles below the famous city in Jerusalem. I was in awe of the flowing clear water that was waist deep for a majority of our journey through this ancient man-made tunnel. I found it hard to comprehend that Hebrew soldiers with only chisels and hammers were able to produce such a masterpiece tunnel project hundreds of miles below the surface of the land during ancient times. I recommend to everyone who visits the city of Jerusalem to take the time to explore this fascinating, well-constructed (located in the depths of the earth) tunnel built by soldiers under the order of King Hezekiah.

The next morning, I went to the dining room for breakfast and saw my friends again. Dr. Praveen was sitting next to a young vivacious, attractive woman and so I asked him to introduce me to his friend. I learned that her name was Micaela. (not her real name) This young lady was living on the British Isle and she'd traveled to a few countries before coming to this prayer conference in Jerusalem, This Jubilee Conference had drawn two thousand people from nearly one hundred and fifty countries and now they were gathered in one place to hear great teachings and to enjoy special, powerful times of worship. As I listened to this woman share at lunch about her newest idea of a website for businesspeople to connect on, I become eager to get know her better.

I could see that this woman had a gentle, gracious spirit about her and the longer she talked the more I realized she was also an anointed woman of influence. As we sat at the table drinking our coffee, I asked her to share her life story with me. She proceeded to tell me about how she'd struggled as a young adult, and she even had wished that she could end her life one night when she was all alone and far from her home and family. However, God intervened and caused her to look over where she saw a church building with a cross on the top of the roof. After this experience, Micaela decided to wait and go find some people who could help her in her search for truth and for meaning for her life. She eventually returned to her hometown and gave her life completely to the Lord. She is doing very well now and is a strong prayer warrior. I really enjoyed getting to know her that afternoon. Later that same day, she encouraged me to attend a business seminar with her where I learned some valuable keys to how to be a successful person in life and in running a business. I really enjoyed spending time with this amazing and very intelligent woman.

CHAPTER EIGHTEEN

Today, after having to delete an entire chapter of my manuscript, I felt discouraged. I wanted to crawl into a dark room and give up on this challenging book project. To be honest, I was starting to doubt if I would ever finish this manuscript. After all these months of working on this book, I still had to fix the numerous mistakes my friend had found as she critiqued my writing. Plus, I needed to keep working on the necessary rewrite as well. Now, on top of doing the rewrite project, I needed to find something else to replace those empty pages. As it was, I'd already invested long hours into this writing project and now I was looking at more effort on my part before I could submit this manuscript to a publisher. I was at a low point in this challenging endeavor.

My first intention in this book project had been to share my life story with my family and our grandchildren. However, last week I needed to stop this editing project in order to drive a few hours away to stay with my daughter and her young children while her husband, Paul, was out of the country for two weeks. Then my son and his friend from Wisconsin were scheduled to arrive here and stay for a ten-day visit in April. After spending ten days with our son, my other daughter and her two young children were coming here and stay with us for the entire month of May. All this family visits meant that I wouldn't have much time to spend on this rewrite and I was feeling a real sense of frustration and weariness in my soul.

Then I remembered that my second reason for attempting to write this book was to testify of all the miracles that have happened to our family members. I couldn't give up in my efforts to record these marvelous events and to share them with other people. Even though I was reminded of the reasons why I'd started this book, I didn't know how I was going to accomplish this goal without some divine help. I was really struggling with this difficult new challenge. I wasn't sure I could over-come my discouragement and feelings of inadequacies. I lay in my bed bemoaning my shortcomings as a writer and wishing I could hide in a cave to avoid this newest challenge. A few minutes into my pity party, I recalled the story of a prophet in the Old Testament named Elijah.

I had heard a friend mention that the prophet, Elijah, had found a cave to stay in for a while. I was curi-ous as to why this mighty man of God had chosen to hide in a cave and so I decided to grab my Bible and read about this prophet lived in the Old Testament days. I learned how God answered this prophet's prayer request to show up and display the power of God to the false prophets of Baal. This event on Mount Carmel occurred during King Ahab's reign over Israel. The prophet Elijah gave a challenge to the false prophets by declaring that his God would display a great sign or wonder with fire upon the altar sacrifice. The other prophets agreed to join in with his strange challenge. Elijah asked God to bring down fire from heaven upon the stone altar where he had placed the meat offering and wood. Next, he had men pour pitchers of water three different times all over the offering and the wood beneath it to prove that his God was stronger than their gods. This next verse revealed the results of Elijah's challenge to the prophets of Baal, "Then the fire of the Lord fell, and consumed the burnt sacrifice, and the wood, and the stones, and the dust, and licked up the water that was in the trench. And when all the people saw it, they fell on their faces: and they said, "The Lord, he is God; the Lord, he is God." (1Kings 18: 38-39 KJV) The next thing that happened was that Elijah and his men seized the false prophets and killed them all.

Upon hearing this grievous news, Queen Jezebel was furious and sent a message to God's prophet to beware since she planned to have him killed by the sword. Elijah fled to a cave situated close by mount Horeb to avoid the queen's death order. Let's suppose for a moment that Elijah might've felt depressed and alone like I was feeling right now with my writing problem. He may've even suffered from fear of being killed by a surprise attack during the night as he lay there in the dark cave. I began to ask myself this question. Why had Elijah contemplated the idea of giving up? After this prophet had watched God defeat the false prophets on Mt. Carmel why was he so afraid? I would have to venture a guess here and say: It's possible he may've considered for the first time his own mortality. Had this servant of God forgotten about the mighty miracles he seen in his lifetime? Did he feel like giving up on being a messenger of truth to the Jewish nation? It was a possibility since he was on his own without any type of self-defense.

Have you ever felt so alone and discouraged by life's challenges and disappointments that you may've felt as if God had forgotten you? I can sympathize with you. For I have sat in a gloomy cave of despondency while asking this question, "Where are you, Lord? Why do I struggle in this or that area of my life? I think that Elijah might've asked these same questions. It is in times like this when we must turn to God and allow Him to give us a better perspective on our plight.

In 1 Kings, God came to Elijah while he sat in his cave and asked this prophet a question. "And there he went into a cave, and spent the night in that place;... and, behold, the word of the Lord came to him, and he said unto him, What doest thou here, Elijah?" (1 Kings 19: 9) Towards the middle of this same passage, Elijah was given new instructions. In verse fifteen of this chapter, Elijah was told to leave and go anoint two new kings. As I studied this story about Elijah, I began to understand that he was probably in the wrong frame of mind after running away to live in a cave.

If I find myself struggling or feeling discouraged about my own inadequacies as a writer, I 've learned to stop and take a break from the project. Instead of feeling discouraged and not wanting to tackle the task facing me, I cried out to the Lord for more insight about my dilemma. Listen my friends; God has an answer for every problem you and I might be struggling with. He is right by your side every time you feel discouraged or think about quitting. Ask Him what to do next and wait for his guidance and answers. That very morning as I was bemoaning my situation and weariness, I heard this verse come into my spirit, "God is our refuge and strength, a very present help in trouble." (Psalm 46:1) So right then, I called on the Lord to help me in my weary state of mind and to enable me to continue with my writing project. By this time, I realized it was nearly seven o'clock, so I shut down my computer and decided to tackle this problem after a good night's sleep.

As I sat in front of my computer the following morning, staring at those empty pages, it felt like I was in over my head. I felt discouraged by the daunting situation. After taking another break from typing, I decided to call my friend for her insight. Sherry has been a godsend to me for the last ten years. She is a mighty woman of faith and has encouraged me often throughout this last year, especially in my challenge to finish this book. She prayed for me, and I felt better that day. So here I am sitting at my computer again and I'm working on replacing that deleted chapter. I've turned this writing challenge over to God and I shall believe that I can finish this manuscript in a timely manner. Just like when I picked up the phone to call my friend for help and she offered me some excellent ideas to consider, I think God loves it when we call out to Him for help as well. I have attended college, received my four-year degree, and acquired certain abilities and yet, I must acknowledge this one thing to be true in my life, it is God who has always been close by and waiting to guide me when I ask him for assistance.

***

In the last twenty-five years in America, I have watched numerous TV commercials informing its viewers about the large percentage of people who suffer from depression or anxiety and these statistics are frightening. I recall reading a true story about a woman who suffered for five years with depression even though she was the wife of a minister. I wondered back then why she couldn't get free from her depression and despair. What do the scriptures say about depression and anxiety? I started wondering if God had an answer for people suffering from discouragement or despondency.

I recall many years ago when my husband was dealing with money debt and a struggling business. My husband normally kept all his money troubles to himself. One late evening he arrived back home and told me that he couldn't stop the negative thoughts from crowding into his mind and he didn't know what to do except ask me to pray for him. I was very surprised and taken back by his strange statement and so I followed him into the next room to lay my hands on him and then I prayed fervently. I did what came natural to me at that moment and rebuked the demonic attacks. Then I spoke peace over him in the name of Jesus and began to pray one more time for my husband to be safe and have a sound mind. The next morning, I called his brother-in-law. I informed him about my concerns for my husband and asked him to contact my husband's father.

Since my husband's father had spent many years advising pastors in various churches throughout the United States, I figured he would know what to do to help his own son who was running a business and struggling with his thought life. I was glad to hear that his father, who was then living in Missouri, had called my husband and recommended that he take plenty of walks to clear his head and to improve his mindset during this diffi-cult time. I am sure that his parents began to intercede daily for him to recover from this disparity. Gradually, things began to improve in our business situation and with his thinking. My husband still knows the value of taking walks outside in the fresh air in order to clear his mind. He also has turned his finances and the business over to the Lord and it quite possible that this has helped him deal with the oppressive malady which folks label as depression.

A person suffering from depression usually doesn't see how their troubles may be affecting those around them. My husband didn't talk to me or anyone else about his troubles and this wasn't healthy. I believe that getting wise counsel and emotional support is important step for people who suffer from bouts of despair and feelings of hopelessness. Going to a counselor for practical insight or prayer can be a valuable way to deal with this type of trouble. Sometimes when life brings us several disap-pointments, we can feel discouraged and alone. I realize that depression can also be a result of a person suffering from the loss of a child or failure in a business venture or maybe from losing a job. These kinds of losses can be devastating and debilitating for the individual. There is also the other aspect which has to do with a lack in the brain functions (chemical imbalance) or even hormonal imbalances which can contribute to a person feeling depressed too. I don't hesitate to advise these people to get medical help in these situations.

The Bible states that when a person is overly stressed or worried about their future then they can become depressed. When an individual feels as if things will never change for the better then it can overwhelm them. It might be very helpful for them to talk with a counselor more than one time. A person can also focus on what the scriptures say about them. I believe God's word can bring true help and hope to a person's troubled soul and mind. "Fear thou not; for I am with thee: be not dismayed; I will strengthen thee; yea, I will help thee; yea, I will uphold thee with the right hand of my righteousness." (Isaiah 41: 10) It is important to realize that we are not to live by our feelings. Scripture tells us to not entertain anxious thoughts and that we can have a renewed mind by reading the Word of God.

A wise pastor of my former church used to say this expression about faith versus feelings, "first, there is fact, then faith is applied, and then the feelings come." By this statement, he meant for us to apply truth located in scripture to our lives and believe the promises of God. As we perceive the Word of God and its promises as truth and base our faith on this truth, we can be confident that our soul will eventually acquire the desired feelings of hope, peace, and joy which has been promised to believers. I've chosen to walk by faith and to believe that time spent reading God's word can produce a renewed, positive way of thinking. As I take walks in the scenic outdoors, I end up praising the Lord and thanking my heavenly Father for all our wonderful blessings and victories. This is living in kingdom principles! If we walk in the truth found in the Bible, we will learn how to become people who live with real joy! Think for a moment about what it is like in heaven to be with the Lord. Believers who've died are there right now. Now consider this marvelous idea: His will is for you and me to experience heaven invading our lives daily as we chose to follow his leadings. There is no worry, fear, or disbelief in the heaven's realm. I can certainly carry His presence with me as I give my day to the Lord and take time to acknowledge his presence in my life. As an experiment, try doing this very thing for one month and see if you don't get a better result in you thought process.

In a world full of job stress, money problems, and pain, depression can cling to anyone if they let worry and doubt seep into their thoughts about their uncertain future. An individual who is in despair might consider the possibility that they could be focusing on the negative aspects far too much. I have a good friend who admitted to me recently that she'd suffered from depression a few years. She'd eventually sought medical advice from the doctor for the imbalance in her hormones and the subsequent body troubles. She was given an anti-depressant prescription for one year which enabled her to better manage her thought life and emotions. After that year, she felt like she had her life back to normal. She shared with me that she was able to quit using the meds and I rejoiced with her. My friend also gave God praise for answering her prayers and setting her free from this malady at the end of that long difficult year.

God sincerely wants us to be people who know how to handle challenges and discouraging struggles. I have experienced disappointment and discouragement in my living situation and after complaining to a friend, she encouraged me to be thankful for what the old country house we had. When I changed my attitude and words then things changed and eventually the house problems were fixed, and I could rejoice. I like to encourage young people to remember to daily put on the whole armor of God which will enable them to defeat the enemy's strategies. The devil comes to us to remind us of our lack, our sadness, and our failures. When we place our focus upon the disappointments and struggles then we tend to feel discouraged or defeated by life. First, try this idea of being more thankful for the good things in your life like family, friends and good health; and then release the grief and disappointing problems to the Lord and trust him to either change your attitude or the situation.

CHAPTER NINETEEN

L ife can become difficult and trying for many of us. This world has plenty of sadness, grief, disappointments and pain. However, I want to encourage you that there is an answer! Try asking God to give you His perspective on the matter first. Then, it is always good to put away complaining which only feeds negativity into your troubled soul. The Bible mentions the importance of not murmuring or complaining about life's hard challenges or trials. Instead, let's try going to our Father God with our troubles and disappointments and allow his Holy Spirit to renew our mindset and our attitude.

Sometimes we can slip into a state of hopelessness or feelings of defeat when things in our life keep going from bad to worse. It is extremely helpful at this time to determine if we might be blaming God for not delivering us. In my own life, I made the choice to ask God to forgive me for my wrong thinking after a friend confronted me. We were sharing our feelings about losing someone we cared about. Our family had lost a good friend (a single mom) when she died suddenly a few years back. Her four-year-old daughter had to go live with her biological father. One day, months later, my mentor friend asked me if I was angry with God after the tragic loss of this friend. I thought for a moment and then my reply was yes. I'd been upset and grieved because I hadn't been forewarned by God in a dream about our friend's discouragement. If you recall, I've had numerous warning dreams about loved ones and this gift would cause me to pray much for their protection. When this didn't happen before her death, I was disappointed. My daughters and I were all in disbelief when our dear friend died so suddenly and left her young child without a mother. My mentor/friend had asked the right question to me that day and now I needed to repent for blaming God for not intervening in this situation. This nurse friend's untimely death wasn't his doing and so my frustration towards God was unhealthy and unjustified. Therefore, I needed to turn from my own understanding and allow God to heal my heart in this matter and that is what I did that afternoon.

God can be trusted to take care of us and show us what is more important in life. Often when we are going through a difficult challenge or exhausting time, we don't respond well to platitudes or scripture verses. Sometimes we just need a good friend to listen and to tell us it will work out and that they are praying for us. I've had times of disappointment and pain in my life like most people. I've tried this idea of taking time to pour out my grief or frustrations to the Lord and I feel better after so doing. I am assured that He is close by to listen to our troubles or complaints because the Bible says God cares for us. He will direct us in the best way to walk through life's troubles or challenges.

Take a moment to ask the Lord this question, what is the truth about my struggle or my pain and what do you, Father God, advise me to do about this problem? He is waiting to show you how to live in his truth, his freedom and his remarkable joy. I will stop and take a moment to remind myself to change my outlook or attitude and then find something to be thankful for instead of bemoaning the hard realities of life. No one likes to live with a complainer type. It gets old fast. Let's review the story of Job.

In the forty-second chapter of the Book of Job it mentions that Job changed his thinking to align with the Lord God and then prayed for his misguided friends. In the next few verses, it says that God accepted his change of attitude. There are specific scriptures which instruct people how to live according to God's ways. "And the Lord turned the captivity of Job, when he prayed for his friends: also the Lord gave Job twice as much as he had before." (Job 42:10) I believe this counsel from the Bible gives us the right perspective on how to handle life's disappointments and grievances, so we don't allow depression or despair to enter our hearts and thoughts. Negative thoughts and wrong attitudes can only promote more bad thinking and troubles for our soul. For a fact, I've experienced the benefits of praying and blessing people as Job was instructed to do in the Old Testament. In every situation or frustrating relationship, when I turned the problem over to God and allowed him to direct my thoughts, I've had good results.

***

As you may recall from the previous chapters, I'd been contemplating the idea of traveling to Israel. I'd shared these travel plans with my good friend who had moved to California. I told her that I'd finally purchased my plane ticket and was planning to leave by the end of September of 2017. Surprisingly, she asked me to look for the man of God during my fourteen-day visit to Israel. She wanted me to ask the prophet man when I found him for a word of knowledge about her life struggles. I thought to myself that this was probably an impossible feat to accomplish since the ancient prophets like Isaiah and Elijah were no longer living in the land of Israel. However, I was wrong. One day while I was waiting for an elevator ride to the ninth floor of the hotel in Israel, I bumped into an African man in the hall. He was a white-haired, handsome gentleman with a pleasant disposition. I felt drawn to this man as I introduced myself. We spent the next ten minutes talking and getting to know one another. Since his first and last names were long and very difficult to pronounce, I asked if I could just call him an easier name like that of Isaiah. This elderly gentleman didn't seem to mind my request since he replied with a yes and we continued chatting in the hallway.

Finally, I shared with this new acquaintance in Jerusalem about a friend of mine living back in the states who needed a word from a prophet. This African gentleman, Isaiah, pointed to two chairs in the hallway so we could sit down. I asked him to pray for my friend from California. After praying for her, my new friend, Isaiah, shared what the Lord had spoken to him for me to share with her. "You are to go home and tell your friend from America that there is a 'neighbor' person who has troubled her soul. When you share with her what I've told you about her situation, then God wants you to show your friend how to get free from this trouble and difficulty!" His comments caused me to begin to pray for more wise insight before my next phone conversation with my friend. I wanted to be accurate in my counsel and words of encouragement to her.

I was amazed that I had met and talked to the man of God who was a wise prophet while I was traveling in Israel just as my dear friend had asked me to do. I thanked this kind African man for his insight and prayers. I looked forward to sharing his counsel with my friend and when I returned home to the states that month, I called her and shared about my recent encounter with the gentleman from African and of our time of praying for her. I had been praying for God to enlighten me with a clearer understanding of this word 'neighbor' and who this person might be that had troubled my friend back in America. After we talked on the phone, I told her to forgive that person who had caused her so much grief and trouble. I knew in my heart that it wasn't a next-door neighbor since she'd just relocated to a new area. A week later, my friend understood of who had troubled her life and she made the important decision to forgive that individual. I was grateful for her change of heart, and I believe that long term hurts and offenses with people can cause us great distress and unhappiness if left unresolved. I appreciate my friend's heart to do the right thing. I believe she will be blessed if she decides to heed the wise counsel of this kindhearted prophet man whom I'd met in Israel.

***

We must also believe and speak out this truth: We have the mind of Christ Jesus as specific scriptures teach us. Do you understand that you have been given the right to be called a son of God? Yes, indeed, you and I have been adopted by the Father God and He has given us the right to be called his beloved son or daughter. When we accept the truth that the Father sees us as 'sons of God' and co-heirs with Christ then this understanding will give us enough courage to face life's challenges and to learn how to be overcomers. I have also chosen to make declarations that I am a victorious woman. I have been set free! Jesus abides within me, and his great power is at my fingertips to use! I like to declare scriptures over my life that speak success and abundant life. I have chosen to no longer see myself as a weak person, but instead I now make this type of declaration: "I am an over-comer in this world because of my testimony and what the Lord says about me; I can count on God's promises. There is no question in my mind that God's Word is the abso-lute truth and I know from experience that I can depend on the promises which I've read and believed from the scriptures!

Sometimes I try to imagine how a person suffering from chronic pain or back injuries must feel everyday as they attempt to get out of bed in the morning and struggle through the long, arduous day. I know a couple of people who are suffering like this. They finally had to turn to using pain meds prescribed by their doctors.

As I pondered the fact that some people suffer more than others, I recalled a previous time when I'd been pray-ing and these words from the Spirit of God came into my heart. *Put your finger in the nail holes in my hands.* Well, at that very moment, I decided to do this act by faith, and I imagined myself placing my fingers in the deep nail holes in the Savior's hands as if they were extended out in front of me. I had to believe that God was trying to get my attention about something important at this moment. At first, I thought maybe I needed to really grasp the full extent of deep pain he suffered during the crucifixion. I began to consider how much excruciating pain a person might experience from thick metal spikes being driven into the flesh of his hands and feet. This visual made me become more aware of the agony which the Lord must've endured that day on the hill of Golgotha.

As I discussed this with a good friend, she reminded me of doubting Thomas who was told to place his finger in the Lord's wounds (nail prints in his hands) Next, she turned the conversation around to ask me this question. "Do you have some doubt that God will one day intervene and change someone's physical pain or difficult circumstances? I pondered her question for a moment and then replied with this answer. "Well, I suppose I've doubted that God would ever heal my friend's injured lumbar discs since she has suffered from chronic back pain for such a long time." It's not easy for me to look at my own shortcomings and yet, it seemed that God already knew my thoughts of unbelief that God would ever heal her injured body. In that instance, I stopped and chose to believe for a miracle for this hurting person. We sent a prayer of agreement towards heaven as we spoke life and restoration over this woman's physical pain and disabilities. I shall continue to praise and thank God until we see her fully healed of her physical pain.

CHAPTER TWENTY

While I was traveling overseas in September of 2017, I spent time with some wonderful people and pastors from several countries. I met a pastor who now has an underground church in a Muslim country where they don't allow the preaching of the gospel. He was very gracious and kind to allow me to have an interview with him that day. He didn't mind that I wanted to share his testimony in my book, and he gave me his permission to share how God protected him a few times in his life. I need to mention here that I had let the young people whom I'd met during my travels in Israel and Uganda call me "Momma Cathy" and they love it when I refer to them as my newly adopted son or daughter. I pray for these new friends from Israel and Uganda who I care about and we still are in communication ever since my visit to their countries.

This is my new friend's true story. Adam (not his real name) was born in India, and he was under the influence of the Hindu religion for most of his youth. Later, his father put him into a Christian college. After graduation, he had a very good job working in an insurance company. It was a great life and he made plenty of money during this time. However, he wasn't a happy man. His background history consisted of a grandfather who was an idol worshipper and his father who was an army officer in the military in India. Despite this family lineage, Adam was searching for some meaning for his own life. He went to a Pentecostal church one day and he decided to follow the one true God of Christianity. He gave up his great job and the monetary security to instead become a destitute individual. He had no place to live, and he had to sleep on the floor with eight Muslim men. This was in 1997, and he was extremely grateful to these kind people for sharing their apartment and food with him.

That same year while attending a Pentecostal church, the pastor invited him to have the infilling of the Holy Spirit and to receive power from God. He responded with a yes and then he did in fact, receive the baptism of the Holy Spirit of God. Then to his surprise, the spirit of the Lord told him to leave India and go to an Arab country. He began to understand that God was ordaining him to preach the salvation message by this commission, "Whom shall I send?" In that moment, my new friend, Adam, responded with an answer to this question by saying, "Here I am, Lord, send me." At this time, he needed two hundred dollars to pay for his sleeping arrangement and so he knelt on the floor to pray for provision.

He had no family members in this new country, no friends, and he felt totally alone in this distressful situation. All he knew was that he needed to pay this rent money. Some people he didn't even know came and knocked on the door to give him the money necessary to pay his debt to the landlord. This was a miraculous provision that continued for the remainder of that year.

Every day he was fed by the people there who weren't even part of his own family. The more I listened to him talk, the more I realized that I was hearing about miracles surrounding his unusual life story; within minutes, I realized I needed to get some paper from the front reception desk to record his words as I sat there in the hotel in Jerusalem listening to him share.

Since the preaching of the gospel was forbidden in an Islamic nation, he didn't know what to do while living in this place. Adam asked God this question, "Where should I go Lord?" Then in reply, the Spirit of God told him to go to a hospital. The next thing he discovered was that he could visit with men who worked on a construction site and even housemaids coming out of some of the Arab homes as well as cleaning personnel who worked in the local hotels. As he continued to pray about sharing God's love and truth with these people, he heard the spirit of the Lord tell him to *"go to the streets and you will find connections and God will help you in this new endeavor."* After a while, he remembered the idea of going into the hospital to pray for the sick folks. When he prayed for people there, they'd get healed and then they would ask him this question, "Sir, without medicine, how can you heal us?" His response to these folks was this, "It is not me healing your bodies; this healing has been done in the name of Jesus." The next thing they asked him was this: "Who is Jesus?"

Pastor Adam would then introduce Jesus to them, and they wanted to receive Him as their own personal savior. He told me that there was a total of one hundred and fifty souls that became Christian believers that year as he shared the good news of salvation through Christ

Jesus with everyone he met on the streets. He had to meet with these new Christians at ten o'clock in the evening as he preached the good news in this underground church in a major city since there was no safe place to worship. If a person talked about Jesus or Christianity in an Arab country, that individual will be put in prison and even killed there. As I sat there in the hotel lobby listening to his story, I felt a shudder of dread go through my physical being and I wondered what would occur to this man and his family if he continued to preach about Christ in this foreign country.

Then my new acquaintance, Adam, motioned to me to write down about the first miracle in his life and so I quickly picked up my pen and turned to the next blank piece of paper so I could adequately record his next statements. He shared with me about his father and how his parent had donated five acres of land to his village which needed a water treatment facility plant in India. His father had received a large amount of money to finish this project, but he spent the remainder of the grant money. He was now in debt and was sending a letter to his son in order to get help to clear this debt. In the letter he asked his son to clear his debt and then to send him money to build a house for his parents in the city instead of having to live in the country. My friend told me to write down this response which he sent to the demands of his father, "I have no money to be able to give to you, father!" Then this man from India went to his knees and asked God what to do about this letter.

Adam heard this response, *"Follow me and I will make you fishers of men."* He tore up his father's letter and threw it into the wastebasket. Two weeks later, the next letter came from his father asking again for financial support from his son. He dad had written in the letter that they would commit suicide to escape this debt and shame. My new friend continued sharing that he realized he needed to respond to this letter somehow and so he once again made his petition to God as to what he should do about his parent's dire situation. This time he heard a phrase from the New Testament, which states this truth, "He that loveth father and mother more than me is not worthy of me:... And he who does not take his cross and followeth after me is not worthy of Me." (Matthew 10: 37-38) After hearing these words, Adam tore up his father's letter once more. It was very difficult for him to not follow the traditions of his culture which is to bear the responsibility of taking care of your parents. He sat down next and cried in the time of waiting upon the lord and then he heard the spirit of God tell him this, *"Son, you do my heavenly business by preaching the kingdom of God to the unreached souls and I will take care of your parents, the problems, and their needs will be taken care of."*

Adam didn't hear from his parents for eight months. The next thing that happened in his life involved his past employer, Mr. ——. The owner of the same insurance company he'd worked for before hadn't cancelled his visa. Even though he was not working while living in this Arab country and should've been deported back to his country of India, nothing like that happened to my friend. His former manager at the insurance company called him and offered him his original job again. He told Adam that he would pay him five thousand American dollars as a salary for each month along with a commission fee. As my new friend continued sharing his story with me, he recounted how he started to pray more about this new opportunity. He felt that this invitation was orchestrated by Satan in order to tempt him. Since he needed plenty of money to live, he continued to ask God for guidance and to help him make the right choice about this new job offer. He sat quietly waiting upon God and then he recalled this scripture from the Bible, "But He answered and said, "It is written, 'Man shall not live by bread alone, but by every word that proceedeth out of the mouth of God'." (Matthew 4:4) Then he got a message from his previous boss informing him that there was a letter waiting for him in their office and to come there to collect his mail. Adam told me that he travelled to his hometown in India to retrieve his letter and while he was there, he informed his manager that he will not be coming back to work with this same company, but he will pray for his supervisor. The man responded with this: "Thank you for your prayers, my door is always open to you."

As soon as Adam saw the envelope, he recognized the handwriting was from his father. He rejoiced that his father was still alive, and he had great joy within his heart. Upon opening and reading the letter, he learned that his parents were very sad and didn't know what to do about their debts as they stood on the city bridge that crossed over the river in a certain town in India. Then the next passage said these words, "Your God sent two angels to protect us. Do you want to know who those two were? They were the local policemen who came and grabbed our arms to stop us from our plan to be in the cold river waters below." Then these two men took his parents to the police station, and someone there called the news media and gave the information of this incident to the reporter. Since his father had been a military offi-cer in the Indian army, this was big news. The article in the newspaper stated that this well-known military per-son was so disturbed because his only son, Adam, who now lives in an Arab country did not support his father with enough money to solve his financial troubles. The reporter put a photo of his father with the information into the newspaper for the entire city to read. Once his father's sister had read the article in the newspaper, she rushed over to the police station to pay the fine so they would release her brother and his wife. Then his father went home. Later he decided to sell his property and to pay off his own debt. God provided a way of deliverance and Adam didn't have to be the one to save his parents. The living God saved them! Then his Catholic parents went to a Pentecostal church and received the truth about Jesus. In 2013, his father died and went to heaven. He now looks after his mother who is still alive.

The second miracle that my friend, Adam, wanted to share with me involved his new life as a street preacher while living in a Muslim country. I hurried over to the reception desk of the hotel he was staying in and asked for two more blank pieces of paper to write on and this is his next true-life story. One day after preaching in his night service in the underground church at about one o'clock in the early morning, Arab policemen found this pastor and they asked him to open his bag so they could inspect the contents. When they discovered his Bible inside the bag, they confiscated his money offerings from the church members, his passport and other items and they pushed him into their police vehicle and took him to their jail building. He had to stay one night in a cell and the next morning they informed him that other officers would come to take him to court.

While he waits for this next process, he shares the gospel with the prisoners, but since they are all of the Islamic faith, they did not accept this new belief. Later, the police officers interrogated Adam and because of his Bible and his mobile phone, they looked into his eyes and then surprisingly the man said, "I don't know why, but someone is telling me to release you. I am not going to register your case and you will not be going to court. You are free to leave here. Take your Bible, your phone, passport, and the money in your bag and leave." This was the favor of God upon Pastor Adam. They had the authority to prosecute him and even physically beat him, but they did neither. Instead, they gave him a cup of hot tea and released him the next morning. He was a free man again. When he returned to his place of residence he asked God a question, "Why did you bring me here, God?" The answer back to my friend was this: "*I am preparing you for a greater glory and for more miracles and my provision which you will need to go to many countries and to be my witness where it is prohibited to preach about my son, Jesus. The* peace of God was upon Adam that night and he had no more fear of man after that first experience.

The third miracle that he told me about is even more amazing. Adam was sent to the country of Azerbaijan to share about the good news of the gospel. He was told by the spirit of God to visit a Muslim priest in a mosque. So he decides to obey this commission by getting his visa and a plane ticket to fly to this country. He lands in the capital city during the nighttime. He didn't know where to go in this new city. He was standing outside of the airport, and he didn't know their language. No one spoke English around him, and he wondered what he must do. A policeman in the airport area came over to him and asked him this, "Where do you want to go, sir?" His reply was to say this: "I don't know where to go." Then the man asked him, "Can I take you to a hotel?" This pastor friend replied with these words, "Take me to a hotel that cost twenty-five dollars a day. This was in 2003, and the man replied with a simple word, okay and he called for a taxicab. Then he also accompanied this foreigner in the cab and spoke with the hotel manager to help him complete this money deal. The officer paid for the taxi fare and wanted to meet with Adam the next day. They had breakfast together along with the same taxi driver while the pastor from India shared the gospel with them. These men didn't totally reject the gospel, instead they told him thank you for the story and breakfast and they exchanged telephone numbers.

After this visit, he used the phone directory to locate a translator. A pastor in this country replied by sending someone who could be an interpreter to help him at the hotel. The translator person worked with Pastor Adam to translate his gospel tracts from English language into the country's national language. Then they printed three hundred gospel tracts to distribute to people on the street in many other towns. On the second day of doing this effort, he asked the translator man to take him to the biggest mosque in a large city. They travelled by taxicab, and he asked the Holy Spirit this question, "Shall I go to the mosque and preached about the Son of God?" He recalled a verse from Matthew 28: 19-20, which states, "Go ye therefore, and teach all the nations, baptizing them in the name of the Father, and the Son, and the Holy Ghost, teaching them to observe all things whatsoever that I commanded you: and lo, I am with you always, even unto the end of the world." When they arrived at the place, with the help of his translator he learned what the words said on a plaque on outside of the wall of the mosque, "non-Muslims shall not enter into our mosque." This determined pastor decided to rely upon the leading of the spirit of God in this instance and so the two men entered inside of the mosque. Once again, my pastor friend felt strongly impressed to speak about his Lord and savior, Jesus. When he mentioned the name of Jesus, the priest became very angry and said these words to him, "How dare you come here in our mosque and speak of this Jesus. You will be killed soon. Although he was upset and he'd threatened this visiting foreigner, he still allowed the pastor to pray for him.

At the last, the Muslim priest shouted in an angry tone of voice, "Get out of this mosque. If you speak anything of Jesus, we will kill you." The pastor/evangelist said thank you to the priest and left the mosque with his translator friend. They both headed for the metro train to purchase tickets for the next town. The local police arrived at the train station and told him to stop and come with them and to ask no questions. Then they placed the pastor and his new translator friend into a dark room in the jail house. They opened his blazer jacket and removed his passport, the gospel tracts, his wallet, a small Bible, and his flight ticket to go back home again. They told him to wait there while they made a phone call to the higher authorities. A different officer put him through an interrogation process with many questions. Even though he was in this new and very cold country, he was hot and sweating as he sat there in the police station room in a foreign country. Then this time he had recalled a passage in II Timothy 1: 7, "For God hath not given us a spirit of fear; but of power, and of love, and of a sound mind." *Why are you afraid?"* He became more relaxed. A police officer came to his room and asked this question. "Don't you know this is an Islamic country? There is to be no preaching or distributing of gospel tracts or Bibles here. The punishment for these crimes is lifetime in prison, so do you want to stay in prison for several years?"

The pastor's response was to apologize for disobeying the laws of this country. He continued to talk as he also stated this to the officer, "I'm sorry, but I will have to obey my God, sir!"

"Who is your God?" The Muslim officer asked him.

"Jesus is my God and my Lord who died for me on the cross and rose again after three days. He is alive now and is coming back some day to this world!"

The policeman yells out to him, "How dare you talk about your God in front of me in our jail?"

"The Lord's spirit will help me!" The hopeful man replied.

The officer looked over at him and laughed as he made another comment. "I don't know what this is in me. Something is troubling me in my heart. You are different person and I'm forced to release you. I don't understand why, but this is on only one condition. You should not preach but instead go back to your own country within twenty-four hours from now. If any police officers here catch you in the future, your case will come to me again and I will not release you the next offense. This is a final warning to you!"

"Thank you so much, sir. Thank you for your good heart!" He replied.

The two men, the pastor and his translator friend, both got their wallets, passports back from the police. This evangelist/pastor also received his Bible and the gospel tracts along with his plane ticket too. They shook hands with the man and the guards and bide them good-bye. The police officer escorted them out of the jail house to a gate and to their freedom. God surely rescued this evangelist. I kept writing his story down on paper as he finished sharing with me his testimony of the miracle of protection and deliverance from prison. He explained as he smiled over at me holding my pen and ready to keep writing. "I believe in God whose name is also Jesus. He is alive today and still does miracles every day for people."

Then this new pastor friend of mine went on to talk some more by saying, "My translator said this to me once we were free from the jail,"

"Let's go to the hotel so you can pack your bags and go to the airport!"

"No not yet, I want to still travel to another town first." The pastor said.

The translator man got upset and replied to the pastor with this, "If you don't obey the government police authorities, then it will bring me trouble and even prison possibly."

"If we get caught again, just tell the police that you are only a translator."

He unwillingly accepted the pastor's request and so they travelled to a different town where they stayed for ten days handing out gospel tracts to the people. Then they returned to the city and its large airport. He flew home on the plane unhindered by the police and full of a heart of rejoicing at how God took care of him on this trip. These were his exact words as he motioned for me to continue writing his testimony.

"The Holy Spirit is a real helper for me. The spirit of God is a gentle companion who abides in us always. I was released from the dangers of imprisonment and able to continue freely preaching about the love of God in other countries. I give praise to our heavenly Father God!"

The next day, I met with my new friend from India to listen to another true miracle story of protection which he was willing to share with me. I was very intrigued with this man's faith and his life of dedication to preaching the gospel wherever he was sent. As we both sat in comfortable chairs in the hotel's lobby, I began to record his next story onto paper. The following statements are the remainder of his true story.

"One day, as I was in fasting and prayer, the spirit of the Lord asked me to fly to Iran. I thought I didn't know anyone there!" My friend stated as he smiled brightly to me.

He continued sharing about his experience as I hurriedly tried to write and keep up with him. Next, he shared with me that he went to apply for a visa permit and a plane ticket to obey God. When he arrived in the country of Iran he went to a hotel where he fasted and prayed. He asked the Lord, "Where should I go now". Everyone in this country spoke in the Persian language and didn't understand English.

The next day, my friend, Adam, asked the hotel manager to help him find a tour guide and a taxicab driver who could speak the English language. They locate a man called Abdulah who could drive him anywhere he wanted to go as well as help him translate. He thanked the hotel manager and left to go outside and get into the taxicab. The driver asked him, "Where do you want to go, sir?" The traveling evangelist/pastor replied with this, "I want to go to the biggest mosque in your city!" The driver started the vehicle and drove down the street and asked this question. "Are you going for prayer of Ramadan?" This is the time of thirty days of fasting from food for the Muslim people. He replied with a resounding, NO! Then the driver asked him, "Are you not fasting then?" No came his reply again. "Well, if you're not fasting and wanting to pray today, then why are you going to the mosque?"

"I have a word from the Lord Jesus." The pastor replied to the driver of the taxi.

"Who is this Jesus you are referring to now?"

"I am a Christian believer and a servant of the Son of God, Jesus, who is the God of all creation and of whom I believe on for salvation." He said with strong conviction.

The taxicab driver asked him this, "What are you saying to me? So once more this brave man presented the gospel to this man in the car. The driver stopped the car and then said, "Don't you know you're in the country of Iran? Christians are not allowed inside of Iran to preach. Tell me why you want to go to our mosque?"

"I have a message from the Lord Jesus for this people!"

"Are you going to tell the story of Jesus to this high priest in the mosque too?"

"Yes, I am."

"Then they will stone you to death on this Friday in front of the Muslims or maybe even hang you in the city."

"I am not afraid of dying." He replied.

"They will give me trouble for bringing you to the mosque, so I can't come into the building with you."

"Don't worry they will not harm you, sir! Just tell them you're only doing your job as a taxi driver and a translator for me. You are doing nothing wrong. If they catch me today, you can run away and be safe. I will pay you a little more for your services today." He replied.

The driver of the taxi agreed to take him to the mosque. When they pulled up in front of a large building facing the street, he told the visiting pastor that this was the biggest mosque.

"Go get a person and ask him for permission to enter the mosque. Tell them a tourist from India wants to visit you today." Pastor Adam stated.

His translator returned with the necessary permission, and they entered the building. Once inside the mosque, this pastor saw police, government officials, high priests and reporters from a national television station standing around. His driver learned from a man standing nearby them that this was a special day in their city. It was a National Day of Remembrance for all the freedom fighters for Iran. One person came over and gave a short welcome to this man from India visiting their mosque. He responded with these gracious words.

"I'm from India as a tourist to Iran. I came here to establish a friendship with you all because my friend, Jesus, sent me here today to convey a message to you."

His taxi driver translated the English words into the Persian language for all the officials standing there listening. The TV media reporters were filming this conversation on live television at that moment. As I was writing down his words, I thought, how amazing is the timing of the Lord to send him to this large mosque to deliver his message to so many people in Iran. Then the priest spoke and told him to go ahead with his message.

"Jesus is the Son of God and he died for you and me. After three days, he rose alive again and this same Jesus is coming back."

Everyone there began looking at Pastor Adam with angry faces. It was the grace of God upon him that day. "And God is able to make all grace abound towards you." (2 Corinthians 9: 8) He had stood there and testified of Christ Jesus to these Muslims and high priest by the grace of God. The power of the Holy Spirit helped him to have the words to share in the mosque. Then the priest replied, "We don't believe what you have said."

"No problem, sir. Iran will receive prosperity in the name of Jesus."

"Thank you. Please come to my house for lunch." Next thing that happened to this visitor from India was the priest showed him the visitor's book and told him to write down his name and the message in this book. Adam wrote the message in the English words and his translator friend spoke the words in Persian for the people to hear on the live filming for TV his message. The Islamic priest thanked him for coming to Iran and then the two men were guided to high priests' home situated next to the large mosque. As they sat down in this place, the man spoke and told them today was a fasting from food time for them all. They gave their visitors some apple and orange juice to drink instead.

"Can I offer a word of prayer before leaving your home?"

"Yes, you can."

My friend, Adam, from India prayed for peace and blessings upon this man and his household. Since there were two priests in this home, he asked if someone could take a photo of him with the priests. They took pictures and he said thank you for this time together and left. The taxi driver took him to the hotel for a rest time and then returned by five thirty to get him and drive him to a five-star hotel for dinner meal. As they entered the restaurant area, they saw fifteen priests sitting together at a long table. They saw Adam and recognized him from the televised film earlier in the day and they stood up and welcomed him. With the help of his translator, he was able to share the gospel with these men. He thanked the men and said goodbye and then he left for the night. He told me that it was the anointing of God that helped him to be able to share the good news of the gospel each time that one day in Iran. "There was absolutely a protection from God upon my life as I spoke to the Muslim people. It was the plan of God for the Iranian people to hear the gospel." He declared with much fervor.

The traveling pastor had asked his driver to come back to his hotel in the morning. The driver returned to talk with him in the morning and he said, "Pastor, please come to my house today to bless my home and my family." He said yes and they drove across the city about ten kilometers until they reached their destination. Before he even had left the hotel, he told me that he'd a concern, "should I go to this man's place, Lord?" As he waited to hear some counsel or wisdom from God, he heard this response, *Do not doubt, I am with you, servant of the Most High God, go! Remember the words in Romans 8: 14, "For as many as are being led by the Spirit of God, they are the sons of God.* So that was the main reason for him continuing with this taxi driver that morning. He had a feeling that something good might happened during their time together.

The man opened his door into his apartment. He welcomed Adam and motioned for him to sit down on his sofa. Then he went into another room and came back out with a Bible and started to cry. He said this to his new acquaintance, "I am a missionary in my country of Iran. I lived in a different town before coming to this place. (This revelation and truth came as quite a surprise for my pastor friend that day). Then he hugged this newfound brother in the Lord. This man went on to share with Pastor Adam about how he'd been all alone in this apartment building and his family lived away from him in that other town. It was a marvelous ending to a dramatic story for sure. The Lord had provided the right person and interpreter for Adam while he was visiting Iran. He shared with me about a scriptural promise and protection as he related this last time of fellowship with his new friend in Iran. (Psalm 34:7) Surely there were angels that had come to help this traveling pastor/evangelist to be able to share the gospel in this Muslim country of Iran. He learned that day that he did not need to be afraid to go to any Islamic country to preach the gospel. He has been living in a Muslim country for twenty years now and he mentioned to me about an important scripture promise where God declares that when He is for us then no one can prevent us from being safe and doing His will.

I rejoiced with my new pastor friend as we sat together in the hotel lobby in Jerusalem that day. I was excited to have his permission to include in my book his true testimonies about all the miraculous protection and victories. We still correspond by email messenger now that I am back in the states. I really have enjoyed listening to his recent audio video and learning about his mission trip back to India. He just sent me a short video clip about his trip to Uganda, Africa because I had shared my hope to travel to Kampala, Uganda one day. Recently, I sent my friend a second message by email stating that I was praying and planning a ministry trip to Kampala this coming March of 2018. He responded by informing me that he was now praying for my travels to Africa and that he had also been to Kampala, Uganda last year. Pastor Adam, who I'd met in the land of Israel, is in my estimation a very good man and a trustworthy friend. I was thrilled to make his acquaintance while staying in the same hotel in the city of Jerusalem last year. I am considering the idea of going to visit him and his family someday. If it is God's will then I shall go to stay with Pastor Adam when the time is right.

CHAPTER TWENTY-ONE

How would you like to partner with God? What if you could be called a friend of God like the patriarch, Abraham? I would like to be a person who operates out of a strong faith-based life like Abraham and Joshua. My new friend from India was not afraid to go into countries where they threaten to put Christians in prison for preaching the gospel. There were men and women in the Bible who walked with God so resolutely and powerfully that the inspired authors of the Old Testament books included those testimonies in those biblical writings. One such individual was Enoch who walked so closely with the Lord that God chose to take him in a moment to heaven to live with him. Enoch did not taste death like the average person living here on earth. Enoch had a close relationship with God, and this must've pleased his heavenly Father.

Deborah was a woman who lived during the Old Testament days. She was so anointed and favored by God that she became a well-respected judge during the time that Israel needed wise leadership. In Judges 4: 4 it describes this woman. "And Deborah, a prophetess, the wife of Lapidoth, she judged Israel at that time. She dwelt under the palm tree…and the children of Israel came up to her for judgment." Then she called for Barak and instructed him about how to win the coming battle when she states with great conviction that God would help him have a victory. "And Barak said unto her, if thou wilt go with me, then I will go: but if thou wilt not go with me, I will not go." (Judges 4: 8)

Barak goes on to believe for this victory as Deborah predicted and he defeats the commander of the Canaanite army. I believe it is possible even today for an individual to follow godly principles, to have a closer relationship with Him, and to become a true friend of God. I desire this in my own life and so I'm learning to trust in the Lord's more each day. I believe that these heroes in the Bible learned to spend quality time with God and this produced great victories in their lives. I also believe there is another part to why they were successful people. They may've heard a directive from the Lord, and I believe they obeyed God's counsel instead of their own ideas. In my life, I've experienced the blessing and favor from the Lord when I obeyed his counsel and instructions.

I also have a passion to see people healed and delivered from cancer and other diseases and afflictions. I desire to understand God's principles more fully in the area of praying successfully for people who need a healing touch. Allowing God's truth to change our attitudes and actions must go hand in hand with a person's prayers for divine healings and miracles. Faith sometimes looks like this: We must stand on the promises of God no matter what we see or feel until we receive the answer or the healing which we need. On the other hand, God can certainly use the doctors and their medical expertise to help people get well too. However, even though I believe in divine healing and miracles, I will still encourage people to go to a doctor for serious problems and get a proper diagnosis first. I have a plaque on my wall that says this, "Prayer Changes Things" and it reminds me to first go to the Lord with my needs. And if necessary, I will of course make an appointment with the doctor. I like to call this idea a 'balanced lifestyle plan.

***

I'd like to share an event that happened to me one summer day in 2016 and which has had a significant impact upon my life. I had bought a train ticket in order to travel from my hometown to the city of San Francisco to meet a friend and his kids so I could join them and watch a Giants MLB game at ATT Stadium. During the eighteen-hour train ride, I'd gone up to the observation deck to view the scenery and to play a couple of my favorite DVD movies on my laptop (PC). When I returned to my seat the person who'd been sitting next to me had disembarked. In his place was another man. This person was the exact opposite of the first occupant. Instead of a rather thin body shape this next man was bulkier, of a different ethnic background and skin color, and he had several dreadlocks in his dark hair.

His initial words to me came out like this: "Where have you been, I've been waiting for you." This caught me off guard slightly, but I responded with this answer, "Well, I was up top in the observation deck of the train watching two of my most favorite DVD videos, "Sahara" and "Days and Nights" since my trip will last for eighteen hours total.". After I settled myself in my original seat next to the window and introduced myself to this friendly person, we chatted amicably for the next hour or so. He told me that he was thinking about writing a book about his life experiences and I replied that I was working on a fiction book myself. He mentioned the idea of writing about one's own life experiences and I gave this idea some consideration as we talked. We became more acquainted, and I soon began to realize from his conversation that he was also a believer. During our entire visit that afternoon and into the evening, I was amazed at how loving, caring and attentive he was towards me. It was as if this stranger was thoroughly engaged in our conversation, and he genuinely cared about my life.

Feeling more and more comfortable with this new acquaintance, I shared my concerns about this weird problem with my eyes. Ever since I had spent an afternoon diving into the pounding ocean waves of the Pacific Ocean two months before, I'd noticed these thin, black circular lines on both sides of my peripheral vision. Some folks might say that this is the result of a degenerative eye disease. However, I decided to not accept this report, but instead I chose to seek God for complete healing for my eyes. I asked this man to pray for my eyes to be restored and healthy again. He laid his massive hands over my eyes and prayed for me. Then he made the curious comment that I would see the Glory of God. I accepted his interesting insight and pondered it in my heart from that day on. Next, I asked him to pray for my daughter who was still struggling with some residual side effects from her bout with cancer years earlier. His next statement gave me great hope for her complete recovery and well-being. He shared with me what he saw in the spirit. He told me he had a picture of a young woman in his mind's eye, and she was being held in the Lord's arms and she was healed. His prophetic insight gave me great hope for my daughter to be completely healed and well. Then I continued sharing with him about the plot of my fiction novel since he'd expressed the same desire to write a book. I found myself feeling at ease and very comfortable with my new traveling companion.

Eventually I suggested we ought to head up to the observation deck where we could talk more freely. He liked that idea and so we headed up to the train's upper deck. We spent the next few hours talking about the goodness of the Lord and what I wanted to see happen in my life. Then, since it was quite late and he had to depart at two in the morning for his destination, Bethel Church in Redding, California, we headed back to our original seats. I didn't want my new friend to miss his final stop, so I told him to get some sleep. Before he dozed off, he mentioned that he was going to walk the streets and pray for healing for the people he might encounter in the city of Redding. I mentioned that I'd love to get off and visit Bethel Church as well. His immediate reply to me was, "Well then, you should come join me in praying for people in this city." I wanted to join in his evangelist efforts, but common sense kicked in and I reminded him that I had a friend in California waiting for me to arrive that next morning. I thanked him for the invitation and wished him much success for his time of doing the street ministry. I feel asleep for a couple of hours and then awoke to see the empty space next to me. Even though this stranger was gone, I will always hold our conversation and time of praying close within my heart. He blessed me and left me feeling encouraged and hopeful about my future and confident that God was caring for my daughter's health issues.

The amazing thing for me, as I looked back on this marvelous time spent with this caring, soft-spoken individual, was that my heart had burned within me the entire time as we talked. It was as if I was walking with the Lord like the disciples had done centuries before on the road to Emmaus in the land of Israel. Now as I reflect upon this wonderful time of sharing and praying with this larger-than-life individual who'd sat next to me on the long train ride, I wonder if I had entertained an angel unawares like it says in the Bible. "Be not forgetful to entertain strangers: for thereby some have entertained angels unawares." (Hebrews 13:2) It really didn't matter to me if he had been an angel or not, I believe that I shall see the glory of God like this man had stated and that my daughter will be fully healed as she is held in God's loving embrace like he'd mentioned.

And one more thing I just realized while writing about this experience; maybe this man on the train ride had come into my life to plant a seed in my heart about the need for me to write a nonfiction book about my own life experiences. It is true that God cares about the details of our lives, and He has a wonderful plan for each of our lives. You see, some months after being home from my trip to California, I started feeling as if God's was trying to get my attention. It was as if I needed to lay aside the fiction novel work for a while. I decided to comply with this nudging from the Holy Spirit. Instead of working on the fiction manuscript, I sensed that I was being given a new assignment in the area of writing. I felt compelled to share about the powerful miracles and healings that had happened to my family members over the last ten years. This writing project has been challenging and yet, rewarding for me. I believe that it is important for us to remind our children and grandchildren of the miracles we've experienced so they can believe for healings and miracles to happen in their lives as well.

I also have a great hope for all my children to become powerful prayer warrior like their grandmother. I have tried to impart a certain truth to my children which I learned from my mother. Later in her life, she'd discovered the key to living a life filled with an amazing faith. She also taught me how to appropriate God's promises from the Bible. Before this, I would simply read the scriptures and enjoy them, but I've learned from her mentorship that I can apply a scripture such as, the 'abundant life' promises and then see the fruit of my declarations. I now make scriptural declarations which are powerful and have the amazing potential to produce fruitfulness and abundant life in my life. I've been transformed by believing and speaking forth these biblical truths. I have chosen to share this same insight with my own children and my hope is they will carry on this legacy by teaching their children how important it is to appropriate God's promises for their own well-being.

There are many times in my life where I needed strength and so I've called upon the Lord to infuse me with His abundant life and to give me a renewed mind. I must confess that I've also desired to gain more knowledge about the supernatural realm that our Lord walked in while on this earth. There are some verses in the New Testament which had previously been difficult for me to fully understand and apply to my own life such as the one where it talks about the transformation and the renewing aspect in Romans chapter twelve. I believe in this promise for all believers and yet, there were days when I found it hard to look past my own inadequacies to be able to understand and apply a scripture truth. Why couldn't I seem to understand this concept or apply it to my own life? A transformed or renewed mind seemed unattainable for me. Plus, I didn't have a mentor/friend to call for insight or teaching about this concept back then.

Even though I'd read this scripture several times in the past, I didn't have a clue as to how to apply this scripture truth from the Book of Romans to my own life and to see some actual change. How could quoting this verse create a renewed mind for me I wondered? I was feeling frustrated with my lack of understanding in this matter. Then, just this morning I came across a verse that opened the eyes of my understanding. "For to be carnally minded is death; but to be spiritually minded is life and peace." (Romans 8: 6) I started saying this simple prayer for a while, "Holy Spirit, come and be Lord over my attitude, my actions, and my appetites." I call this prayer declaration the three valuable, life changing A's. Once you invite the Lord to be in control of your thoughts, attitudes, and actions, then you can come under His divine influence and favor. God will perform the changes and the renewing of your mind and soul. He is the expert in this area of changing people with His grace and love.

The art of being content in whatever state I found myself wasn't easy for me either. I do understand the importance of readjusting my perspective about life and about how I view God. However, there have been a few times when I was upset with God for not answering my prayer requests. For instance, it was especially hard to praise God since I was still driving an older Nissan car (1997) that could break down any day. The car's paint had started to peel off and therefore, it looked unsightly to my dismay. I was embarrassed to own an older car and wished I had the ability to purchase a newer car. I've retired from a part-time job and so I couldn't rely on that extra income any longer. Now I had to learn to trust God to provide for my future needs.

To date, after praying for a newer car for many years, I can joyfully report that my husband just purchased a 2009 Toyota Corolla vehicle for me. I am thrilled beyond words to have an excellent-running vehicle that looks super clean and well maintained. I like the way this newer car looks as I drive around town. I feel cared for and honored by my husband since he chose to buy this car through the bank and build up his credit in the process. The idea of purchasing a newer car from a car lot was something my husband had decided many years ago he would not ever do. He believed in buying a less expensive car through the newspaper ads and paying cash at the time of purchase. I think this is a good plan and yet, I always wanted a beautiful new car. This vehicle has a much better engine and four new tires and so I feel safe as I drive on the freeways. I am also grateful to the Lord for providing a car that had only one previous owner and plus, it had low mileage.

***

As a believer, I have come across this good news: God delights to show people how much He truly cares for them. He is a God of kindness and mercy. He is willing to show favor and blessings to an individual who worships Him with a thankful heart. Not only does God want us to be successful and to prosper as we learn more about His ways, but our heavenly Father also wants to extend kindness and mercy to people in their time of desperation and lack. Take for instance, the wealthy woman living in the town of Shunem during the Old Testament time. She took in a prophet man named Elisha and fed him. In return, the prophet asked this woman what she desired from him, and her reply was to have a son. He promised her she'd have a son within a year's time, and she did. However, the next time she needed Elisha it was because her son had been very ill and had died. In her grief and desperation, she called for him to understand about her loss. (2 Kings 4: 14-17 & 18-20)

This grieving Shulamite woman needed consolation like any loving parent would want. When she traveled to Mount Carmel to visit this prophet she shared about her son's death and her great sorrow. Elisha came back with her to see the boy and when this prophet asked God for direction about this problem, God showed him how to believe for the boy to recover and live again. The prophet of God, Elisha, placed himself upon the child's dead body and breathed into his nostrils and then he had to do this act one more time before the child sneezed seven times and came back to life. (2 Kings 4:34-35) Another time there was a widow and her deceased husband had left her with heavy debt and she was in desperate straits when she asked Elisha the prophet for assistance. There was a certain woman who needed the prophet's advice in Book of 2 Kings. "Then she came and told the man of God. And he said, Go, sell the oil, and pay your debt, and live thou and thy children of the rest." (2 Kings 4:1 & 4:7) This is a great example of how God directed the prophet to bring provision and protection to a widow lady and her sons. Just like in this biblical account of the woman getting a word of knowledge as to what to do exactly, I believe that God will send us specific insight or counsel for success as we also cry out for his guidance even in this present-day world.

CHAPTER TWENTY-TWO

As I've already stated in a previous chapter, I travelled in September of 2017 to the Holy Lands. There were numerous breathtaking wonderful sites which I encountered while traveling on a tour bus in Israel. On the third day of traveling, our tour bus parked on a hillside, and we all exited the bus to get a view of the ancient city of God. I had a better vantage point-view of this awe-inspiring city of Jerusalem from where I stood on a steep hill called Mount of Olives. The pale, light-yellow limestone walls of the city with its tall stone gates really caught my attention. Then a few days later, my friend and I visited the inside area of this same city called Jerusalem. As I approached the famous Western Wall after passing through the Israeli soldier's check-point, I couldn't help but feel a powerful drawing to this place. It was a magnificent sight to behold. The tall, white and tan colored limestone structure captures one's heart, emotions, and senses immediately. As I turned around to walk to the next area of this huge courtyard, I glanced up to see the most glorious sight of the flag of Israel with its Star of David symbol placed in between the two distinct blue borders. I have this scene ever etched into my soul; the flag of God's chosen people fluttering gently in the breeze and the aquamarine-blue skies in the background. I have a great affinity to this holy land, and I love the Israeli flag and what it represents. I purchased a replica of the beautiful flag, and it hangs on my bedroom wall today.

As my friend, Esther, and I walked the cobblestone streets of Jerusalem, we saw a small group of rabbi's walking together on the cobblestone street. They wore long, blue and white prayer shawls draped over their shoulders and if seemed as if I had been translated back to the ancient Hebrew days. I also saw a few Jewish men wearing somber black attire as they strolled past us on their walk down the same cobblestone streets. These Jewish individuals never looked our way as they passed by. I took a few photos of these people to show the family back home. It was as if ancient history and the Jewish culture had come to life right before my very eyes. My impression of these people is that they have a gentle, reserved nature; as well as a desire to be left alone by the tourists who flock in multitudes to their sacred city. I wonder if they would prefer to live in peace and quiet within the high walls that surround this noble city of Jerusalem. One gets the impression as one walk around the different sections of this famous city that the inhabitants would be happy to not have to deal with the constant attention from the multitude of onlookers who daily frequent their ancient city. After viewing the many historical sites within the ancient city of David, I still only wanted to return one more time to see the 'Western Wall' and all its majestic, but sublime beauty. I left my small pieces of paper with the many prayer requests from friends and family members inserted into the cracks of this gigantic wall that day.

This famous site was one of my favorite places to visit. I felt very close to God as I approached this venerable wall to stand in awe and pray for the peace of Israel and the surrounding nations in the Middle East.

I sensed God's presence while standing at the base of this huge wall built of century old limestone and mortar brickwork. I knew the God of Abraham, Isaac, and Jacob was still present in this ancient city of Jerusalem. While I was traveling in Israel, I met a lady named Deborah who shared with me her own experience while standing next to the Western Wall section of the Old Jerusalem area. She told me that she had sensed the holy presence of God there during her visit. This area is located near Solomon's Temple or what some Israeli people call the first temple mount place. She then told me about the verse located in the Book of Chronicles, where God answers King Solomon who had just completed the building of the temple, "Now mine eyes shall be open, and mine ears attentive to the prayer that is made in this place. For now, have I chosen and sanctified this house, that My name may be there forever: and mine eyes and mine heart shall be there perpetually." (2 Chronicles 7:15-16)

I looked up the word, perpetual, in the dictionary and its meaning is this: continuing for an endless amount of time. This scriptural truth that God's presence is still there and will remain continually upon the temple ruins is truly amazing. As I read this passage, I was thrilled to see the written word as a confirmation for what I'd experienced as I sensed the actual presence of God's as I stood there admiring the front portion of the Western Wall in the ancient city of David. My heart's desire is to experience God's presence more and more in our worship services at church as we, like King Solomon, offer up our worship and thanksgiving to the only true God, Yahweh.

The passage in seventh chapter of Chronicles told of what had occurred after Solomon had finished making his long prayer to God that day. Then fire from heaven came down to earth and it consumed the priest's offerings on the altar in the temple. The next thing that happened was that the glory of the Lord filled the house. There are verses in the Old Testament which describe the glory of God resting in the sanctuary among the Israelites. Just think about this, God's presence is still there in that same area of the old city of Jerusalem. I have walked by the ruins of that temple, and I have experienced the reality of a divine presence and beauty in that place. I wish for God's holy presence to come and fall upon us during worship times in America so that we will also experience the cloud of God's glory in our midst like the Jewish people did back in the ancient days of Israel. This might only happen as we all determine to worship the Almighty God as the Holy Spirit directs us to do.

My second favorite place to visit in Israel was the Jordan River area where hundreds of people come daily to be baptized. For many folks this sacred act of identifying with the Son of God can be a life changing experience. This colorful river water is a brilliant greenish hue which literally captivated my senses. The foliage and slender trees surrounding both sides of this beautiful river were amazing to behold. Everything I took in at first glance seemed to invite me to come closer still. I felt like an artist who needed to have my easel, paints, and apron tucked under my arms so I could sit down by the river's edge and recreate this mystical, magical scene onto canvas and then take it home on the plane to America.

I wished I could have stayed there longer and enjoyed the idyllic and peaceful scenery. It felt as if I was seeing a glimpse of heaven's beauty and peacefulness as I stood in the waist deep river watching fish swimming around my legs while two doves flew over my head to land on a tree branch nearby. I closed my eyes for a minute and tried to imagine the Lord being baptized right there so many centuries ago. Then I recalled how the Spirit of God came down in the form of a dove and rested on the son of man as he came up out of these same waters. The sight of a white dove flying there is a reminder of the peace that God has bestowed upon this Hebrew nation. The dove is also a symbol of the anointing of the Holy Spirit which is a gift for all believers. The Book of Acts describes how the Lord instructed the disciples to wait in Jerusalem until they received this gift from heaven. The same Holy Spirit that enabled the disciples to do mighty works is available today to all who ask for it. One of the benefits of this heavenly gift is that you will have more boldness to share the gospel wherever you go. The first chapter of the Book of Acts declares this blessing for us, "But you shall receive power, after that the Holy Ghost is come upon you: and ye shall be witnesses unto me both in Jerusalem, and in all of Judea, and in Samaria, and unto the uttermost parts of the earth." (Acts 1:8)

My next favorite spot to visit was the empty tomb of Jesus. This place had its own special aura and sublime beauty. As I walked through the peaceful garden scenery with its many majestic colors and historical significance, I felt as if I had stepped into an ancient venerable era.

Next, I sensed an awe-inspired serenity hovering over this beloved garden site as I walked throughout it. Towards the end of our short journey, I stopped to marvel at the peacefulness and the historic truth which captured my soul as I gazed into the open tomb. The truth that He is risen and is alive forever more began to well up within my heart as I beheld the empty grave. I could almost envision the two women in the Bible, Mary of Magdalene and her friend, Joanna, walking down the same garden path and stopping by the same wine press before taking the stone steps which led down towards the entrance of the tomb. I rejoiced with my new friends, Esther, Adeline, and a friend from India as we walked up the stone step and then reverently entered this sacred, empty tomb which shouts for the world to acknowledge the power of resurrection life in its full reality.

Once we were back outside of the tomb, I walked around and marveled at each area that contained lush vegetation with roses lining each small stone pathway. The second time I explored this historic site I found it to be even more peaceful and pleasant than the first visit. It felt as if I was standing on holy ground, and I wondered if there were angels hovering nearby us. This sacred tomb site is supervised by American and British folks who gladly guide tourists to each portion of the garden settings as they answer everyone's questions. As I walked about the entire garden that day, I stopped this second time to view again the ancient empty tomb which had been carved out of a large stone formation. I was amazed at how few tourists were there this time. I was enjoying the quiet solitude this time around and so I began to take more photos to show my family back in America.

Earlier in the day I had been told by my friend, Esther, to be sure and bring my passport to enter and leave Jerusalem to not be detained by the soldiers who guarded the checkpoints. So, I was wearing my light-weight fanny pack under my shirt which held my passport, my American ID card, and a debit card. After taking several photos with phone camera, I would insert my phone back into the zippered purse. I took a few more pictures of the ancient wine press area with its unique stonework and then headed across the courtyard to use the restroom facility. On my return from there, I walked along the final stone pathway to reach the gift shop building and meet up with my two friends. A British personnel member who was one of the guides in this famous garden site happened to see me coming down the pathway and so he came closer to chat with me. He held in his hand a small, flat looking wallet with a photo ID displayed through the clear plastic window. The next thing he did was to ask me what he should do with this lost item. I answered the man with, "You could take it over to the gift shop and then the person who lost it might stop in there to ask about their lost ID card." He kindly smiled over at me and held the small piece of identification closer to my face. I suddenly recognized my own face staring back at me! "Oh, my goodness," I exclaimed to this kindly gentleman dressed in the normal employees' khaki-tan outfit, "That's my American driver's license/ ID card; it must have fallen out of my fanny pack while I was taking photos today. Thank you so much for finding me and returning my wallet!"

I was so glad to have my small wallet which also contained my debit card back in my possession that I decided to go into the gift shop and purchase a small banner gift there. I intended to give this banner gift to my daughter to hang in her new home in North Carolina. I was eager to share with my friends about this amazing mini-miracle which happened for me while visiting the garden site. Now I could leave Israel and board a plane heading for my homeland without being stranded in Istanbul, Turkey on my return flight. I had been so confident that if I kept all my important documents in this zippered pack around my waist that I wouldn't have any trouble traveling in Israel. This was not the case for me as I nearly lost all my identification documents that very afternoon while taking photographs. So, for any trips in the future, I plan to carry one pack for my important passport and my ID card and a second smaller purse for my camera/ phone. Please remember, I was travelling by myself to a foreign country for the first time in my life and I was not an experienced traveler. After that scare however, I will make sure to keep my camera separate from my ID and my important bank debit card.

Towards the last few days of riding a bus with our capable tour guide, we headed to Judea, Samaria, and finally, to the beautiful city of Nazareth. The heavily loaded bus rumbled along the steep, dirt road until it reached a high ground region that overlooked the valley below. We could see for miles around us. There was a rich, fertile region and it displayed many different crops and vegetation growth in both directions. The last spot of interest we visited was an area called Mount Carmel. As the afternoon sun beat down upon this high elevation, I went in search of tree shade. To the left of a picturesque church structure, I found a quiet place to sit and meditate. I decided to stay in that grove of trees and boulders for a while in order to relax and rest on one large boulder which also gave me a grand view of the valley below.

I was not interested in just looking around this site with our tour group. Instead, I was hoping to sit and commune with the Lord on Mt. Carmel that sunny afternoon. Resting on a smooth, creamy colored boulder, I prayed to the Living God for my own destiny to be fulfilled. While resting there under a grove of trees, I knew for sure that God was sending me to Africa soon. I needed to get a hold of God's directives or insight for the next travel dates to fly across the ocean to the continent of Africa. At that time, I just didn't know which region in Africa I was being led to visit exactly.

I stopped briefly to reflect on the battle that Elijah had to fight to prove who his God was to those standing against him on Mount Carmel. While relaxing in the tree shade on this same mountain spot, I sensed a strong presence of God right then. Like Elijah's younger apprentice, Elisha, I too needed the power and anointing of God upon my life to accomplish all that God wanted for me in my future travels. So, I called out to God for his blessings on my life while sitting there on the hill area of Mount Carmel in Israel. The large smooth boulder I was resting upon that day had a mixture of white and light brown colorings. I had never seen anything so beautiful as those large rock formations and I was taken by their simple smooth surface. I would love to have a few of these boulders situated in my back yard to sit on and show off to my friends. I decided to pick up a few small rocks lying on the ground nearby to bring home to my friends so they could experience a tiny bit of the grandeur of Mt.

Carmel. As I sat there asking the Lord to guide me and to give me his courage, I felt his gentle loving presence again and his words of encouragement resounded within my heart. That special time in Israel when we stopped on a famous mountain area is one memory that I hold dear to my heart. I am so grateful that God's spirit had directed me to travel to the holy lands and experience this rare place of beauty. I shall never forget this experience of being in Israel. I loved the fact that I could walk in the land that holds so much amazing historic significance for all the world to see and enjoy. God's plan for me to go there was perfect!

I want to share a unique experience with you. When I was going to a community college in my hometown, I went with my mom and her friend to a Full Gospel Businessmen's meeting. After the dinner meal, people were going over to wait in line for a man who would pray for them. I asked my friend, Eunice, what was happening there with the people and her reply was that this Episcopalian preacher was expecting God to baptize people with the power of the Holy Spirit with the evidence of speaking in new tongues like the bible talks about. Well, I gave this some thought and then I responded with these words, *"I want all that God has for me and so I shall go over there and wait my turn too!"*

The preacher man laid his hand on my head and prayed for me to be filled with God's love and power. Then he encouraged me to start telling God how much I loved him and to thank and praise the Lord in English to begin with. I complied with his instructions and then a strange word came out of my mouth. He asked me if I knew what that word meant and I responded with, "Ah, no, I don't have a clue as to what this word means!"

He told me that the word, 'Abba', is the same as the English word of 'father'. I went back to my seat at the table and relayed my encounter with my mom and her friend. Eunice shared with me that I was to not allow the enemy to lie to me with thoughts about this experience being not from God, but instead she encouraged me to keep practicing and using my heavenly prayer language often. Her words stayed with me through the next few years of college, and I continued to pray in my new language until I had more words and more understanding of this gift of the Holy Spirit and why it is so important for believers to use. My experience with hearing the gospel, receiving the baptism of the Holy Spirit and then being introduced to the concept of water baptism two years later was like the story I found in the Book of Acts where Cornelius heard the disciple Peter sharing the good news, he believed on the Lord shortly thereafter, and then received the gift of the Holy Spirit and evidence of speaking in new tongues that day. And then he was later baptized in water to profess his faith in the Savior. "While Peter was still saying these things, the Holy Spirit fell on all who heard the word. And the believers from among the circumcised who had come with Peter were amazed, because the gift of the Holy Spirit was poured out even on the Gentiles. For they were hearing them speaking in tongues and extolling God. Then Peter declared, "Can anyone withhold water for baptizing these people, who have received the Holy Spirit just as we have?" And he commanded them to be baptized in the name of Jesus Christ. Then they asked him to remain for some days." (Acts 10: 44-48)

CHAPTER TWENTY-THREE

Our family has encountered the merciful kindness of God in four different occasions when some of our family members have been confronted with the possibility of dying. The first time was when our oldest son's life was almost taken by a hunter's bullet as a teen. The second time was when God kept our daughter from dying from a disease (AML) and the third miracle involved our other daughter, Kristina, who been rushed to the ER one scary afternoon. She was fortunate that a second doctor who was her obstetrician before this was able to finally solve a serious bleeding problem for her and she recovered safely. Lastly, there was another big miracle when the medical team discovered what was wrong with our sixteen-year-old grandson, Benjamin's heart after many months of him under-going different tests. By the time he was seventeen, he needed to have open heart surgery. The doctor had to repair a life-threatening problem which had previously caused our teenage grandson's right atrium section of his heart to be dangerously enlarged. I've been praising God ever since for His miraculous protection and timely intervention in all our family member's lives. A year before this all occurred, I was given a frightening warning dream about our grandson, Benjamin. In my dream about my grandson, I'd sensed that something dreadful had happened to him, and it shaken his father terribly. I couldn't even share the awful dream with my son, Robert. I had to rely on a close friend to pray with me about it for a long time. Then I decided to tell my son, Jonathan, so he could pray for his nephew, Benjamin's' safety while he was attending a public high school. At the end of that year, we were all so relieved to learn that the doctors could resolve a very serious heart issue problem for Benjamin with the surgery and a closely watched medical plan of recovery and rest. I tend to pay attention to my dreams now.

I have come across other stories in the Bible that tell of the merciful kindness which the Lord has shown to people. One example of God's kindness towards people can be found in the story of Jonah. God had asked this man to go to the people of Nineveh and proclaim God's disappointment with the wicked folks living in this great city. Jonah didn't like this request and so he chose to not obey but instead he ran away by boarding a ship that was headed for the open seas. The Lord God caused a big wind and storm to prevail which created a serious problem for the crew of this ship. They were afraid for their lives and so they questioned Jonah about why he was fleeing from God. Jonah informed them of his mistake and the only remedy to this impending disaster was for them to hurl him into the ocean. They complied and then God stopped the raging sea waves at last. After being swallowed by a huge whale, Jonah cried out to God for mercy with these words, "But I will sacrifice unto thee with the voice of thanksgiving; I will pay that that I have vowed. Salvation is of the Lord." (Jonah 2:9-10)

God delivered Jonah from the belly of the whale and showed him great mercy and kindness despite this man's disobedience. Then God commissioned Jonah to go Nineveh again and to proclaim this statement, "… Yet forty days, and Nineveh shall be overthrown." After hearing this verdict through Jonah, "So the people of Nineveh believed in God, and proclaimed a fast, and put on sackcloth, from the greatest of them to the least of them." (Jonah 3:4 -5) As the people of Nineveh repented of their wicked ways and all violence, then God relented of his judgment and showed His great mercy, kindness, and compassion to the entire city. I am grateful for the fact that our Heavenly Father shows great loving kindness and forgiveness to those who turn to Him with a humble and contrite heart. His mercy endures forever. Thank goodness God wants to bestow favor and goodness towards people as they turned around to obey Him. What a cruel and sad world this would be if God judged us by our wrong actions, mistakes, and foolish decisions and did not give us a second chance. Fortunately, the New Testament speaks of a better covenant, one he calls a covenant of Grace and not of man's works. I am thankful for this better provision which comes through God's Son, our Savior.

***

I'd asked my one friend who has moved recently to a different community if she minded if I shared about her battle with cancer in my book and she thought about my request for a moment and then she replied with a yes. Jessica is married and has a young son who likes to play baseball. When she was thirty-five years old and her son was only two and half, she was a very active woman. Since she enjoyed exercising and running often, she tended to pay close attention to her body. One morning she detected a lump in her right breast which began to concern her. Her husband reminded her of the doctor on TV who had a brain tumor and how he managed to prevent it spreading more by going into the doctor sooner than later. She went into her clinic to have this checked out. The physician's assistant who saw her requested a mammogram test done even though the doctor didn't think it was a problem.

Because she had just turned thirty-five and seemed very healthy and active my friend, Jessica, decided to listen to the doctor and go in for the mammogram. The day of her appointment the I5 freeway was backed up some distance from the bridge and so she started thinking she'd turn her car around and go home. However, before she could carry out her plan, the traffic began moving again and she made it over the bridge into Portland. Once she was situated in the clinic, a tech person took two pictures with the machine. Then twenty minutes later a guy in a white coat approached her and asked her a question. "Is there any breast cancer in your family?" Her reply was no. "Well, here's what I see, there are some lumps which look suspicious. And you're taking this rather well!" Now normally a radiologist doesn't come in to tell the patient about the results, but instead this matter is usually left up to the patient's doctor to set up an appointment first. His next statement scared her. "You're young which means this is an aggressive type." Her initial thought was *Oh my goodness; this cancer could be spreading everywhere. I could die!"*

The radiologist mentioned that he was going to see about scheduling my friend an appointment for her necessary surgery. She told me that she immediately called her husband and told him the awful news. When the nurse came back to talk with her, she asked if she was going to die. The nurse tried to console her. Then the nurse informed my friend, Jessica, that the doctor needed to sit down with her and give her this personal information. She was feeling upended and later she told me that this was unprofessional of the medical personnel to give her the frightening news without waiting for her own doctor to relay the pertinent facts first. I heartedly agreed with her and try to console her as I listened to her story. It would have been more humane if they had made sure that her husband was with her at the next appointment so he could comfort and support his wife. It's been five years since her surgery. Even now as I'm doing this interview with Jessica, I could tell she was still upset with this radiologist person. She continued sharing with me her story. While she was driving home from the clinic that day, some five years earlier, she had cried out to God, "I'm scared to death, I need your help!" A well-known gospel singer came on the car radio with the song and her beautiful music filled my friend's car and her heart. During her darkest hour, God had come into her car to give this friend the comfort and security she desperately needed to be able to face this horrendous ordeal.

A week later in November, Jessica went for the scheduled biopsy and four days later they received the test results. The doctor told her she had invasive ductile carcinoma which was in stage 0. She was told to have an MRI body scan to check the lymph nodes. The scan showed that her lymph nodes were enlarged, and this naturally freaked my friend out. At first, the doctor planned to remove the lump in her right breast, but then he determined it was best to do a single mastectomy. At this time, she felt strongly impressed to have a double mastectomy even though the doctor had advised her to wait on the second surgery. Her husband supported her right to decide in this critical situation. She insisted that the doctor's honor her decision to have the double surgery and that's what eventually happened on December 5, 2012.

The doctor told my friend that she'd to make another hard decision going into her surgery. Since the doctor doesn't want his patient to go through two separate surgeries, she needed to let him know if she wanted to have implants or the actual spacers placed into her chest to allow the implants that might come much later. The only problem with doing this procedure the doctor said is that when a person undergoes chemotherapy it can result in your body rejecting the implants some seven months down the road. It could turn out to be a nightmare experience and so she declined to have the procedure. This must have been a very difficult decision for her.

Jessica was trying to figure out what was normal and to not be afraid every day as she waited for the surgery. She expressed to me that day as we sat in the coffee shop chatting that she had felt as if her life was out of control, it was as if she had no say in what would happen next. All she could do at this moment in time was to lean on God's big shoulders and trust him for the future. This same day she showed me her journal book and graciously allowed me to read the entries to get a better understanding of how she'd felt back then. She had tears in her eyes as we talked about how she wanted to live to be a mother and raise her young son and see him graduate and get married someday. I told her she was a brave woman.

When the doctor told her about his plan to remove the lump, he mentioned to her that normally when they do a test on a person's two main lymph nodes and there is no evidence of a problem, they don't need to remove nodes or muscle tissue. In other words, with my friend's situation, the doctor found clear margins around the cancerous lump area, and this was a very good sign. Her chemo treatment was scheduled for every three weeks. The doctor decided to do a hand-pushed style of injecting the chemo into her hand and not the drip method. He explained to her that if she had the drip of chemotherapy, it was only allowed once in her lifetime so it would be better to go the other route. She was finished with the last dosage of chemotherapy by July 15, 2013.

I learned exactly how this journey had affected her family and how she learned to cope with and overcome fears or anxious thoughts during her chemo treatment and surgery. My friend was quite transparent and real with me as I interviewed her and so my hope is that her story will speak to someone who might be going through a similar experience. My friend allowed me to read her daily log journal as she went through each process of dealing with the cancer. The journal writing was gut-wrenchingly real and transparent and as I read every page, it gave me a glimpse of her daily anguish and fears as well as her desire to live.

During our chat at the coffee shop, she mentioned this to me: "When I received the phone call from the oncologist's office telling me to make an appointment, I was told that I should do chemo treatment. I wondered if my body was strong enough to handle the chemo. This is not what I wanted. God, even though you didn't perform my exact idea of a 'miracle', I will trust in you. Your ways are better than mine. But I want to see your miraculous works throughout the rest of my journey to health. Right now, my young son is my priority." Jessica finished telling me her story and smiled.

I had been writing down her words as best I could that day in the coffee shop. It has been five years since she finished the chemo treatments and has been declared free of cancer in her body by her doctor. One day, my other friend, Alisha, myself, and this young woman, Jessica, were all spending some time together in her home and I learned some more about Jen's family history. I had a strong desire to pray for her again. After our time of praying for each of our families, we all set a date to get together again. I had a desire to continue praying God's blessings and divine health over her entire situation and future well-being.

A month later, all three of us were sitting in my dear friend, Alisha's lovely spacious, country home and I felt compelled to pray/declare over our friend that the cancer disease would not ever attack her body again. After I was finished praying for Jessica, she thanked me profusely and shared more of her family background with me. I felt that she had an issue with being afraid of the cancer coming back again one day and so we prayed against this fear. From that day on my heart has been strongly connected with this dear woman. I look forward to every opportunity that I may have to meet with her at a coffee shop and share our lives. We will grab a coffee and visit for a while and then go into her vehicle and pray for her family and for her concerns. I value this young woman and her ability to believe God for her health and for the strength to take care of her family.

Jessica is grateful for the doctors, the medicine, and for a loving God who does the final healing and deliverance from any disease. My prayer is that God can use her story of healing from cancer and each time she shares her testimony it will bring hope and strength to others. It takes great courage to face the horrible disease called cancer and to believe for one's own healing. People who go through this kind of battle need a group of friends praying for them who can declare God's truth and promises on their behalf. I have made a commitment to intercede for those who are going through this kind of health challenge.

There are two inseparable truths I've learned about God: The first is that He loves people, and the second truth is that He desires to heal people. Apostle Paul makes this statement about what the Lord had shown him to share with all believers, "Bless the Lord, O my soul, and forget not all his benefits. He forgives all my iniquities and heals all my diseases." (Psalm 103:2-3) "I cried to the Lord and He saved me from all my trouble and distress. He sent His Word and healed and delivered me from my disease." (Psalm 107:19-20; Luke 17:19) This is God's heart for people everywhere: he wants people to live with good health, to be free of worry, anxiety or fears and to be thankful for all His mercies and loving kindness. For sure, it's hard to be thankful during extreme difficulties such as sickness or a battle against cancer and yet, when we cry out to God, he hears us. If we determine to fully trust God by placing our lives, our health, and our time in His hands, then who knows, we just might encounter the soft whisper of divine love resounding within our hearts. Your miracle might be right around the corner and so don't stop believing for your healing and for an answer from God.

CHAPTER TWENTY-FOUR

I believe in my heart that God wants to bring a powerful wave of the Father's love to believers in such a new way that they will be changed dramatically. I really believe this move of God has to do with believers praying more fervently and more often for our region. My friend, Debbie, and I have determined to meet every Tuesday to do a prayer walk around our community and we have seen good things happen as we share God's love with folks we meet on our walks. one day as we sat on a bench by the waterfront area enjoying the view, Debbie felt impressed that she should use social media to invite women in our community to join us in praying at three o'clock every day for families living in our community. Since that time, we've seen more and more people connect on her Facebook page to state that they want to intercede daily at three o'clock for Clark County Washington and for the nation of America.

When we ask for the 'more' of God, I truly believe He will answer our heart's cry and infuse us with an overwhelming new experience that contains more of the supernatural, divine blessings. I am convinced that God wants us to return to our 'first love' with our heavenly Father as we move forward in our quest to know Him better. One night in my room, I asked God to give me more supernatural abilities. After that I told God that I would allow Him to do whatever was necessary to bring this about in my life. I was surprised the following morning when a good friend who lives in Phoenix, Arizona called me to share something important. She said that she felt God was asking me to share my true-life story in a public setting with women. I was taken aback by her insight because I knew this was the one thing I did not want to do. She encouraged me to not worry about what people might think of me or if I might break down crying in front of a group of women. Instead, she asked me to do the one thing that I was very hesitant to do, she wanted me to speak about my pain and shame of sexual and physical abuse issues to a group of women.

She went on to ask me to consider practicing by telling a couple of friends at first until I could feel more confident in sharing my story of childhood abuse. As she was talking to me, I remembered making a certain promise to the Lord the night before. Wow, was God really asking me to do this difficult thing? He'd taken me at my word and now I needed to keep my promise to Him. The following day I spent a half an hour walking around in my house trying to verbalize my story of how I'd been abused as a young girl. The hardest part of this new challenge would be for me to admit to others about my childhood experiences and my feelings of shame and embarrassment. My friend understood that this would be a huge step for me. It had only been a year since she'd challenged me to even write about the sensitive childhood issues and how it had made me feel to be abused by my own parent. I realized finally that this step towards being real with people was not about me, but rather about doing what God may be asking of me. But would my huge mountain of shame stand in the way of sharing about my dysfunctional family and the abuse I suffered? Could I trust God to help me be able to truly share my story with people? In other words, did I really trust the Lord in this matter? One thing I knew for sure; if I was ever to share the entire story about my childhood abuse and how it had affected me, I would need the courage to be honest and forthright about my pain.

***

I would like to share here something that my good friend, Doug, had advised me to consider doing while I was traveling in Uganda. He'd told me to ask God what I should do each day while I was traveling in Uganda. Now to be honest here, I hadn't been accustomed to taking the time to do this on a regular basis. However, I kept his advice in mind as I headed for Uganda to spend fourteen days with two leader friends. During the second week of my stay in Kampala, I remembered my friend's counsel and it proved to be very valuable advice for me while traveling in this foreign country. I had prayed a couple of mornings about getting divine appointments while staying in the pastor's home and I felt like my trip was going well thus far. However, the following day things began to get complicated. I had made plans to go with an African youth leader when he mentioned that he wanted to take me to Lake Victoria. I love to swim in lakes and rivers and so I agreed to this outing with his family. Early in the morning I sensed God trying to get my attention as I was waking up. I heard these words come into my spirit, *ask me if you are to go to the lake with this leader today!* I became more awake and alert at this moment; I asked God if I was to go swim in Victoria Lake with this adult youth leader in Kampala. The reply was a definite NO to going to the lake. I told my pastor friend, Anthony, to call this individual and let him know I was not available to go on this excursion.

This happened one more time at the end of the week and I really believe God was teaching me to rely more on His daily guidance. Even though I missed doing some things on my schedule that week, I really believe God had a better plan for me. I ended up staying an extra four day more in the pastor's home. Anthony and his beautiful wife were gracious and hospitable as I asked them if I could extend my stay with them. The first day in his home, I played with his youngest boy during the morning and then in the afternoon, I relaxed and read a book. The following day, Pastor Anthony invited me to spend the day at his church office. I enjoyed my quiet time in their prayer room where I could read an English Bible and spend time worshipping and praying for the Ugandan people. As the days progressed, I slowly began to recognize that God was setting up divine appointments for me. Each day a different young adult showed up in the front lobby of Anthony's church office. I would ask if I could pray for them, and they always said yes! As I began to pray for each person, I was led by the spirit of God in how to bless them and give them a word of encouragement. Each one of those African young adults thanked me profusely and it seemed they were very happy to call me Momma Cathy'. I was blessed beyond measure and all because I had given my days and plans over to the Lord.

Just the other day in my hometown, I was relaxing in the sun and visiting with my dear friend who is the wife of a prominent local pastor in our city. She had travelled to Uganda this last year and was telling me about her recent trip to Kampala. She mentioned Lake Victoria and then went on to describe what had happened to two different people who'd went swimming in this lake in Africa. She informed me that these two same men who she knew about were not warned about the parasite that inhabited the bottom of the lake area. they had stood in the shallow water of Lake Victoria and somehow a nasty parasite had managed to work its way into their feet, and it had gradually travelled up into the spinal cord causing them to be paralyzed. This was very sad news to hear. I shared with my friend that I'd almost gone on a day excursion with an African person to go swimming in this same lake near Kampala when I stayed in Uganda in 2018. I was very thankful to the Lord for His divine intervention and marvelous protection over my life while I was staying in Africa. I love to dive and swim in any kind of water especially on very hot days and it was by the grace of God that I'd chosen to avoid going to Lake Victoria with the African youth leader that day.

I have a marvelous true story to share with you. My friend, George, from church told me about an elderly friend he knew. His friend, Gregory, had become very ill and was admitted to the hospital one morning. The doctor informed him that he was dying. So that very day, Gregory, who was a strong Christian believer, decided to make a list of about twenty-four people in the hospital that he wished to share his faith with during his short stay there. After spending a certain amount of time with the medical staff, this dying man told my friend that twenty-three doctors and nurses in this hospital had prayed with him to receive the son of God as their savior. This was marvelous to hear. During the last few hours of his life here on earth, the twenty-fourth person, an older nurse, had been sitting by his bedside and she told someone what she'd observed about this elderly gentleman. After this gentleman had passed onto his reward in heaven, she'd told the other nurses that she'd observed his peaceful and glorious transition from this earthly life of pain onto his next eternal home with the Lord. My friend George learned that this same nurse was so astounded by this amazing death bed event that she fell on her knees and cried out to God to receive this same eternal salvation the rest of the medical staff had received as well. I loved hearing this powerful story of how one person, close to death's door, cared enough for others that he was determined to share the truth about salvation with every one of the medical staff before he died. The marvelous part of this man's testimony is that he helped bring others with him to heaven right up to the day of his passing. This is a powerful example of a person who'd learned how to yield his life to the heavenly Father. God used this individual in a mighty way to bring others into his glorious truth and the joy of His eternal life provision.

***

The greatest gift a parent can impart to their child is to tell them how valuable and loved they are. Our Father in heaven is a good caring father. He truly loves us without reservations. God has refined the very 'art of romancing' people. He is no respecter of persons; in other words, it doesn't matter to our heavenly Father what a person's status in life may be or how much money they've earned or what they look like. He sent His words of love through the Bible and then, years later, He sent His only son to die in our place to show His profound, unconditional heart of love and acceptance for humanity. All we must do is believe on His son and the sacrifice he did for us and then accept this gift of eternal life. I have flourished under my heavenly Father's loving, watchful eye all these years. I am grateful for the Father God's desire to romance us and to remind us often of the fact that he is the author of love; there is no darkness, evil, hatred or injustice in God's nature. I believe that if God was to visit you in your home right now, He would tell you how truly important you are to Him and that he wants to spend time communing with you.

You might be asking a question right now concerning my family dysfunction. How can a person like me truly be able to express love when as a young girl I was raised in a dysfunctional family and my parents were sadly lacking in the ability to show affection, and words of affirmation? This is a good question for sure. And you would be right; I did have difficulty expressing or showing love to my own family as an adult. Since my mother and father struggled in maintaining a peaceable relationship with each other and with me, I grew up feeling confused about family relationships. I seemed to struggle with feeling insecure and nervous as an individual and it's possible that this came from living in a volatile environment as a child.

I need to mention here that my mother eventually became a true believer when her friends, Eunice and Jeri invited her to a Full Gospel Businessmen's dinner in a small town in Washington. I was nineteen years old back then. I remember sensing that my mom had changed significantly and so I wanted to go with her and my younger sister to see for myself why this new gathering of friends had so impacted her life. As the years went by, I saw a big difference in how my mother related to me. She became kinder and more gracious in her attitude and actions. I saw her becoming a mighty prayer warrior over the next forty years and our relationship became even better too.

My mother prayed often for us and for the grandchildren. She even came to stay with my sister and help take care of the kids for a while and impart the love of God to them. My sister was going through a difficult struggle, and she needed help with everything. Mom was a wonderful cook. and this took some of the household duties off my sister's shoulder that year. She taught me about faith and to believe for things to change for the better. I commend her for her unselfishness and her faithful walk with God. Our mother became the rock for our entire family throughout her remaining years on this earth. She lived to be in her nineties, and she was a blessing to all who knew her. Nearly one year after she passed, I had a vision in which I saw my mother running joyously through a field of grass. She had black hair again and she was running freely in this quick scene. I was blessed to receive this vivid glimpse of her in God's heavenly realm where I believe everyone is young and healthy. I cannot recall one time when I saw my mother running while she was alive on earth. She wasn't athletic at all and towards the last twenty years she had blood pressure problems. The BP meds from her doctor had caused her legs to hurt and this problem even slowed her down even more. This vision of my mother gave me great joy and I'm thankful that she is in heaven now rejoicing with her family members, her beloved Canadian relatives, and her lifelong friends.

CHAPTER TWENTY-FIVE

I liked to share a few things about my close friend, Debbie Z. One sunny day we'd decided to meet at Lake Merwin with our kayaks to enjoy some time on the water. We had a wonderful time kayaking and exploring the immense waterway and then about a mile into our trip we turned right to explore some more areas and came upon a stunning waterfall spot. Once we'd arrived at this hidden waterfall, we could climb out of our kayaks and enjoy the quiet, peaceful scene. We sat down on the warm boulders by the water's edge where we could lean back to relax and watch the waterfall as it cascaded over the larger boulders. Then, twenty minutes later, as we continued paddling back, I needed to glide on the water's surface in order to rest my arms from paddling. During this restful moment, we took time to pray for our family members. It is very relaxing to just sit in our kayaks and admire the quiet wilderness around us. I could feel my soul being restored as we stopped there to take in the beauty of another idyllic lake spot.

After we'd eaten our lunch that same afternoon, we swam for a while. This is my favorite thing to do at the lake. Feeling refreshed and cooled off by the lake water, we both rested on the sandy beach after our swim. A lazy osprey flew overhead and then circled once more and disappeared among the tall, stately evergreen trees. We were hoping to catch a glimpse of a bald eagle that day, but none came our way. The summer sun was beginning to dip behind the tall row of trees in the far distance and the wind was beginning to pick up a bit. I glanced up for a moment to my right side to enjoy the gorgeous view and noticed the wind playing with some falling leaves until they'd landed gracefully onto the gleaming waters' surface. In my mind's eye, they looked more like twirling, lively water sprites dancing or performing before my very eyes. The lake area is my favorite place to visit on a summer day. I've spent many weekends camping here and I always want to stay longer in this vast wilderness with all its glorious beauty and tranquility. Both of us were feeling quite happy and renewed after spending the day on the lake. When we are not kayaking in the water, we like to hike the splendid trails and forest area which circumvents lake Merwin / Cresap Bay Campground.

That afternoon I asked my friend to share one of her most difficult experiences of her life. This is her heart-wrenching experience. In the early years of their marriage, this couple had lost their first child, a four-year-old boy, in a horrific accident. A friend of this family had asked a chaplain to come to support them in their time of deep grief at the funeral. He was a very caring man who knew the power of prayer. She told me how this chaplain person had held them up in prayer as he believed for God to comfort them through the healing process. Within six weeks, this young mother gave her broken heart and this awful loss over to the Lord. God kept her marriage together during this difficult time.

Then when she was twenty-six years old, she needed a physical healing for her body. She had two young daughters by this time. She shared with me that she was working at a dental office, and she would take her two girls to the babysitter and then head off to work four days a week. Nearly a year later, she caught a flu bug and was feeling miserable for the next three days.

This feeling of being sick lingered on for another seven days for this mother of two young girls and she had still not regained her strength. Then after eight months of feeling poorly, she knew something was not right in her body. After dealing with extreme fatigue, she was forced to work only three days a week. She went to the doctor to get his expertise in this matter. Finally, some thirteen doctors later, my friend learned she had Epstein Barre which is an auto-immune disease. My friend began to seek God to be free of this dreadful illness. The more she prayed to God the more she began to realize that she needed to try a different avenue for her health's sake. She spent an extra amount of money going the naturopathic route with this doctor located in Oregon. He put her on a strict food diet and certain vitamin supplements to help her body recover. His medical prognosis was that he couldn't heal her of this disease, but he could help her get healthier with time and with homeopathic supplements. She felt as if her life was falling apart again, and she worried that she wouldn't be able to work long term and help with paying the family expenses.

My friend, Debbie, continued to pray and believe God for healing for another few years. One summer she was told about a Jesus Northwest conference coming to the area where she lived. She attended these meetings where she signed up to hear Dutch Sheets teach on intercessory prayer. After listening to his teachings, she decided to incorporate his style of praying into her own life. She also became involved with Youth for Christ which is an offshoot branch of Campus Crusade for Christ. This branch of the ministry works with high school youth. Later they were trained in child evangelism. Then they went onto work for ten years in Youth with a Mission and its program called King's Kids ministry in local churches. During this time of intercession and involvement in God's purposes, she didn't experience the same type of fatigue and weariness as before. She was now living a normal life and praising God for his healing mercies towards her. We've been friends for nearly twelve years now and since I've known this woman, she has been the picture of excellent health and strength. She kayaks, works in her garden, and takes care of their four active grandchildren. I am blessed to be her good friend. She has become like a sister to me, and my children call her auntie now. So even though we are not related by blood we are now sisters by our special bond of love. We've shared many wonderful experiences and memories over the last seven years.

During our last kayaking experience, I also learned more about her childhood. Her father was a long-haul truck driver, and he was gone on trips for ten days at a time and back home for only two days. When he was home, he made the family uncomfortable or anxious. She remembered how mean and angry he would be around her mother. She hated feeling unhappy during his few days with them. When she was only eight years old, she would hear that her father was coming home, and she'd get very excited. Then when he arrived and climbed out of his truck, she'd run over to him only to be disappointed each time. To her dismay and sorrow, her father would ignore her and continued into the house to collapse on the sofa and growl at the family members. Finally, after becoming a believer my good friend realized she needed to forgive her father for his wrongdoings and unkindness. Even though she'd released her father from her resentments, she still needed a deeper healing for her wounded heart. This kind of healing came some years later for her while she sat in a church service in Redding, California.

The last time my friend made the long ten-hour drive to Bethel Church, she was ministered to by a sweet lady and an older gentleman during a time of prayer. They spoke a word of knowledge to her that this would be the final trip to Bethel Church. They said God was healing her heart and she wouldn't need to be concerned anymore about this grief. They encouraged her to release her father from her judgment and she chose to do this. After this prayer of releasing the judgment against her father, the healing process could begin. Then the kind-hearted gentleman spoke a 'father's blessing' over her which replaced the lack and wounding she'd experienced from her earthly father. For years I'd felt justified in holding onto bitterness towards my own father. As my friend shared this experience with me, I too realized that I needed to let go of the judgment I'd held against my father. I chose to release my father as I asked God to forgive me for holding onto my anger towards him. Then as my friend prayed over me, she sensed the Holy Spirit telling her that a stronghold of offense was being broken off me.

Our time of sharing at the lake gave us both such encouragement and joy. What we experienced that day reminded me of this scriptural promise, "Oh Lord my God, I cried to thee, and thou hast healed me." (Psalm 30: 2) I am thankful that our heavenly Father doesn't ignore us or leave us in our own weakness. But rather He comes to our rescue when we humbly cry out for help as we face our own lack or a need to change.

This one thing I know to be true: God has an ideal blueprint for people's lives. I believe that He lovingly inserts a desire in each person for the heavenly realm and we are not satisfied until we find Him. I'd been searching for this kind of personal love and a reason to live since I was fourteen. My quest for truth had begun the day I questioned why I was born. What I really was searching for in my life turned out to be the Son of God who had come to earth to demonstrate His love and to give us a divine purpose.

As a follower of God our earthly goal ought to be to know God and to discover what our divine purpose is as we journey through this life. The first man named Adam walked with God in the cool of the evening. He was able to talk freely with God and enjoy an unhindered fellowship with the Father who loved him tremendously. God desires to walk and talk with us each day just as He did with Adam in the first garden. I desire a more intimate relationship with my heavenly Father so I can enjoy the fullness of his love for me. In the Bible we can read about a woman named Mary of Bethany who had chosen the best thing by sitting at the Lord's feet and learning everything she could from him. Can we do less than this dear Jewish woman? I have chosen to seek God more than ever and to not be apprehensive of what He may say to me or ask me to do. When I've taken the time to ask God to give me a divine appointment during my day, it has happened. And after I've shared what I sensed was God's word of encouragement for that individual I'd just met for the first time, I've seen their face light up with a smile. Being led by the Spirit of God can be an interesting and fulfilling way to live.

***

During the wintertime, we decided to join our son, Robert, his wife, and their two girls for lunch and then the plan was to buy tickets for a family movie later in the afternoon. We had an hour before the show started so we all walked from the theater area to a local Starbucks Coffee Shop. While we were waiting for our hot drinks, the girls and I pulled out a kid's game of Sequence to play. After three rounds of this fun game, grandpa and Natalie won the competition. Finally, it was time to stroll back to go inside and watch our fun movie about fire jumpers and a family of three kids. Once we had driven back to our son's house, we sat for a while chatting in his vehicle. His wife shared a marvelous testimony of God's divine intervention in a family's situation recently. Robert is in law enforcement and a part-time pastor in his church, and he received a phone call from one of their parishioners asking him to come to the hospital to pray for a neighbor's ten-month-old boy in ICU. This young child was struggling to live and breathe properly after a bout with pneumonia and complications.

The doctor had told the parents that they didn't expect the baby to survive the night and if he did somehow live, they were concerned about the lack of oxygen to his brain and if he would be able to function normally. Our son, Robert, began to describe to us that on a Tuesday normally he'd be at his day job, however, because the electricity went out, he had to stay home to resolve the problem. When these church friends called with a request for him to come to the hospital and that it was urgent, Robert went to prayer immediately, He felt a strong sense that he was to write out a prayer directive to use in the hospital and to give the same instructions on the paper to this mother for her to pray daily over her child. He went on to explain how he'd chosen to make a strong declaration that this child would receive a miracle healing from the Lord as they prayed in faith over him. On this piece of paper, our pastor son wrote down a scripture to declare, "Death and Life are in the power of the tongue." (Proverbs 18: 21)

That evening as Robert entered the hospital ward, he had to use the wall phone to get permission to be in the intensive care unit. Our son mentioned to the receptionist that he was a pastor and he wished to come into the child's room. The attending nurse finally agreed to allow him to come into the ICU area and pray for the very sick youngster. Next thing I learned from our son was that the young child was hooked up to IV tube for fluids and to a ventilator machine and tubes; he could tell that the situation was extremely serious. Then he laid hands on the child and expressed words of life over the youngster such as you are loved and a child of God, you are blessed with supernatural strength and healing, you will live and be prosperous and glorify God's name above all other names!

Then at the end of his time in the ICU room, our son made this powerful command in faith as he stated: "In Jesus mighty name, I rebuke the spirit of infirmity and death from this young child and we ask that complete healing and physical restoration come upon you right now in Jesus' name, amen!" The child's mother agreed with this prayer.

After this brief time of praying for the youngster in the ICU room of the children's hospital, Robert proceeded to go out to the waiting room to meet with his wife, Karina, the neighbor friends, and some folks from the church. He encouraged the group of visitors to continue praying for the parents back in the ICU. Rob also pulled up the video from Youtube.com that was on his phone's music playlist which featured the worship leader from Bethel Church in California who had sung the amazing lyrics called "I Raise a Hallelujah" and everyone joined in as they sang this song and worshipped the Lord God.

That evening as we listened to our son shared this testimony, we saw how he'd played a pivotal role in praying as the Spirit of the Lord had led him to do. I was thrilled to learn how he'd risen to the occasion as a young leader and pastor. He told us that the following morning he'd learned that the child was still alive. Then he showed us a photo of the youngster lying in the hospital bed hooked up to IV and the breathing tube. After we saw that first picture of the sick child, our son then showed us a different video which had been taken and sent to his phone a few days later; we could watch the child playing and hitting a child's mobile toy and kicking his legs. The sight of this youngster alive and responding to everyone's prayers was exciting. I can imagine that his parents were overjoyed with the amazing turn of events for their child.

After hearing about this wonderful testimony, we left to drive back to our home in the country. An hour later my son called me to share some news about the family. The young child had been released from the hospital that very afternoon while we all had been at the movies. This was great news, and we gave God the glory for this marvelous intervention in a very ill child's life.

What a thrilling example of a pastor listening to the Spirit of God and being bold enough to share a prayer idea with the mother who had been given no hope from the doctors. Ever since our son was a teen, I've witnessed his powerful faith and his strong belief that God could heal people. One time, he'd asked our family to pray for a friend who'd been stricken with bone cancer, and we saw her healed completely. He has this confident trust in the scripture promises about healing and therefore, he believes God will perform miracles and heal people. And that is one of the main reasons why I tend to go to my son and ask him to pray for family members. I am thrilled to say we've seen marvelous answers to our prayers of agreement.

CHAPTER TWENTY-SIX

Today I was watching a show on the TV Channel 39 where a woman was sharing her story in an interview. She had been diagnosed with tuberculosis in 1940 and the doctor told her she'd died from this illness. She cried out to God to give her some more years on this earth and if he did, she'd serve him and go wherever he asked her to go with his message of love and healing power. She was touched by God's power and delivered from a dreadful disease. She kept her promise to the Lord by serving him faithfully for many, many years after that dramatic healing experience. At the time of this interview, she was one hundred years old. She informed her audience that she had travelled to Africa and had started church plants there. I saw the photos of her standing alongside her African friends in those churches. Then later back in the states, she even started a church in a large city near the east coast where she was the main pastor, and her husband supported her efforts. This church flourished with many parishioners for years. She and her husband adopted a boy when she was fifty-eight years old. When their son grew up, he took over as the pastor in this same church. I loved hearing this fabulous story. This woman's testimony is a marvelous example of how God answered her prayer of faith.

I have another true story to tell you and yes, it's about blessings and miracles. As a Sunday school teacher, I have the privilege to work with a great couple. My friend, Troy, is a kindhearted individual who loves to help with the children's ministry at our church. After class one day, he sat down with me and shared about his battle with cancer. This is a marvelous testimony, and I am thrilled to be able to share it. He met his wife in 1996 and they got married. He was happy and he worked on restoring old antique automobiles and selling them. At the age of thirty-six, he was struggling with numerous sinus infections. Since his wife worked for the school district as a bus driver, her husband could be put on her medical coverage. So, he went into the doctor to get some relief from this affliction. The doctor prescribed antibiotics to help him get well, but the doctor informed my friend that he couldn't solve the reoccurring problem permanently. Then his doctor asked if there was anything else he could help Troy with that day Troy responded by telling him about the concern he had with blood in his stool. The doctor insisted that he have a colonoscopy scheduled soon.

During this exam, they found two polyps in his intestines. His doctor then scheduled a surgery date for him. During this procedure, he was watching the monitor screen and he saw something leave his intestine at that moment, it was purplish in color, and it left his body. When they were finished, they wheeled him out of the operating room and he felt this strong impression and words come into his spirit, *there will be no more occur-*

rence of this problem in your intestines. The doctor sent the biopsy to their lab for review. They found what they had suspected, he had cancer. During that next month, he received a few certified letters from the doctor informing him that their recommendation was for a removal of twelve inches of his intestines and to undergo radiation treatment as a safety factor. He felt the cold hand of fear embracing his heart and mind during this time.

At this point in his well-documented, Troy mentioned to me that he had been a part of the Vineyard Fellowship in Oregon and they had been experiencing renewal that had originated in Toronto, Canada. He had been attending a Wednesday night life group gathering in someone's home and this evening he recalled standing in the group as he worshipped the Lord. Then suddenly, he saw with spiritual eyesight, the Lord Jesus standing right in front of him. Next thing that happened was he realized was that he was presented with a question in this vision. *Who do you believe?* My friend replied in a whispering voice with these words of faith, "I believe you, Lord." Apparently, God was doing something magnificent in his soul and his body because he continued to kneel and laugh for another fifteen minutes or so. Then he went home rejoicing in the Lord.

His primary physician called him into his office that following week to discuss his future medical plans. My friend then told the doctor that he'd had an encounter with God. These were the doctor's exact words in response to his statement of faith. "I'm inclined to believe you since I studied medicine at Oral Roberts University for a number of years." My friend finished telling me his miracle story of healing by giving me a further conclusive statement of victory. "Five years later I had another colonoscopy which showed there was nothing wrong in my intestines" In other words, he no longer had any evidence of cancer in his lower intestines. It was quite clear to him that Jesus of Nazareth had healed his body completely. His testimony reminded me of the woman who pressed through the crowd to reach and touch the hem of the Lord's garments as she believed for her healing deliverance. Jesus spoke to this woman in the New Testament Gospels and asked who'd touched His garment, for He sensed virtue flowing out from His body at that very instance. The women in the Bible replied that it was her and then He spoke to this woman that her faith had made her whole and well again.

My friend, Troy, had to walk in a courageous decision of faith and trust in what he was hearing from God's spirit in this battle against cancer. He decided to not allow the physician to schedule that surgery to remove a large section of his intestines. It has been several years since that last dramatic "five-year mark of good health" for this man of faith. He looks remarkably healthy and happy each Sunday when I see him worshipping at church. Now he and his wife pray for people to be healed when the pastor invites people to come forward for prayer.

When a person is faced with a negative report from a medical doctor, they may experience some fear at first. Some people may even feel as if they're facing an enormous giant who can literally take them out of this world with one tremendous crushing blow from a disease called CANCER. Believing God for a miracle can be a real test of one's faith. If a person decides to trust in the Bible's scriptures for healing, then they can also ask the elders of their church to anoint them with oil and say the prayer of faith like the Bible mentions in the Book of James. In some situations, it is important to get a 'Rhema' or a 'now' word or divine insight from the Lord before you decide to not follow the doctor's directions like my friend did. I believe that a person needs to be wise and make sure they have documented proof of their healing as they stand in faith for a completed work. One thing I truly believe is this: When God heals someone, it's very beneficial for that individual to share their wonderful healing story. I'm of the belief that if you receive a healing from the Lord then it pleases the Father God if you ask him this, "Lord, I thank you for healing the pain in body or delivering me from an evil disease, now what would you have me do for your kingdom and with my life here on this earth?"

Troy's story of a miraculous healing is an example of an individual receiving a word of knowledge or divine insight from the Holy Spirit in order to be able to believe the report of the Lord and not the report of the doctors. I am thankful that this gentle individual is still here on this earth helping others to see God's power and mercy in action. He recently joined our Spitfire' intercessory group and he brings his guitar to play as he sings his original music for us. He is very talented and fun to listen to once we are finished praying. I am inclined to call his deliverance from cancer a real miracle from heaven. I rejoiced with Troy and his wife for this wonderful healing and together we all shout to the world that our God is a loving Father in heaven who loves to heal people. Yes, indeed, miracles do happen when you believe and keep expecting them to happen for those you love and pray for.

This conviction about miracles reminds me of a movie called "the Miracle Season," which I watched yesterday. There was a teenage girl who was a star player on her high school volleyball team name Caroline. One night as she was going to visit her sick mother in the hospital, she crashed her motorbike into a tree, and she died. The whole town and her classmates were in shock and grief over this tremendous loss of life. Then two weeks later, her mother passed away. Caroline's best friend was overwhelmed with sorrow and grief which made it nearly impossible for her and her teammates to play this sport. The coach of this same team tried to encourage the group to keep coming to practice and to even play the next competition game; they lost two games and were faced with a losing season if something didn't change soon.

I watched the one teammate (Kelly) wearing the number nineteen on her volleyball jersey spur her team onto an inspiring attempt to win the next fifteen games to go to the playoffs and to compete in the state championships. They managed to motivate each other in a magnificent show of courage and fortitude which finally sent them to the state competitions. These girls were able to come from behind and win the state championship and to celebrate Caroline's life and their own team's challenges with a major victory! This is truly the best inspirational movie I've seen in a long time. Please watch it and get a glimpse of what it really means to expect a miracle until you eventually have the amazing miracle which you've cry out for in faith and true believing!

***

I'd like to revisit the time when our firstborn daughter had finished her Bone Marrow Transplant in 1998. Her doctors had allowed her to leave the hospital a week early to be home for Christmas. We were thrilled to see her released from that dreary, depressing cancer ward. She still had to receive anti-rejection drugs for a year. She needed me to drive her up to the hospital for her follow-up treatment. She had to go to the infusion room and have certain drugs injected into her Hickman Port that was still inserted into her chest. While my daughter sat there resting and waiting for the procedure to be completed each time, I would read or take a short walk around the halls of this immense facility. Yes, I walked and walked and prayed for her and the other patients who sat in the same infusion room. There was a certain atmosphere of gloom and despair that pervaded this sterile room full of sick patients.

This depressing hospital scene would often cause me to feel apprehensive and at a loss for words of encouragement to give to my daughter. One day as we were sitting there leafing through the pages of our reading material, the supervisor announced that a prior patient of this ward was returning to visit and share briefly with everyone in the room. We waited and wondered what this visit would entail. Finally, the woman who was a survivor of the BMT procedure arrived and was introduced to the entire group.

As we listened to this woman's story of what kind of cancer she'd dealt with and how she was now ten years cancer free, I wondered what the fate of the other patients would be and if this person's life story had possibly given them a renewed hope for their own lives. I also wondered what my daughter was thinking after she'd heard this person's survivor story. I tried to be careful about what we talked about while she was going though such a long ordeal that year. I really needed a counselor friend to confide in during this exhausting time. Maybe she would've told me it was okay to ask my daughter tough questions. I wished I had encouraged my daughter to talk about her frustrations and feelings during this time. I felt very inadequate as a mother during her year of recovery. I was able to control my emotions somewhat by walking out of the infusion room at this larger hospital facility to call a friend to pray with me for my daughter. I did the best that I knew at that time. Maybe because I'd grown up with coping skills as a survivor, I could now manage my emotions in the same manner; I pushed the fear and worries down deep within my soul and put a half-hearted smile on my face most days. Overall, I became my daughter's chief intercessor as I reached out and held on tight to God's hand. It was during our time in the first hospital where I had a vision of my daughter, and she was being held in the arms of her Savior. I also saw her arms wrapped around his neck and she seemed to be resting safely there. I felt this strong impression that I was to walk right behind the Lord as if I needed to step into His very footprints. That same day, I called on God to guide me daily as I decided to follow in those same divine footsteps. Then as I prayed about this beautiful scene in this vision, I heard the Lord's spirit tell me that Sharon would become a messenger of hope to hurting people one day. I've continued to declare this promise over my daughter ever since the time.

During that difficult year, I also watched many patients on this unit of the hospital in Oregon as they faced the possibility of getting the dreaded graft vs. host disease after their transplant procedure. Since some of the patients in this ward didn't have a perfect donor match, then they were more susceptible to the danger of their body rejecting the transplant and thus, succumbing to eventual death from this vicious grafting disease. This fact became a serious worry for our family, and we could only trust in God to protect Sharon from this newest threat of death. Our daughter had befriended a patient who was around twenty-six years old and six months after his bone marrow transplant, we were informed that he was dying from this dreaded graft vs. host disease. When Sharon informed me of this sad news, I drove back up to the hospital to stay with him. I relied on the Lord to be with me as I sat next to his bed. My heart went out to this young man. I said a few encouraging words, and then before leaving his room I prayed for him and kissed his cheek with a soft goodbye. I cried and mourned the loss of this young man as I drove home from the hospital that day.

Whenever, fear or doubt would try to enter my heart about my daughter's chances of surviving this procedure, I kept reminding myself of this phrase I'd received while in prayer: *Your daughter will have a successful Bone Marrow Transplant as the people of God joined together and continually pray for her during this procedure.*

I wrote this promise down and held tight to the belief that God would preserve her life. I was visiting my good friend, Patti, one day and I showed her the piece of paper on which I'd written down this promise from the Lord. I read it to her and then asked her to believe with me for this next healing miracle. She did as she has always done which was to pray continually for my daughter to survive this risky procedure. I was encouraged by the continual support of our many faithful friends. One caring friend even put our daughter's name on the worldwide internet with the request for everyone to keep praying for our daughter to be protect from the graft-versus host disease that year following her transplant.

Our twenty-one-year-old daughter did survive the Bone Marrow Treatment and she didn't contract the deadly grafting disease like others did during that long, tiring process. Now it's been twenty years since her awful challenge, and we are happy to report that she has been free of leukemia since 1998. We are all so grateful to God for keeping her alive and helping her to recover emotionally and physically to the degree where she could return to college and get her diploma.

Sharon is working now as a registered nurse. She believes in divine healing because she has experienced God's intervention in her life. Now I am praying for God to heal her from the traumatic experiences which she endured while fighting for her life during the two different hospitals times. We are overjoyed to have this daughter around today. She has become my walking partner as we hike in the beautiful Northwest region throughout the year. Praying for her during that awful time in the hospital has taught me how to persevere with God. I've also learned to seek God's counsel by asking for a 'crafted prayer' from the Holy Spirit as to how to pray successfully for this daughter. I believe in prevailing prayer, and I have seen the results of a person not giving up on expecting a miracle from God. Our family has been so blessed with good health and with answered prayers for our wonderful children and all our grandchildren. We are looking forward to this coming month of June when our one daughter, Kristina, is scheduled to deliver her baby boy, Isaiah. As I finish writing this book two years later, we've just learned that Kris is pregnant again with our fourteenth grandchild which they plan to name him Elijah Josiah. This is amazing and exciting, great news! We love our children and grandchildren so much and we sincerely believe that they are a blessing from the Lord. We love sharing with others about the miracles and healings which have happened for our family. We are truly blessed and happy to have the opportunity to pray for other folks who may be facing certain difficult challenges or health issues.

CHAPTER TWENTY-SEVEN

I was traveling in the northern part of Israel this last year with people involved in the International House of Prayer Conference of 2017. During our three days of touring Israel, our bus driver took us to the northern part of this unique country that was called Judea and Samaria. I found myself riding in a tour bus full of happy, excited travelers who I had met just a day before. as I traveled to each area where the Son of God had walked thousands of years before this, I tried to picture Christ Jesus ministering to everyone he encountered. Our tour guide was a wealth of information and facts about this country and its rich heritage. Along with the other travelers on tour bus, I enjoyed listening to the guide tell us about this beautiful land and its inhabitants as we traveled many miles to see each famous site. One of our first stops was in a place called Shiloh. We piled out of our huge white tour bus and filed inside of a beautiful modern styled church that had brilliant colored stain glass windows in the very front of the sanctuary. A Jewish man named Mr. Rubin stood up at a wooden podium with a microphone in his hand and began to share the history of this area called Shiloh. As he began to recount the olden stories of this significant city, I began to get a glimpse of what the Hebrew people must have felt as they travelled to this very location.

Mr. Rubin informed the audience that the name, Shiloh, signifies a beautiful place and the exact meaning of this word translates to express the word, Messiah. Mr. Rubin went on to share with us that the city of Shiloh was the same place where the prophet Samuel had lived. He mentioned how the distraught and barren woman named Hannah went to Shiloh to worship God in Moses' tabernacle. Eli the priest had heard her petition to God as she asked the lord to open up her womb and give her a child. Hannah became pregnant and had a son whom she called Samuel. She chose to keep her promise to God by leaving her first born son, Samuel, with the priest to help him in the duties of this Shiloh tabernacle sanctuary. Sitting with my tour group in this beautiful sanctuary, I enjoyed hearing about this biblical history in reference to the ancient Israelites who once lived in this region. He told this gathering of people in the small church setting that he was of Jewish descent and proud of his heritage as he continued recounting another story from the Old Testament pages.

"When Joshua blew the Hebrew Shofar horn instrument outside of the city of Jericho, the walls came crashing down to the ground. Then fourteen years later Joshua the servant of God brought the Hebrew nation to stop at Shiloh. They were told to take possession of the land in the name of God and for Israel. After a time of exile of two thousand years, we have taken command of this area. Seriously, we stand here today, and we stand with the Israeli people for this land of promise." Mr. Rubin informed the captivated audience.

I was thrilled to be there in that dwelling place listening to this authentic Jewish person as he told of his love for this land. Then he went on to describe an actual story which occurred to him many years ago. A militant terrorist group attacked him as he drove from the city of Jerusalem to his home. We all sat in our seats spellbound as we listened to him recount that horrible day. Later, we sat on the only spot of green grass to the right of the dwelling place to eat our lunch. I felt so honored to have met him while traveling in Israel. He graciously stopped and took the time to chat with me after our lunch break that afternoon. We had been standing outside of the Shiloh Church as the hot dry sun beat down upon our heads when I asked him if I could share his testimony of divine intervention in my book. Mr. Rubin graciously gave me permission to include the frightening events of that horrible day. The following paragraphs tell his true story about his unfortunate encounter with angry militants and how he managed to survive.

On December 17, 2001, this guest speaker, Mr. Rubin, and his three-year-old son were heading home when a hail of terrorists' bullets slammed into his car. With a wound in his leg, he thought he was the only one in the car who'd been hit. Later at the hospital he learned from a doctor that his son had sustained an injury too. The terrorists were still shooting their AK-47 machine guns at his vehicle and his car had stopped running thus, causing him great distress and worry for his life and for his son's well-being. He frantically tried six times to start his car and leave the roadway to find a safer place. It wouldn't turn over and start. Our guest speaker cried out to his God like this, "Father God, please help me get this dead car to start running again." Miraculously, the engine turned over and he was able to drive away from that horrific attack. He drove about one hundred MPH as he raced to the nearest hospital for help. When he reached the next community of people, he shouted at the guard standing at a military gate section of this town. The guard either ignored his cries or didn't want to leave his post. So our guest speaker from Shiloh began to panic and yell loudly by this time. Finally, a young woman walking on the street started yelling too for an ambulance to come help this distraught man who had blood on his pant leg.

This loud commotion on the street brought other people around who finally approached him and his vehicle. One individual handed this man a phone so he could call his wife. They all heard his exclamation as he shouted into the phone. "I've been shot in the leg. Meet me at the hospital soon." Then an ambulance arrived on the scene. Two paramedics ran over to his car and worked on getting the straps free from his young son and then they lifted him out of the car seat. This Hebrew man could hear the bystanders' comments through the fog in his brain. "This man's son has been shot. He is bleeding and we need to place bandages on the boy and apply an oxygen mask over his face to help him breathe better."

After two years of operations, post-trauma therapy, and doctor's visits which culminated into more healings for both him and his young son, this father began delivering his heartrending testimony to people and tourist who visited his city of Shiloh. He is committed to telling the truth about what is happening in the Land of Israel. He asks folks to help him be able to support and care for the children of his land by donating a few shekels or dollars to the Shiloh Israel Children's Fund in order to promote more youth programs, summer camps, and playgrounds and post-trauma therapy programs for Israeli children who have suffered from the violence and hatred of the terrorists in Israel. His website is here: www.shilohisraelchildren.org please visit this site and learn more about how Mr. Rubin is dedicated to bringing some healing out of pain for children in need. I was fortunate to spend some time with this wonderful man and I give God thanks for sparing his life. He was very happy to have us visit his city and learn more about his country and people. I was impressed with this gentle, caring giant of a man from Israel. Then when we were done talking, I asked him if he minded if I included his miracle story of how God had saved him and his son from death. He answered me with a yes, you can share my story with others and ask people back in America to pray for the peace of Israel and for our children. As I shook his hand and watched him walk away on that hot, dusty day in Shiloh, I was reminded of the man of God called Jeremiah the prophet who walked this dry, rocky land so many thousands of years ago and I asked the Lord God to bless this man (the guest speaker) and provide for all his family's needs. I continued to ask God to protect the Israeli children from any more deadly attacks from Hamas or Isis militants. Whenever I pray for my country of Israel, I also add a prayer for the peace of Jerusalem and the Jewish people in Israel.

One evening almost eight days into my visit to Israel, I met a young man who was also staying that week in the same hotel in Israel. This chance meeting was a divine appointment that took place on September 28th, 2017.

Let me explain what I mean by this encounter not being just a chance meeting with a stranger in a foreign land. I felt like I was supposed to obey God and take a trip to his Holy Land, and I'd prayed often about this decision and my plans. My first thoughts about going to Israel involved the idea of either working in a small school in the West Banks region or possibly visiting an orphanage where I might be able to help and pray for children there. Even though I had certain concerns for my safety, I knew I needed to put them aside and obey God's leading to go there. Before I even decided to purchase a plane ticket for overseas, I had been at a prayer meeting at my friend, Trish's home. As I sat in her living room praying about such possibilities, I felt impressed upon by the Holy Spirit that I would meet some Israeli people with these names, such as Sarah, David, Isaiah, Isaac, Elijah, Samuel, and someone with the name that began with the letter H. In my mind, I thought that a few of these names might possibly belonged to some Hebrew children who lived in an orphanage in Israel. I had heard about an orphanage located in Israel from one of the women at Trish's meeting and it was on my heart to go stay there for a week, help somehow, and bless the children while in Israel. I was looking forward to being introduced to the ones who were called by these Hebrew names. Since I didn't know anyone in this country it would have to be orchestrated by God. Surprisingly, during my fourteen days of being in Israel, I met all the people with these names which I'd been given months before leaving America. It was such a marvelous confirmation for me of the fact that I was supposed to fly to this country by faith and to pray for the Israeli people while I was there.

So, keep in mind that I had asked God for divine appointments months before I left America to travel to Israel. However, as the months went by, I had forgotten about this specific prayer request. When the date of my departure came around, I was scheduled to fly to Tel Aviv and spend fourteen days in the Holy Land. So now picture me staying in a room with three other travelers who were excited about attending the same prayer conference. One day as I was waiting for the hotel elevator to take me up to the ninth floor of this very tall hotel where I was staying, I happen to greet a person from India standing next to me waiting for the hotel elevator as well. As we chatted briefly, I felt impressed to ask him his name. He told me his name was Elijah. I mentioned to him that I'd been shown back in America that I would meet someone with the same name when I arrived in Israel. I asked him if I could pray for him and his family since he was a believer. He replied yes, please! As I started to place my hand on his shoulder to believe God to bless him, he interjected with a second request when he mentioned that he and his wife were struggling to agree about having another baby since their only son was now five years old. So, without missing a beat, I included both requests into my prayers at that pivotal moment. As he was heading to his hotel room, he shared with me that he was a pastor of a church fellowship in the country of India. When I heard him make this statement, I informed this gentle individual that I had a heart for pastors and then I asked him if I could pray for him a second time. He gladly invited me to pray some more. After this we parted company, and I went to the ninth floor and my hotel room to get changed and ready for the evening meal. I felt that this encounter by the elevator had been a divine appointment from God and an answer to my early morning prayer.

As I entered the large hotel dining room for the evening meal, I noticed how crowded the place was. Hoping I would find a place to sit down for my evening meal, I headed for the food line. Seeing my favorite vegetables in heated containers, I scooped up a few potatoes, some juicy red beets, and a generous helping of humus onto my plate and turned to scan the dining room area for a vacant seat in the packed room. Finally, seeing a few of my new acquaintances at a back table I made my way over towards their table. I grabbed an empty seat next to this same pastor from India and three other men whom I had met earlier in the hotel lobby. While we sat there enjoying our evening meal, I asked this pastor to tell me more about his life. Srihri—or as he is called today by his new name of (Elijah) related to me how he had been born into a Hindu family. His family had wanted him to become a Hindu priest. His father enrolled him into a type of religious school at the age of twelve. He spends three years under this priestly tutelage training.

When my new acquaintance, a Hindu teenager, Srihri ———, was fifteen years old, he started questioning things that were happening to his relatives. He couldn't understand why his father and some relatives were beginning to argue about money problems. He didn't think this was the right way to act if a person knows God. He soon found out that a relative had done something wrong in a business matter. The next thing that occurred was that his father couldn't pay for his school fees at the temple. Another problem occurred where a person stole money from him, and this really disturbed this young Hindu lad named Srihri. Why would these people who served all these 33,000 gods in India do these kinds of wicked sins? He asked this question often, "If there is a god in my country why do my relatives treat us so poorly? His response to all this trouble was to think that everyone here is just living for making or taking money and it seems like there is no god. He finally said this, "Since there is no god in this land, I might as well just live as I chose to and try to get wealthy for my own self. Also since there is no god to serve, why would I want to perform all these Hindu rituals?" During this time of reflection and wondering, he also said this to himself as well, "I want to know for sure if there is a God or not. In his time of searching for a true reality of a God to serve, he withdrew to stay alone in his bedroom for a few days. He stopped talking to his mother and the family.

After his takes some time of introspection and silence, this teenager called Srihri decides to start chanting the words, Hari Krishna repeatedly. He sits on the carpet flooring and tries to meditate. Soon his mind forgets stuff and his brain becomes nearly like a blank slate. He tried to chant some of the idol names he remembered. Shortly after this he quit chanting in frustration. Then the next day, his auntie (his mom's sister) came there and asked her nephew this profound question. "Do you know Jesus?" Who is this Jesus, he replies to his auntie since he'd never heard anything about this man while growing up in a Hindu family background. His auntie tells him this, "Jesus is the real true God." Srihri answers her back with this statement. "I don't know your God, but I want to know this, is there a God for sure?"

His aunt begins to share with him about her experience of discovering who God is in her own life. She shared with him using these words, "I was doing idol worship like the rest of our family and then God appeared like his son, Jesus in my home". Before this happened to her, she had mentioned how she'd married a Christian man who prayed for her. How this marriage came about was interesting to me as I wrote his words down on paper that day. Then, this same man, stopped in his story to explain to me about the caste system in his country. There are tribes in India and so this is how it worked out for her. Her grandfather decided to give this man to wed his granddaughter since they were both in the same caste level. Then my new acquaintance continued telling me more about his auntie. At first, she told her nephew, Srihri, that she had opposed her husband's faith in God and his son, Jesus. She later learns that his Christian parents have been praying for her to know the truth about their God. She encounters the son of God herself and she relates to him of her real experience. "Jesus appeared to me that day. He sat with me and spoke words of life to me." Her nephew continued sharing with me as I wrote feverishly each thing he spoke as we sat together forgetting about our meal then. "My auntie told me that she received God's son by faith, and she was very happy and full of peace. Then she came to talk with me because she heard I was visiting my parents for the weekend." Srihri stated.

At this point in my interview with this pastor from India, he informed me to write down his new name. I recorded his new, legal name on my paper and waited for him to explain this to me. Elijah informed me that he had decided to stop using his given names after becoming a Christian. He told me to now record his new name at this point in his story)

Then this pastor who changed his name to Elijah continued telling me his story as he mentioned making this request to his auntie, "Give me a picture of this Jesus so I can worship him too."

His auntie replied to her nephew with this: "Jesus is not an idol; he is alive like you and me. He is like a good friend, and you can ask Jesus for whatever you need, and he will give it to you!"

"I don't need anything from God, but I want to know for sure, is there a true God?" He asked. "Please pray for me, auntie; I don't know how to pray."

"You ask God to show himself to you in a real way." Then his aunt prayed these simple words, "Lord God bless my nephew and save him." Then her nephew understood how to make his own prayer words after this. He went into his bedroom and made his request unto God.

"Lord God if you are real, I want to see you." He waited and waited, but no one came into his room that time. Later, his auntie gave him a Bible to read. "Read this book, if you seek the living God, He will come to you."

Elijah experienced a glimmer of faith as he read the Bible. Again, this nephew asked God to appear to him, however, no one came that next day to his room. He cried out while sitting in his room alone with his thoughts, "Does anyone hear my prayers or am I speaking only to the air?" No answer came to him at this time. He decided to open the Bible one more time and his eyes fell upon a verse, "The Lord looked down from heaven upon the

children of men, to see if there were any that did understand, and seek God." (Psalm 14: 2 KJV)

Then he understood that there is a God who lives
in Heaven who is hearing his prayers and looking at him
and listening to his heart. On the third day of waiting on
God, my new pastor friend, Elijah, made another request
with all his heart of the Lord. "Lord, come and appear to
me here." Then he saw a great light come into his room
and he was filled with joy. His exact words to me as I sat
and listened intently to his story went like this: "That
light came near me and I felt that I could barely handle
the strong shining light." After this amazing experience
he came out of his bedroom to tell his dear mother about
this amazing experience and her response to him was
profound, "God is light." The next morning, he felt a
strong desire to know God even more and so he looked
for a church to visit and to learn more about this Jesus.
Elijah found a church where the preacher was referring
to the first chapter in the Book of John. "In the beginning was the Word, and the Word was with God, and
the Word was God." (John 1: 1) After hearing this statement he thought if he could read the words in the Bible
then he might discover the truth about who God really
was. As he read this next verse, "But the Lord is the true
God, he is the living God, and an everlasting king…"
(Jeremiah 10:10) He had trouble digesting this statement
since he was now faced with a choice. He'd have to leave
the thousands of Hindu gods and follow and serve the
God who called himself the one and only true God. This
became a battle within his heart – who indeed was the
one true God. As he contemplated making this decision,
he decided to ask again this request of his aunt's God.

"God, I want you to come in my house and appear to me like a real person and then I will believe in you."

The next week while at this same church service, Elijah heard a man's testimony. Most of his life this man who was sharing had served many gods or idols in his country of India. Then his wife began to attend a Christian church and she becomes a believer in the son of God. She asks her pastor to visit her home and pray for her husband to accept her faith in God. Her husband did not want to listen to this pastor. The pastor asked the husband to do one thing for his wife that very night. In order to have the pastor leave him alone and go away, the man finally agreed to say the name of Jesus before he falls asleep. After speaking out the name of Jesus, the nonbeliever slept until around one o'clock a.m. Suddenly, Jesus appears in his room with angels. The man fell to the floor from his cot and says these words, "Lord, forgive me for I am a sinner." Later he wakes up completely and he realizes that Jesus is really the one true God. The next day he takes all the idols out of his home, places them into a box, and hauls them in a rickshaw buggy to the railroad tracks. Then a train comes down the track, runs over the boxes, and smashes all the idols When Elijah heard this man's true story of salvation and repentance, he believed in his aunt's God, and he rejoiced.

The next week, he read the passage about doubting Thomas who was the one disciple who didn't believe he'd seen the risen savior alive again. He wanted to believe in Christ even though he had not even seen Jesus appear in his room like that other man had. He chose to trust God and he didn't want to test God by asking him to appear in the flesh in his home. A few more years went by and now Elijah had turned nineteen years old and was studying to be an industrial engineer in the university. One day he left his college classes to go spend some time with his auntie. They went to visit her church where the pastor preached the word of God from the Bible. Then afterwards this pastor asked the people if anyone wanted to be filled with the Holy Spirit. If they wished to have this new gift from God, then they should come to pray with him in the back of the church. Even though he was already sitting in the back of the church, he still stood up by himself and asked God to baptize him in the Holy Spirit.

I needed to ask pastor friend now going by the name of Elijah to pause for a moment while I caught up to him in my writing. After we resumed the interview, I continued to write down his words as fast as I could. This portion of his story had to do with a second glorious experience. He mentioned to me that he stood there waiting in the church expecting God to answer his request. Then he felt the love of God in strong measure, and he was filled God's spirit and he began to speak in a new, unfamiliar language. He told me that for three days he continued to speak in this prayer language called 'new tongues' which is found in the Book of Acts, and he told me that he'd slept very little during this time. If he dozed off for a short while, when he woke up, he was still speaking in an unknown language just like the disciples did in the second chapter of Acts.

At the end of the third day, Elijah was feeling like he was surrounded by the presence of God and then he was given the gift of interpretation of his 'new tongues' language. He went to visit his auntie and they rejoiced and prayed together. She saw a vision at this time which she described as like seeing the wind and a flood of the Holy Spirit coming to her. He prayed for his auntie to receive the gift of the speaking in tongues, and she also received this marvelous empowering gift right then. They were both elated and together they praised God for granting them this joyous experience with the Father God. At the beginning, his auntie had shared the truth about salvation with him and then later he was blessed to be able to share the new truth about being baptized in the Holy Spirit. This was a great true story of redemption for a man and his family who live in a foreign country steeped in idol worship. I was thrilled to hear his amazing salvation story and to call him my new pastor friend from India.

CHAPTER TWENTY-EIGHT

I have learned about this remarkable pastor who has a great church in Texas. He started out by feeding the hungry and poor of his city and eventually, miracles and healings began to take place and they had to rent a building and establish a church group. He shared his vision with folks on TV one Sunday while I was visiting my friends in Phoenix, Arizona. I was impressed with this pastor's generosity and heart of compassion for the needy folks in his city. This pastor also spends plenty of money, his own time, and great effort to rescue young girls from brothels located in foreign countries. This dynamic leader shared an amazing true story about how he was involved in a recent rescue. While he was in another country on a speaking assignment, the Spirit of God captured Troy's attention and showed him in a vision some insight about a young girl who would be wearing a white dress. He felt a strong impression that he needed to rescue this child.

Pastor Troy finally managed to convince an Uber driver to take him to this rather undesirable section of the town. He knocked on the door of this brothel house and asked to see one of their girls. After a few minutes of discussing this matter with the lady of the house, he requested a younger girl. The woman in charge of this brothel brought out a six-year-old girl who was wearing a white dress. He insisted on purchasing this child. It took a lot of convincing before they would accept his money offer, but once he'd completed the purchase of this child, he left the place in a hurry and jumped into the Uber vehicle with the youngster, and they raced away from that vicinity with her. This young girl was transported to another location and eventually to a safe house in a different country where the older girls (who'd been saved by this same kindhearted pastor too) could minister love and compassion to this hurting, abused girl. I loved this story of how an American pastor helped rescue a young hurting child from sex traffickers and who later came to accept Christ as her personal savior and is on the road to healing and a new life. This dedicated pastor from Texas had decided to become like the church of Philadelphia and now God has richly blessed this leader's heartfelt endeavors and it seems to me that he is storing up treasures in heaven.

***

One Saturday while my daughter and I were visiting Bethel Church in Redding, California, I went into a large room to receive prayer from the prayer team that morning. I wanted everything that God had planned for me to experience there, and I was not disappointed. After being prayed for by a team of three caring young adults, I went down on my knees because of the presence of God's Holy Spirit resting heavily upon me. I sat there on the floor and focused on listening to what God wanted to impart to me. I have learned through the years to wait for him to finish ministering to me in these quiet times. When I eventually stood up, they gathered about me and prayed for me one last time. During this time one of the young adults shared a word of knowledge with me, "You are a freedom fighter for God." Since that time, I have pushed forward to believe and operate out of this new concept or blueprint for my life. For the past few years, I've determined to quote the first ten verses of a true biblical way of life often which are found in Isaiah 61. I find that as I declare this passage over my life, it is easier for me to believe I can be a victorious freedom fighter and a mighty prayer warrior. I also believed because of Christ's indwelling spirit and this authority given to every believer that we can walk in His anointed purposes while here on earth. Let's look at the first two verses and how it applies to a believer and the way we minister to others.

"The Spirit of the Lord is upon me; (insert your name-here in this place) because the Lord hath anointed me (insert your own name here) to preach good tidings unto the meek; he hath sent me to bind up the brokenhearted, to proclaim liberty to the captives, and the opening of the prison to them that are bound;…" (Isaiah 61:1)

This entire passage of Isaiah 61 continues with wonderful promises from the Bible for all those who can believe this applies to them as well.

Before I continue sharing about my quest to become a 'freedom fighter' for God's kingdom purposes, let's go to the dictionary for a definition of the word freedom. The term, 'freedom' means to be released from the Old Testament law and the Jewish religious traditions. Webster's Dictionary states that the word 'freedom' implies the absence of constraints in a person's actions or choices. Most people desire to be liberated from the enslavement or control by others upon their life. We've all heard this concept spoken to us, 'the truth can bring you freedom'! Some people might be kept from experiencing real freedom and joy for their lives by either believing a lie or by not understanding the truth. In my journey to see people set free, I usually will find a specific scripture which could've been meant just for them. God has been faithful to show me how to pray for that person more successfully when I depend on receiving his valuable insights.

There is one more aspect of freedom that needs to be shared here. We were all born into sin and have fallen short of the glory of God. Therefore, we have all lived under the control or bondages of a sin nature at one time in our past. People generally need to be set free from their own ways and the slavery that sin produces. Most of us desire to walk in liberty and the only true way to gain freedom like the Bible refers to is by changing our thoughts and ways to align with God's instructions. Have you ever wondered how to achieve true freedom? Let's look at this absolute truth: God loves you and He wants you to be free! He has given us the Word of God to show people how to achieve freedom and we must search out what God's promises mean for each of us in our quest to discover this type of victory. In the Book of Romans it declares that we need to incorporate this concept into our thinking, "Being then made free from sin, ye became the servants of righteousness…" (Romans 6: 18) When we quote this scripture verse and declare that we are free from the power of sin and that we want to serve God then he will empower us to live a fulfilled life because

Christ has the power to make us free to serve the Lord in righteousness instead of doing things our way. In my own journey I continue to ask God to teach me how to stay living in true freedom!

Let's look at another key to obtaining more freedom and the abundant life provision. For me, it involved learning how to surrender to God's plan for my life. As a young twenty-one-year-old, I decided to hand my life over to God in a commitment to serve him fully when I said this, *"God in heaven, today I surrender my future to you, and I make you Lord of my life and my decisions!"* God wants us to look in the Bible for guidelines to health, wisdom, and success so that we will find freedom and joy while living in this world. Without biblical keys to success and victory we are merely human beings striving for perfection and the hope of being free from sins, guilt, shame, and depression. It is only by turning our lives over to God in true, complete surrender that we discover this much desired liberty and fulfillment. Surrendering our plans and dreams to God and walking in a spirit of humility is the opposite of what the world teaches about achieving success and taking care of the number 'one person', yourself. Another aspect of obtaining true freedom comes when we renounce guilt or shame or negative words from our past which can plague our minds. I have seen the benefits of yielding my life to God daily. Have you considered the idea of making Him the Lord of your entire life and you decision making? I made this decision as a young adult, and I have no regret all. The Lord can be trusted to lead everyone who calls upon his name in his marvelous ways of peace, joy, success and fruitfulness.

Truth is a powerful weapon which will break any lie or deception. I'd believed a lie about myself because I thought it was my fault that my dad molested me. One thing I've came to understand from the professionals in psychology is that I could be categorized as a victim of molestation and abuse. Yes, I now understand more fuller that I suffered a great deal and I lived with a lot of pain and anguish as a child. Yes, I could refer to myself as a survivor of physical and sexual abuse. However, even though I survived the trauma and grief of abuse and wished I could die or live in a different family, I still found God and he redeemed my life from destruction and turned my sorrows into joy. This is how it all culminated for me one dreary, depressing day as my children were napping and I lay on my bed bemoaning my miserable life with all its grief and heartaches. At one point, I said a simple prayer of surrender. "Lord, my life story is really messed up! I hated my life with all the shame, pain, grief, and bitterness of soul but if you want to use my depressing life story to help someone who has been abused like me, then it's okay. Have your way, Lord with my life. I give you my pain, my shame, and my hurting, grieving heart. Help me to tell my story of redemption and healing to anyone who will listen. There is hope for anyone who has been abused and feels unloved or forgotten. My prayer of relinquishment turned out to be powerful turning point for me that day.

My life has not been the same since I surrendered my hurting life story to my heavenly Father. It keeps getting better and whenever I share my pain and shame with someone, it allows them to feel safe to share their sad story. I have had the opportunity to hold women who were distraught, inconsolable, and weeping over their own painful stories. All I could do was hug them in a caring way and tell them that God loves them. There is hope for a survivor of childhood abuse. God truly cares for the brokenhearted and He understands your anguish. The Son of God was beaten viciously and horribly mistreated by men. He suffered a great deal for all of mankind and then he died while hanging on a wooden cross in order to take upon himself the sins of the world. I was set free from my own sorrow and anxiety the day I said yes to the Living God. It is now my heart's desire to pray for people to be healed and set free too.

Now that I know more truth about my life history, I am willing to share my testimony with others. God has truly healed me and set me free from the emotional pain, the awful despair, and the shame of being abused as a young girl. Of course, this newfound freedom came at a cost! I had to be willing to be transparent, to be honest with my friends and the trained counselors, and to be willing to face my fears. Eventually, I discovered there was a light at the end of my dismal tunnel of anguish and sadness. This light of truth came shinning into my soul when I turned to God and experienced such love and kindness from His heart to mine. The Father God was there all the time even during the times when I felt alone. He was with me when I felt like giving up on my soul-searching and lengthy journey to be made whole and well. Of course, during this process, I had to be willing to face the truth, to allow God to heal me from all my pain and trauma, and to change my way of thinking and how I see myself.

Today, as I was walking on our gravel driveway that leads up to our home situated in the countryside, an American bald eagle flew overhead and perched on top of a tall Evergreen tree next to the barn. As I gazed in wonderment at this American symbol of freedom I was struck by the grandeur and beauty of this fascinating animal. Then I recalled the first time as a young adult when I'd watched an eagle swoop down over the bay waters of Hammersley Inlet and how that scene had caused me to believe for my future. This time around, I asked the Lord what this magnificent sight of a close-up sighting of an eagle could mean for me. As I waited and listened, I felt as if this was a sign of good things to come. Then I had a strong impression that I was to use the idea of a flying eagle for the front cover design of this book. Next, I headed inside to look up online for the significance of the eagle and this is what I found. "The bald eagle was chosen June 20, 1782, as the emblem of the United States of America, because of its long life, great strength and majestic looks, and because it was then believed to exist only on this continent. ... The eagle represents freedom."

This website referred to the following as a reason for the choice of the eagle as a symbol for our nation by saying, "It is said the eagle was used as a national emblem because, at one of the first battles of the Revolution the noise of the struggle awoke the sleeping eagles on the heights and they flew from their nests and circle about over the heads of the fighting men, all the while giving vent to their raucous cries. "They are shrieking for Freedom," said the patriots." —Maude M. Grant

As I reflect on the unusual sight of the rather large eagle flying into view and landing on an Evergreen tree nearby my country home, I am reminded to not give up on my goal to be a better writer. I believe now more than ever that God has a good, good plan for my life, and he will sustain me in my writing endeavors.

***

I have learned through the years that I need to pause and ask the Lord to show me some important insight for a person I am praying for. Just this last Sunday during my drive to our church, I was asking God to give me a word of knowledge for the folks who might come up for prayer after the church service. While driving in my car, I heard the spirit of God mention that there was a person who would be coming for prayer, and they would have tears which needed to be wiped away and I was to believe for this person to experience a breakthrough. I said a quick prayer for help in this matter as I drove into the parking lot of our church. Sure enough, after the service had ended and the pastor asked folks to come forward for more prayer, a young woman walked up and asked me to pray for her. We knelt there on the carpeted floor, and I prayed for her needs which she couldn't even express with words right then. I was sad for her pain and sorrows as she wept in my arms. I prayed and expressed one of God's promises to her and then I motioned to my good friend to come and join me in praying for her too. He felt impressed to pronounce a 'father's blessing' over this young woman. This was exactly what she needed that day. I rejoiced with my prayer partner as we watched our heavenly Father God perform his wonderful loving touch upon this broken-hearted woman. I am trusting that she will begin to truly understand that she is loved and very important to God. God desires for a believer to walk in humility with others, but we really need to ask for the Lord's help to accomplish this goal. Then there are the other times when we find ourselves waiting and waiting for a break-through victory. It is during these difficult times of waiting for an answer to prayer that I had to trust God and all I can do is offer a sacrifice of praise. For example, when I decided to obey God by flying to Israel, I learned the value of obedience and trust. I gained so much more peace in my heart as I chose to put my faith in God's plan.

Let's get real here for a moment! Things don't always go the way we want them to in life. Sometimes life presents us with a paradox. Someone may get healed of a dreadful disease while another person languishes for a long time and then dies. One person might lose a child in a tragic accident while another family may see their daughter or son survive a bad illness and be released from the hospital to go home. If you have suffered a grievous loss of a loved one, then my heartfelt compassion and empathy goes out to you today. I am truly sorry for your loss and for the empty hole' in your heart. I believe we will one day understand more about our time on this earth and what God's divine wisdom involves when we sit at the feet of our Savior one day. Until that time, we can only put our trust in the Lord and continue to believe for God's will to be fulfilled in our lives. He does want to heal our soul and restore our hearts as we give him our grief and losses.

What do you do when your miracle doesn't happen? First thing I'd be inclined to do is to surrender my desire for a healing or miracle to the Lord. In other words, I would say this, 'not my will, but yours be done in our family member's life. Secondly, I would tend to ask God to show me as I'm waiting for my miracle or healing if there is something hindering this answer from heaven from happening. There was one occasion when I needed a breakthrough and I realized there was an individual I needed to forgive. I prayed and blessed that person just like Job was instructed to do. The Bible showed us Job relinquished his anger and rights and then he was in a better place to receive a supernatural provision and blessing. The other thing I'd do is to ask the Father if there needs to be a change in my heart attitude or to show me His perspective about this matter or situation. God is ready to give us an answer when we sit and listen in quietness and rest. When my daughter was in the hospital for a month, I called the 700-club phone line (800-700-7000) and prayed with a CBN partner. Then I asked the person I was talking with to put my request in with their chapel prayer team for a week. There is a tremendous wealth of power and victory when we follow the scriptural promise of agreement prayer with another person who has faith even that of a mustard seed' kind of faith.

There were times when I needed to ask God a question. "Lord, how do you want to heal this person?" Sometimes, the healing looked different than I was expecting; this truth became more evident as I saw a woman's aching heart and soul healed first and foremost before the physical healing was manifested. Since we are a triune people which includes body, mind, and soul we ought to consider asking the Lord to heal our hearts and our memories too and not just allow our focus to rest mainly on a physical healing each time! "But he was wounded for our transgressions, he was bruised for our iniquities: the chastisement of our peace was upon him; and with his stripes we are healed." (Isaiah 53: 5) I believe the healing promises purchased though Christ's immensely painful sufferings and awful crucifixion death reveals a full package deal which includes both salvation and healing for those who call on his name. Therefore, we can also expect to be healed in our minds, in our damaged emotions, and in our wounded, hurting souls as we accept the finished work of the cross. Give it a try and trust that God knows the best way to heal people. I am living proof that God can heal anyone who has suffered from much childhood abuse issues, trauma, extreme emotional pain, past fears, and from physical pain! Miracles do happen! There are two inseparable truths about God I want to share here: God loves people, and he loves to heal people!

CHAPTER TWENTY-NINE

I admire certain strong female teacher/ evangelists like Joy Dawson and especially, Corrie Ten Boom. Some years ago, Corrie lived in Holland with her family. Her father was a watchmaker and she helped him in this business. This family also helped many Jewish people escape the deportation to concentration camps during the 1940's. In February of 1944, an informant turned the Boom family into the dreaded Gestapo, and they were apprehended and sent to a Nazi war camp.

She wrote a book which later was made into a movie called "The Hiding Place". After this project she chose to travel to different countries to share God's love and her experiences in the Nazi camp. This woman has been an inspiration to many, and her life is a constant reminder of the grace of God. Here is one of Corrie's quotes that I'd like to pass onto you, "Don't pray when you feel like it. Have an appointment with the Lord and keep it. A man is powerful on his knees." (Tlogical.net)

While travelling in the country of Uganda this year, I met a dedicated missionary couple. We enjoyed an evening of chatting and I learned that they had originally been in the states until they left Atlanta, Georgia five years before this. They'd been living in a big city in the country of Uganda where he worked in an orphanage and his wife taught in a school. Towards the end of our conversation, this missionary acquaintance shared with me how they'd taken a vacation trip to the Netherlands recently. While there they had seen an advertisement about touring the home of an evangelist and Christian speaker, Corrie Ten Boom. The tickets had been sold out for that day and so they decided to just walk about the city sightseeing. As they approached the same street where this well-known family's house was located, he noticed the line of people which had formed outside of Corrie's childhood home. As he counted the number of people standing in line, he realized that this group of tourists was missing the exact amount by four people. He grabbed his wife's arm and pulled her along with him to stand in this same line waiting to enter the landmark dwelling. Then the group was ushered into this famous home by the tour guide. The guide then proceeded to describe details about the house as he also shared interesting facts about the Ten Boom family to this attentive group of tourists.

Their guide described the events surrounding the Nazi SS troops who had hunted and captured many Jews during WWII. The Ten Boom family had played a vital role in providing a secure hiding place for many Jewish families who were trying to escape the country. My friend continued to inform me about how they were given the opportunity to proceed upstairs to enter Corrie and Betsy Ten Boom's room where the father had built a hidden room behind the wall. To prevent the soldiers from discovering this empty extra room behind the bookshelf wall, her father had bricks brought upstairs. Then with the extra bricks they were able to build a new wall in the girl's bedroom. Using mortar with the bricks, he and his son created a strong wall right behind the plaster wall. Every time the German soldiers wanted to uncover a hidden compartment where Jewish people may be hiding, they would tap on the walls to see if it had a hollow sound effect.

The brick partition in Corrie's bedroom kept them from discovering the original hiding place for many months. Her father had contrived a special pulley system with a slender rope attached to the cover up board located on the bottom shelf area of the bookcase. Whenever they needed to hide some people, they just pulled on the rope and the front wall board would slide up until there was a proper sized gap. This opening allowed the Jewish people to bend down on their knees and enter inside of the second smaller room behind the bookcase. I thought this was a genius idea and it worked for a long time. However, the Nazis were diligent in putting someone nearby to watch this house each day.

Eventually, the German soldiers finally had enough evidence to pull off a major raid on this family's home and discovered the necessary proof showing that the Ten Boom family had been involved in helping the Jews to escape. After this raid, the entire family was sent to concentration camps where some of them died from starvation and cruel treatment. This family's story was eventually made into a movie called "The Hiding Place". The Ten Boom family made heroic attempts to protect many Jews from certain death. By becoming involved with the Jews, her father, her brother, and her sister suffered greatly at the hands of the Nazi soldiers and eventually they died in the Nazi internment camp. I was delighted to hear all these new details about my favorite evangelist, Corrie Ten Boom, her family history, and about this missionary's tour of her landmark home in Holland from my new missionary friends who lived next door to Marcus's aunt in Uganda.

The following day I met a man who was employed by this same missionary couple living next door to this aunt. This elderly African gentleman told me his name and I introduced myself too. I started a conversation with him across the fence since he seemed friendly and talkative. I soon learned that he had become a believer when he was a young adult. He went on to share how he'd surrendered his life completely to the Lord and afterwards he'd spent many years working as an evangelist in Uganda. He told me how he had fasted for a year by eating only one meal a day. After enduring this lengthy and grueling discipline, this Ugandan man received more power from the Holy Spirit. There were many times where when he laid hands on a person and prayed for them that they fell under the power of God and were dramatically healed or set free from demonic oppression. I asked this godly man if he would consider praying over me too. He responded with a yes and so I went inside to change out of my white skirt in case I also slid to the ground like the other people. After changing into some pants, I proceeded to walk next door to this missionary home where he was working. I knocked on the metal gate to gain entrance to my new friend's front yard and the worker man greeted me as a brother in the Lord.

This friendly, kindhearted individual presented me with a chair to sit down on as he prayed God's favor and blessing over me. Next, he went on to ask the Lord to help me to do God's bidding while I was here in his country. He mentioned why he'd given me a chair to sit on; it was because he didn't want me to fall in the dirt as he prayed for me. I laughed and thanked him for his kind consideration and care for my well-being. He smiled and began to speak rich blessings and protection over me. Next, we talked some more about the things of the Lord and about the troubles the Ugandan people were experiencing under their recent president's leadership. I stood up and began to intercede for this country, its political leaders, and the people of Uganda, Africa. I also prayed many blessings and prosperity for my newfound friend and his family as well. He thanked me for praying for him before I left. I was blessed once again to have had the privilege of spending time with a man of God and another wise prophet who lives in Uganda, Africa.

Heidi Baker is another person who belongs in what I like to call the 'Hall of Faith' category. She and her husband, Roland, took their three children to live in Africa. They followed their hearts and chose to serve God in a difficult, struggling third world country. Despite the dangers and the difficulties that they've endured over the years, the Baker family has been carrying the message of God's love to African people living in poverty and lack for most of their lives. They decided to adopt some orphaned children who were living on the streets. They gladly shared their home and food with these children in Mozambique, Africa. The Bible says that true religion consists of people willing to help the widows and taking care of the fatherless and orphans. Heidi and Roland Baker exemplify this kind of true Christian believers. I believe that these folks have truly touched the heart of

God. They have chosen to walk by faith and believe for God's help and provision to be able to take care of nearly one thousand fatherless children in Mozambique, Africa.

Some leaders in my church here in America have said that folks are now calling Heidi Baker this affectionate nick-name, 'Mother Teresa' of Africa. I certainly agree with this statement because she truly has sacrificed plenty of comfort to live in Mozambique and take care of the very needy people in her community. Heidi wrote a book about her experiences while they were living in Africa. After reading her book, I was amazed at how dangerous it could be to live there for Americans and missionaries. Heidi was shot at by some men in the African militia (self-appointed leaders) who felt threatened by these white people rescuing young African boys from their clutches. The militants wanted to keep these young boys and train them to become part of their revolutionary/ military plans and so they plotted to rid the community of the white folks. However, God protected Roland and Heidi and their family from such danger and harm. My daughter who is a nurse has made a trip recently to Mozambique, Africa to help with Heidi Baker's children. I greatly admire this dedicated couple for their sacrifices and their commitment to rescue starving children in that region. While my own daughter was in Africa, she saw the great needs there and wants to return someday to Africa and work with these wonderful kids and with Heidi and Roland Baker's staff in Mozambique.

God is for us! He wants us to successful, to be healthy, and to learn His way of achieving happiness in our lifetime. One key to accomplishing these goals is to keep the Word of God before your eyes and saturate your mind with the promises of God. There is a valuable scripture which instructs all believers to give their worries and future to the Lord as they pray with thanksgiving. (Philippians 4: 6-7) The third aspect of maintaining a way of bringing success to your life and business is to ask this: "What is it that inspires me?" I recall looking at this idea many years ago as I struggled in my first attempt to write a fiction novel. I decided to one day create an inspirational, motivational board to help me accomplish some of my heart's desires or dreams. I cut out pictures from a magazine of things that spoke to my soul. For instance, I choose a picture of woman in a kayak paddling on the lake waters. Another photo I cut out was of a beach house near the blue ocean. Then I cut out a magazine picture that displayed a lakeside home and the dock running out to the waterfront. For some reason I leaned towards the colors of blue and white mostly and so that was what I pinned onto my picture board.

Along with my inspirational picture board, I also wrote down on a piece of paper the goals I wanted to achieve in my lifetime. After I'd recorded a few things, such as going back to college to get my four-year degree, becoming a teacher of elementary students, writing a book, and doing some oil painting again, I stuffed this short list into a tin can and buried it in the ground by a huge pine tree out back of our house. I am happy to say that I achieved all these goals before retiring from my job. I am now free to travel to the nations. This idea may seem a little unusual, but I'd heard a true story of an African girl who'd decided to try this unique idea. After making her desired list of goals, she stuffed the paper into a small tin can and buried it beneath the ground near her village. She wanted to finish college, come to America one day, and become a professor. This woman from Africa reached all her dreams and came to America to get her master's degree and Ph.D. Why not give this idea a try and believe that you too can accomplish your life goals and be happy and fulfilled!

Just the other day, my good friend who makes a living by painting unique wedding signs came to spend the afternoon at my country home. She brought her college age daughter with her to take photographs of wedding signs which they'd placed strategically around my house and lawn. Her daughter helped that afternoon by downloading these photographs of the attractive signs onto her mother's website. After we were done visiting, I shared this idea of writing down a person's goals/dreams with my friend and her daughter. She encouraged her daughter to write down her goals for the future on a small piece of paper. I went inside the house to find my friend a small tin box which had a lid. Her daughter stuffed the list of goals into the small container and then she dug a small hole in the dirt next to our shed and covered up the tin can. This may seem like a rather odd way to expect good things to happen in your life, but I believe it has some merit. In fact, I can say this truth: It worked for me, so give it a try and believe that you will achieve your goals and dreams too!

Another way for keeping your life on the path to success is to follow the example of someone you admire. By this I mean find someone who fits into the category of a hero that you might want to exemplify in your own life, your business venture, or maybe your book writing goals. I have a few heroes in my life that I look to for inspiration and guidance as I write this book. I admire my one daughter who has faced many challenges in her life since she was twenty –one years old. I consider her a real true-life hero. She went through a horrible ordeal as she fought for her life while being given the chemo drugs. She did not give up in her fight to survive. She hung onto her faith in God, and she believed along with her family that her redeemer would show up one day and set her free from this awful cancer. He did! She made a conscious decision to not go into debt and she has kept that commitment all these years. Then she chose to finish her education and become a registered nurse. She worked in the oncology ward at a hospital for a while in Oregon. When this became too rough for her emotionally and physically, she changed jobs and found a better nursing position in a medical clinic in Washington. My daughter has succeeded in staying debt free. She is also a gifted and entertaining public speaker as well. She has inspired many folks as well as several medical students and nurses who have listen to her advice about patient-doctor/nurse relationships.

Another important factor to incorporate into your thinking along the lines of success is to become a person of integrity. Let's refer to a man who was well-liked and successful in his career as a military man and then later as a wise leader of the United States of America. This is what an American president said about how to become a person of influence. "In order to be a leader a man must have followers. And to have followers, a man must have their confidence. Hence the supreme quality for a leader is unquestionably integrity. Without it, no real success is possible, no matter whether it is on a sections gang, a football field, in an army, or in an office. If a man's associates find him guilty of phoniness, if they find that he lacks forthright integrity, he will fail. His teachings and actions must square with each other. The first great need, therefore, is integrity and high purpose." Dwight D. Eisenhower

Whether you are a parent, a coach, a pastor, a husband/leader, or a businessman you need to aspire to gain wisdom. If your goal is to be someone people can trust and a person who truly cares for others, then you will be successful. I'd like to refer here to what is called a Leader's Prayer by Pauline H. Peters, "God, when I am wrong, make me willing to change. When I am right, make me easy to live with. So, strengthen me so that the power of my influence will far exceed the authority of my position." I agree with this woman and her statements. When we decide to become a leader, we can impact young people's lives. For instance, as a coach for my own daughter's soccer team, I made it my primary goal to make each child feel important and appreciated. I also chose to pray before the start of each competition for their success as players as well as their safety as an individual on the soccer field. We became a winning team and I believe they appreciated my efforts and value system that I had tried to impart to them each week. My son, Robert, coached soccer as well and he taught his players more than just ball skills; he shared his faith in God with his team and he showed a great interest in their personal lives as well. These boys are now seventeen years old, and they still desire to work hard at each practice, show good sportsmanship on this grassy field of endeavor, and be young men with godly character off the field too. Through the years, my son has implemented what I call a method of honoring the parents who faithfully come to the games and cheer the boys on to victory. He has taught his team to do this: after the game concluded, these teens all run across the field to stand in front of us and thank everyone for their support. A coach who cares about his team members and decides to pray before each contest is a man who can inspire his players to be high achievers in the game of life as well.

Oh, and by the way, our son's team has made it to four different State Finals Competitions, and they won first place in three of those tournaments. Our family is heading up to Seattle for the fourth tournament this coming Saturday; I expect another grand slam win for Coach Robert and this powerhouse team. We give God all the glory and honor for helping this team to succeed. By the way, after going and believing for the success of my son's team this December, I can now happily report that his team won this recent State Finals and brought home the trophy again. It was a wonderful time of cheering and believing for these young men to succeed and feel encouraged by their team efforts. I would say that my firstborn son is a very successful man, husband, and father of three wonderful children. I really appreciate our son and I turn to him for advice and help often. Here's a quote from another successful man and coach. "Deep down, your players must know you care about them. This is the most important thing. I could never get away with what I do if the players feel I didn't care for them. They know, in the long run, I'm in their corner."—Bo Schembechler, former football coach, University of Michigan

I asked my second son, Jonathan, who'd been a youth pastor for twelve years what he believed makes a good leader. His shared with me that a leader needs to establish an important check and balance method in their life: A wise leader or businessman needs to maintain a balance between getting a task accomplished all the while making sure that you treat your followers and helpers with consideration and kindness as you maintain a healthy relationship. There is an extra point that attaches to this valuable key which is for a wise leader to encourage times of feedback from those under his supervision. When an individual is too focused on the task at hand then they tend to ignore someone's feelings which can cause problems or hinder your goals. On the other hand, if a leader spends too much time conversing with someone and establishing a relationship, the task or job can suffer too. This is a valuable insight for those hoping to be an influence upon the youth. My son also mentioned one last concept which is that young people do not always listen to our words as much as they watch our daily examples, and they noticed if we keep our promises to them. I appreciate my son and all his years of dedication and service to young people. Jonathan Scott is a campus pastor in Syracuse, New York now and his heart is to build relationships and to encourage people to reach their goals in life.

The most important ingredient for success is that we get a vision for our plan so, that despite difficulties or setbacks, we can remain strong and keep going. Dreams that are worth fighting for are the dreams that inspire others. And the dreams and visions which come from God are the aspirations we can believe He will help us to achieve. What is your dream for your future? What do you need to do to take a step towards achieving your goals in life? There are times when we need to write our aspirations down in a prayer journal, to also declare them aloud, and to believe God wants us to thrive and be successful in our endeavor. Do you believe in yourself and your dreams? If the answer is yes, then friend, start speaking out words of life like this." I am a person of worth and value and I will achieve my goals in life!" It's okay to declare that you are blessed and highly favored by God! By doing this consistently, you may just set yourself up to realize your dreams and life goals!

As I read my Bible this morning, I came across another verse that describes why I've chosen to write this nonfiction book. It goes like this, "So we thy people... will give thanks for ever: we will shew forth thy praise to all generations." (Psalm 79: 13) This is exactly why I decided to write about the events surrounding my family's miracles and to also include other peoples' powerful testimonies of healings and divine protection. If my grandchildren ever come to me and asked me what I'd like for them to do in remembrance of their grandmother, I'd give this response: I'd want you to be kind to others, be involved in church life, and be thankful for their many blessings like this verse says, "Those that be planted in the house of the Lord shall flourish in the courts of our God." (Psalm 92: 13) My hope is that this book will be a way of reminding my children about the goodness of God and my words will inspire them to teach the Word of God to their children and for the next generations to come. Oh, one more thing: I want my family members to gather often, laugh together, and enjoy great memories, have fun—a great deal of fun and plenty of laughter. I'm smiling right now as I think about this picture. For you see, I am a woman who loves life, loves to laugh, and to have fun. In fact, I'm all about trying to have a good time and that's why my kids will usually find me bringing a party atmosphere to a family gathering or spending time out in nature swimming, hiking, or biking in the sunshine. For sure being in the great outdoors helps me to relax. Maybe living out in nature for a week or two is what we need to give us more balance and a sense of real peace and true joy. I often wonder if this is what heaven is like! Well, just maybe there is baseball and flag football as well!

CHAPTER THIRTY

I believe it would be beneficial to also look at some successful people in the Bible. We can learn some valuable insight from these men and apply this to our own lives. History is oftentimes a great instructor for future generations. When I studied the life of Joseph, I see a young man who learned humility, trust, and perseverance. Joseph of the Old Testament had to rely on the Lord to see him through the heartache and testing which lasted for thirteen years. That's way too long in my estimation of waiting for deliverance and freedom.

When a person comes to me and they tell me they feel like God has stopped hearing their prayers and they feel hopeless and defeated, I point them to the life of Joseph and all the years of suffering he endured. I finish by giving them this piece of advice as I encourage them to ask God a different question the next time they pray. God has an answer for every problem we face; it just may not look like what we want to hear yet. Try asking this question. God is there something that needs to change in my attitude right now? How can I position myself to receive more of your favor and rich blessings in my life? And then wait and listen for His answer.

For many, many years I felt as if my husband and I were going through a 'Joseph trial' because we were struggling financially. When customers don't purchase vinyl or carpet from our business then we do not have enough money in the bank account to purchase certain food items and clothing. At one point, I had to ask our life group leaders for help with our food needs. We had hungry children, and the pantry was bare that week. This gracious couple responded to my request by dropping off milk, bread, and eggs in a bag on our front porch the next day. I was extremely grateful for this provision. Then a few months later, I decided to go to the social services department and fill out tons of paperwork to show that we needed medical cards and food stamps to take care of our grocery needs for the year. At times, I wondered where God was in all these grievous circumstances, but I learned that God was more concerned about a change in my attitude than he was about rescuing me from those lean years of financial lack. Whenever I'd sing a certain song from the Book of Psalm about rejoicing in times of lack or provision for our family, it would bring a sense of assurance that God was still with me in those difficult times.

Yes, my soul was renewed with hope because I knew the Father in heaven really loved me. I relied on the idea that one day our lives would be better. Of course, there were days when I'd grown weary in waiting for a change in my circumstances. During these lean years I had to stop at least once or twice to cry out to God to change my attitude again. In my own life, I've seen some benefit from not dwelling on my past mistakes or frustrations. I have seen the benefit of obeying the Lord instead of finding excuses as to why I shouldn't follow His instructions. When I decided to be thankful for what I had, then my attitude produced a merry heart regardless of my own sad circumstances. I've seen in my own life that when I obeyed the Lord or gave up what He was asking of me, then He opened the heavens and poured out a rich blessing into my heart and mind. I want to encourage people to follow the example of Joseph's steadfast commitment to the Lord God and his unique story of victory. If, like me, you decide to follow the principles found in Joseph's life story, then my hope for you will be that you turn everything over to the Lord and achieve your heart's desires and your true destiny.

I must share this true story here. After visiting my father and his second wife, I went to stay for a few days with my mom in my hometown. I was still very upset and frustrated with my father for the divorce and for his new marriage. I wanted to call him and yell at him and express my true feelings, but instead I stuffed my anger and resentment. The following day, I came down with a fever and felt miserable. I had to drive three hours to get back home and go to see my doctor. He told me that there was an infection in my ovaries, and I had to take the prescribed medication with fluids. This was impossible since I was throwing up everything. The next day, I asked my husband to go and bring back two leaders from our church to pray for me like the Book of James mentions. They came that very day and anointed me with oil and prayed for me to get well, to keep water and medicine down, and to be able to nurse my baby girl. By later afternoon, I was able to drink some broth, take my medication, and continue to nurse my child that night. I was so grateful to God and to these men of faith. "Is any sick among you? Let him call for the elders of the church; and let them pray over him in the name of the Lord: And the prayer of faith shall save the sick, and the Lord shall raise him up; and if he hath committed sins, they shall be forgiven him." (James 5: 14–15)

Nine months later, I was thinking about my dad and the mess his life was in since his second wife had been disgusted with his drinking problem and kicked him out of that house. I was sad because I could no longer come and let our children enjoy the summer place since she owned it now. I began to realize that I was angry with my dad and this woman. I was harboring bitterness and judgement against my father for his bad life choices. It became apparent that I needed to repent for my sinful attitude and in turn to ask God to forgive me. I was amazed at the mercy of my heavenly father who months before this had granted me forgiveness and had chosen to heal me according to his goodness and the scripture promise found in James 5: 14-15 verses. I look back on this whole experience as a valuable learning tool. The kingdom of God is about love, peace, and joy and righteousness. It was only after I turn to the Lord in humility that I found this joy and peace as a reality in my own life.

***

Sometimes as an intercessor I've had to do what Moses did in his wilderness experience when he needed water from a rock. I too had to speak or declare that a sickness had to leave my body! I've even commanded a spirit of death or cancer leave a person's body as I was praying healing for them. And then I also commanded a release or infusion of the Holy Spirit of God and his healing virtue to flow into this individual's body in the name of Jesus. When our family takes time to gather and contend for a miracle or healing in someone's situation, we've seen a dramatic change in that person's dire situation, and we give him all the credit and glory for this.

In one such situation, there was a friend who'd been told by her doctor that she had twenty-three tumors in her lungs. Janice's (not her real name) prognosis looked awfully grim. One day, after much prayer for Janice, I asked three other women to join me to go over and pray with her in her home. Then I spoke to the tumors to dry up, dissolve, and completely leave her physical body in the mighty name of Jesus. When she went into the doctors to have another x-ray of her lungs, the medical staff informed her that there were only a few tumors still in her lungs. We kept praying for her and declaring that God was her healer and we continued to stand against the enemy as we rebuked those tumors. I also invited her to come to a healing meeting to see a woman who knew how to take authority over the spirit of cancer and death. Our friend was totally healed that night and delivered from this oppressive, evil disease.

After receiving her healing miracle, Janice decided to serve the Lord completely and to be filled with the Holy Spirit. When I spoke to the tumors and commanded them to leave her lungs it was like that of 'speaking to the spirit of infirmity'. I have chosen to make strong declarations over people and situations by commanding the sickness or disease to leave their body in the same way that Moses was told to speak to the rock to bring forth water. I believe that it is vital that we listen to the Spirit's leading, and we obey in like manner as Moses did when he lifted the rod at the Red Sea. I believe He heard a rhema' or a 'now' word of instruction from the Lord as he stood by the sea and prayed for deliverance. God caused the waters to part supernaturally and thus; the entire Hebrew nation was able to cross over onto dry ground. As Moses held up that wooden staff in faith, there was a dramatic change in a very desperate situation. Thousands of Jewish people were kept from death and destruction. "But lift thou up thy rod, and stretch out thine hand over the sea, and divide it: and the children of Israel shall go on dry ground through the midst of the sea." (Exodus 14:16) This is a story of one man's amazing acts of faith. I think that this powerful testimony happened because Moses had previously learned to listened to the Spirit of the Lord and rely upon those specific instructions long before he reached the Red Sea challenge. It is quite possible that he also believed in the God of miracles. Just like in Moses' day, many of our family members have been healed by the Lord and we have seen the goodness of our God in our lives.

There were times that I'd been given a vision or a dream from God and through the years, I've learned to pay attention to them. One time, I received warning dreams in which I saw my son, Jonathan Scott, suffering from a very bad injury and even though I didn't understand how this might happen, I still knew it was important to pray continually for his safety. Thankfully, my prayers were answered, and his life was spared during a nasty vehicle crash. However, he had to have surgery after the speeding truck driver crashed into him and sent him flying. I was thankful that he'd listened to my request to wear his motorcycle helmet that summer.

When I was contemplating a trip to Africa, my family became quite concerned about the dangers which a single woman might encounter while traveling in a foreign country. While I was preparing to travel abroad, I learned about the danger of mosquito bites in Uganda. People get very sick from malaria, and I didn't want to suffer from this horrible illness. I wondered if I'd be safe in this land which had endured many years of poverty, corruption, and conflicts. I worried about my safety as I considered buying a plane ticket to fly to Kampala. So finally, I called my friend and asked her to pray with me about this decision. She spoke a word of encouragement to me as she prayed about my plans. She said that she felt good about my plan to go to Uganda and that I was not to be afraid. I called another friend about this trip, and she also confirmed that I was to trust God and not allow fear to dominate my thinking about traveling to Africa.

My friend also gave me a scripture to rely on which went like this: "Fear thou not; for I am with thee:… I will strengthen thee; yea, I will help thee; yea, I will uphold thee with the right hand of my righteousness." (Isaiah 41:10) After my friend had read this passage to me and I understood that this was a specific scripture from the Lord for my travel to Africa, I chose to push away all doubts about traveling in Uganda. I was grateful to my friend for sharing what she had heard from God's spirit that day. After spending two weeks in Uganda, I saw once again how God cared for me and provided his divine guidance and protection for my life. I learned from this experience that God was faithful to keep me safe from harm just like He had promised me. My God is a promise keeper. My time in Africa was profitable and rewarding for me. Maybe one day in the future I will travel again to Kampala to see my good friends there. My African businessman named Marcus has invited me to return and stay with him one more time in the future. I told him I would consider this idea if he'd build his family a better home to live in with added indoor plumbing. He smiled at me and said yes to my idea. I appreciated his reply of "Yes, I shall work on this next bigger house, my dear American Momma!"

***

Two of our children have received prophetic dreams a few times when they were teenagers. When we as a family began to pray accordingly about their dreams, we've seen God protect the person in those dreams from danger. Sometimes their specific dream came as a divine warning for a certain person in our own family. We have learned the importance of praying much during these situations. I've learned to pay close attention to dreams involving someone I know personally. For example, one time I received a dream about my second son where I saw him involved in a horrific accident while he was living in Indonesia. I asked my family members to pray for him as the months went by because I was so burdened by this awful vision. As it so happened our son was riding his motorcycle to a soccer field to play in an international soccer game when a speeding truck driver slammed into his motorbike. The sudden impact sent him flying for quite a distance until he finally landed on the pavement in a heap. Fortunately, he missed being run over by other vehicles and motorcycles since he'd landed on a safer section of the road. I believe angels were there with our son that day to protect him from serious life-threatening injuries to his spine and neck area because of all our continued prayers. I am very grateful for the warning dream God gave me when we needed to be praying for our teenage grandson, Benjamin. He was eventually diagnosed with a malfunctioning heart, and they had to operate by doing an open-heart surgery when he was only seventeen years old. Benjamin is strong and healthy today. He is enrolled in the University of Washington now and doing fantastic in his civil engineering courses. He was there for me recently when I was in the hospital and needed medical attention for my heart and blood pressure trouble. My grandson, Benjamin, had faith to believe for me to be healed and he prayed a wonderful prayer asking God to heal my heart problems and keep me from dying that weekend. Yes, I am thrilled that all our children and our grandchildren believe that God does answer people's prayers and they've certainly learned that he heals people and he does perform miracles.

I have learned one valuable thing in my lifetime and it's this: without God's guidance and blessing we may fail in achieving our plans. I have chosen to wait and listen for God's insight before going ahead with my endeavors. Seeking the Lord oftentimes involves asking for wisdom, for a confirmation, and for a sense of true peace before making certain big plans. "I am the vine, ye are the branches: He that abideth in me, and I in him, the same bringeth forth much fruit: for without me ye can do nothing." (John 15: 5) I have learned to ask God to help me accomplish an assignment as I commit my plans or writings to him.

The more time I spend waiting on God for his counsel, the more I can walk in victory and rejoicing. We need to obtain wisdom, favor, and a powerful anointing to achieve our goals in life. Moses and Joseph were certainly ordinary people like us. And yet, God was able to use them mightily despite their human frailties. If you want to do great deeds for the Lord, then you must stop listening to thoughts of doubt or unbelief at some point. The Word of God is the tool to use when we need to walk or speak in faith. God also changed people's names at times to influence them or change their way of thinking. For instance, He gave Abram a different name; it became Abraham, the father of many nations. Then he changed Jacob's name during a wrestling match to the awesome name of Israel. Next, he changed Simon's name to that of Peter and gave them all the actual meaning of their new names in order to affect a shifting over their self-esteem and feelings of worth.

As you may recall, God even changed Saul's name to that of Paul and he became known as Apostle Paul, a man who did mighty deeds in Christ's name. As you can see, after these men received a new impartation and changed names, they all responded in a more positive way of thinking about themselves. I believe we have a choice to accept our new identity from God so we too can achieve our destiny. I encourage you to ask the Father God to reveal to you exactly what His written scroll in heaven is concerning your life and your future destiny. The Father is waiting to show you what His marvelous plan is for you. He wants you to succeed and be the best person you can be with His help and divine insight. Remember you've been given all authority and power because Jesus sent his Holy Spirit to live within you. The Word of God (Book of Acts) promises this supernatural provision to all believers who ask for the gift of the Holy Spirit. Once you request this baptism of the Spirit, then you can allow Him to be released more and more in and through your life, especially as you allow your tongue to praise God in a heavenly language. (Which means speaking in a Holy Spirit way of a 'new unlearned tongue') Here is something I say often: Holy Spirit, I want to know you more!

There is a vital key to gaining victory over your problems or getting prayers answered and it involves asking God for specific strategies as to how to achieve your breakthrough or victory. An example of getting divine insight for a breakthrough is the time I was seeking the Lord for healing for my daughter. As you might recall, I'd sensed that I should fast for a week and believe that God would give us a victory for our daughter. As I fasted from food each day that week, I also praised the Almighty God and gave Him thanks for bringing our daughter a much-needed miracle. Our family also chose to believe the report of the Lord and not the negative report (diagnosis) of the doctors in this rather scary time. Thankfully, after the seventh day of fasting, we received a better report from the doctor on Sharon's chances of living. This was such a relief for our family amid a horrendous battle. Yes, I believe that nothing is impossible with God, and we all continued to trust that Sharon would live and have a full recovery that year and she did!

CHAPTER THIRTY-ONE

M y prayer is that people who read this book will come to understand how to walk in the promises of abundant life and wholeness. Like King Solomon in the Bible, we need to ask for the Lord's wisdom, his favor, and his divine anointing to be able to influence people with truth and with grace. To receive favor from God means we've learned to listen to His wise counsel. As you recall, Joseph found favor from God. I feel strongly in my heart that after many months of sitting in his dark, lonely prison cell while bemoaning his horrible existence, this young Hebrew man may've woken up one day and realized he needed to change his thinking. Just maybe it was possible that Joseph may have seen good results from a time when he obeyed God's prompting to be kind to another prisoner or maybe he received a blessing as he obeyed the Lord and shared about the one true God with a fellow prisoner. Eventually, we know that Joseph did finally walk out that prison cell a free man. The valuable lessons and insight learned while he was in prison may've helped him to be promoted to the position of a ruler in Egypt. You might be asking a question here. How does a person receive God's anointing for success? What does this term anointing refer to and why do we need it in today's busy, hectic society? The Bible has some answers about this kind of success.

We have all heard stories of men who had accumulated great riches here on earth and yet, have failed to be someone we'd admire or want our children to emulate. In the Book of Luke chapter sixteen, there is a story told by Jesus to the disciples about a rich man who had everything he desired in life. This poor man named Lazarus lay at the gate of this man's home seeking help. Lazarus died and was carried by angels to be close to Abraham. When the rich man died, he ended up in a certain place called Hades. In anguish and pain, this rich man looked across the great chasm and saw Lazarus who was given a drink of cool, refreshing water. The rich man begged for a drink and for help, he received neither because he had not shown any generosity to this poor, hurting Lazarus back on earth. (Luke 16: 19–31) Didn't the Lord say to his followers if you feed the needy, give water to the thirsty, and clothe the poor, then you have done the same kindness to him? Yes, this is exactly what he told his disciples about how the kingdom of heaven ought to look like here on earth.

Certainly, acts of generosity and kindness are vital parts of the good news which touches the hearts of people everywhere. Last month, as I sat in church enjoying the service a man stood up and shared his wonderful testimony with us. He was a business owner who did house repairs and installed house gutters. He told us recently he had chosen to help a widow lady by not charging her the one thousand dollars required to do the job. Then about a week later, he got a job for twice that amount. Now he plans to help other widows who may hear his story and want to call him to work on their place too. I was amazed to hear of his kindness and generosity towards the less fortunate in our community. I really believe that we can never out-give God ever. He will always bless our giving to others by depositing back into our lives either good health or extra unexpected money. There are many verses in the Bible that talk about helping the poor and how God desires to bless those who care for the needy folks. For me, the idea of being a generous person who helps those less fortunate is a step in the right direction to becoming a successful and influential individual. This scripture speaks clearly as to how God sees human endeavors and true success. "I will instruct thee in the way which thou shalt go, I will guide thee with mine eye." (Psalm 32: 8) My hope for our adult children is that they will walk in godly wisdom and with a liberal heart as they get involved in God's kingdom purposes.

Here is a short prayer for anyone desiring to have more of God's favor in their life.

Heavenly Father, please teach me your ways and show me how to walk in your 'living waters' (the Word of God) and may I experience your wonderful presence in a greater dimension. Teach me your valuable keys to bring about your kingdom principles in my life and in my family relationships. Father God caused me to hunger and thirst after your outstretched hands of love in a greater dimension. Bless me indeed and grant unto me divine blessings, favor, and the unlimited measure of your Spirit and joy in my life! Amen

I'd like to mention a few noteworthy women from the Bible as well. There is Deborah the female judge, Abigail, the woman of wisdom and courage, and Mary, the mother of our Lord. These women believed God's promises and they were all ordinary women who were faithful to God's calling and who chose to accept His plan for their lives. God used these women to become influential people and to fulfill his divine purpose on this earth.

I want to also mention another individual in the Bible who was known for her acts of generosity. Her name is Mary of Magdalene. As I read about her, I wondered if maybe she had a difficult life before her encounter with the Son of God. Did Mary of Magdalene suffer from feelings of rejection and shame at some point in her life? Whatever she may've experienced in her life, she still may've sought after this leader one day. When she did meet this Jewish man, she had a life-changing encounter with the one individual who could truly rescue her from a life of suffering and sadness.

As we can read in the New Testament it says that Mary of Magdalene was set free from seven demons. (Luke 8: 1-3) From the various accounts in the Bible, it seems she spent a great deal of time with those who believed in the Son of God. Could it be possible, I wondered, as I studied this Mary in the Bible, if she may've dreamed of being a part of a caring family before she met the disciples. I've wondered if she may've yearned in her heart one day to find love and acceptance in a world where if you weren't married it brought shame with it. I can also imagine that she may've given up on the idea of ever having her own family. And yet, it may be possible that after she'd spent some time with the early church believers like Susanna, Mary, and Joanna that she may've received the family connection she'd been looking for. It has been said that a dream fulfilled is a tree of life and maybe her lifelong dream was to be in a loving family unit and to feel accepted. Is it possible that the more time she spent with the mother of Jesus that she learned the importance of forgiving those people who may have hurt her in the past? One cannot achieve true healing over one's heartaches and pain unless they let go of anger and judgments against those who have grievously wounded them. I can identify with some of the life struggles which Mary of Magdalene might've dealt with.

Just like this historical Jewish woman named Mary, I too needed to be set free from disappointments and shame. God's loving-kindness and patience with me has produced good fruit in my life. I no longer feel like He is far away from me. I have a confidence that my Savior cares about every detail of my life. I truly believe He wants to embrace me with his arms of love and to empower me with the ability to live with joy and peace each day. Here's a prayer that I've said often throughout the years, and I am grateful for a restored heart.

Oh Lord God, I come to you and ask that you set me free from my past and its painful reminders. Please heal my wounded heart and help me to receive your even more of your love and your peace. I give you my hurts and disappointments to you in exchange for your gracious lovingkindness and wholeness. Restore my soul with your divine touch and love. I asked this in the mighty name of Jesus of Nazareth. Thank you, heavenly Father, for making me whole.

Ephrem the Syrian was a gifted theologian from the fourth century Ca. 306–373 who also wrote commentaries on most of the Bible. He spread the gospel by going into Syria to tell others about the Christ. Ephrem was a Syriac Christian deacon who referred to the book of

Luke when he wrote about this woman called Mary of Magdalene. He mentioned that she brought with her an alabaster flask of oil which she used to pour onto the son of God. I read in his description how he believed she poured this anointing oil in humility and reverence upon the man of God while he sat talking with some Hebrew men. Ephrem the Syrian scholar went on to write in his papers that this woman must have had a heart of gratitude towards the Lord and that she also had been released from demonic oppression. He mentioned in his writings that Mary of Magdalene went on to lead a fruitful devoted life to her Savior.

In my studies of Mary of Magdalene, I went to the specific scripture in John 11: 2 where it refers to a woman who poured expensive oil on Jesus and blessed him. People are still debating whether this was the woman from Magdalene region. I visited Israel and walked in the region and saw the city where she was believed to have lived. I tried to imagine her family situation before she met Jesus. I also learned later that she was one of the first women to go to the grave site/ tomb and talk with the risen Savior. I wonder if the disciples were afraid to go back to the tomb and be questioned because they feared the possibility of being arrested by the Roman soldiers. And yet, it was two women who were brave enough to go there with some burial spices in hand. Therefore, they were the first to discover the empty tomb and that Jesus was alive.

The gospel writers include an account of a woman known as a sinner and they mention that she entered the house carrying an alabaster flask of fragrant oils which she put on the master's head. (Luke 7: 37–39) The man of the house was dismayed that this woman would be allowed to minister to the Savior here. Watch what the Lord says to this Pharisee individual: "And he turned to the woman, and said unto Simon, Seest thou this woman? I entered into thine house, thou gavest me no water for my feet: but she hath washed my feet with tears and wiped them with the hairs of her head. Thou gavest me no kiss: but this woman since the time I came in hath not ceased to kiss my feet. My head with oil thou didst not anoint: but this woman hath anointed my feet with ointment…And he said to the woman, Thy faith hath saved thee; go in peace." (Luke 7: 44–46 & 50) This same account of a woman anointing the Lord is also found in the Book of Matthew. "There came unto him a woman having an alabaster box of ointment, and poured it on his head, as he sat at meat …" "For in that she hath poured this ointment on my body, she did it for my burial. Verily I say unto you, wheresoever this gospel shall be preached in the whole world, there shall also this, that this woman hath done, be told for a memorial of her." (Matthew 26: 6–7, & 12–13) I felt compelled to share this true account of a brave woman who sought to minister to Jesus, the Son of God. I believe it took courage for her to do what she felt was important to do for the Master.

I like to consider Mary of Magdalene as being a person with real feelings and hopes for her future, not just a character in a biblical story. I wonder if some people read about her and just think of her simply as an individual who was mainly involved in the most important case of resurrection recorded in history. I like to believe that she was ultimately and primarily a woman of worth and significance to God because He loved her and wanted to adopt her into His royal family. I wonder what Mary of Magdalene may've been thinking back in those days of ancient Israel when she poured expensive oil upon her beloved teacher. Did this Mary decide to show this act of generosity to the man called Jesus on her own initiative? Maybe, just maybe, this was what might've occurred that very morning before she set out to visit the men who were talking and eating with the Master. Consider the possibility that she may've started her day out by asking God what He would have her do. Maybe she then felt impressed to do something special to honor this gentle teacher who had shown her the more excellent ways of truth and eternal life. Maybe she thought to take some anointing oil with her that morning as she strolled the stone walkways in Jerusalem. Is it possible that she felt led to stop at one certain place where the Son of God was relaxing and chatting with other men? Did she have any qualms about entering this person's home on her own? Have you ever been concerned about what people might think if you did something unusual like Mary did during the ancient times in Israel?

I can't help but think that Mary of Magdalene was led by the Spirit to take that expensive oil and place it upon Jesus in a definitive way to honor Christ before His crucifixion and death. Like many believers, we all face the dilemma of hoping we've heard a directive from God versus the absolute knowing that we have. Maybe she thought this idea was of her own imagination to bring along anointing oil to bless her teacher (Rabboni). I suppose she began to question this idea for a while as she struggled with the idea of going to a house filled with only men. Think about the Jewish culture of her time.

Women were, as a rule, relegated to the task of being keepers of their homes and of bearing children primarily. She was even a new believer according to the gospel accounts and so she didn't have years of religious training to guide her thinking and actions.

Maybe her love for the Savior was stronger than her fears of rejection from the men of that town. Whatever the possible hindrances may have been for this woman named Mary as she dealt with the customs of her day, she was rewarded by Jesus who acknowledged her gift and thanked her for her kindness. Not only did she anoint this Jewish man before his crucifixion, but she also tried to bring spices to the burial tomb after his death. Is it possible that Mary of Magdalene may've sensed something good was going to happen to her that day? I wish I could've been privy to the conversation which occurred between her and her female companion as they walked together in the early morning mist towards the garden area. Despite the potential risk of being turned away by the soldiers, Mary of Magdalene went to the tomb of her beloved master and thus, she is known by many today as being the first person to talk with the living, risen Savior. Imagine the feeling of elation and joy she must've experienced that morning when she spoke with Jesus of Nazareth. Afterwards the two women left the garden area to return home and share the good news with all who would listen to their report. This is such a fascinating story.

For a female even in today's standards, it can be daunting to stand up against the norms of one's legal system. Could it be that this Jewish woman had heard people discussing the possible danger of being arrested by the soldiers guarding the tomb? If this was a problem for the disciples, then it would be more so for a woman to go to the tomb. I commend her for having the fortitude to accomplish her task back in the days of Pontius Pilate, the Roman emperor. In my estimation, this Jewish woman named Mary could be an example of what God can and will do for anyone who comes to Him and asks for divine guidance in their daily life. I admire this woman, Mary of Magdalene, for her dedication and loving care for her Savior's family after the crucifixion event. This powerful biblical account has inspired me to seek the Lord as to what He would have me do with my day just as Mary of Magdalene did thousands of years ago on those two glorious, eventful mornings in the ancient city of Jerusalem.

I heard of another marvelous, caring person who in today's world is determined to help others in need. This woman's name is Gloria. She lives in Nicaragua with her husband. Many years ago, they decided to provide a safe place for street kids to live. The home for girls is called Villa Esperanza. Gloria noticed that the poor children of the area were going to the city dump to find food and items to sell for money. This couple also discovered that the baser elements of their society were intent on taking young girls from this section of town and forcing them to become prostitutes for hire. They prayed to God to enable them to rescue as many girls out of this lifestyle as possible. My friend showed me the flyer that announced the arrival to our city of these young ladies who had been rescued from the human sex trafficking ring in Nicaragua. The flyer spoke of a fund-raising dinner where people could come to meet Gloria and her rescued girls who have found a haven in Gloria's villa. The flyer mentioned that they would be sharing their stories with those who attended the gathering. Gloria has established a website where people in America can also view some photos of the group home and the girls there in Nicaragua. You can also read on this website how to donate to meet their basic needs by becoming sponsors for the girls. I so appreciate Gloria's heart to care for the street kids. In the Book of James, it tells us that true religion begins when believers care for the widows as well as the fatherless children of this world. I have seen God's heart being extended to reach the lost, bruised, and abandoned children of Nicaragua through this woman's' sacrifices of love and generosity. You can go to the website of http://www.forwardedge.org to find out more information about this project of hope that helps girls in Central America.

I met a dear woman named Adeline from Brazil when we both stayed in the same hotel room in Bethlehem, Israel this past September. She had been to Israel with the IHOP conference the year before and this time she was serving the team as a Portuguese interpreter during the week of our meetings. She was a valuable help to me as a newcomer and we became good friends during those fourteen days. After we'd spent ten days together in the same hotel and at the meetings, she showed me a video of a fabulous woman whose life mission was to be an instrument of God's grace and love to all people. This woman's name is Ruth, and she lives in her homeland of Brazil where she shares the good news truths to prison inmates who are sent to large prison facilities located in the same region near her hometown.

I watched a video of this Brazilian evangelist in action that showed some of the men getting immersed in a river or what the Bible calls water baptism with the help of this woman and her pastor friend. Two of the men who were interviewed that day were very happy men. The first man's name was Edson, and the second individual was called Marcos. As I watched their heartfelt story unfold, I saw the group of prisoners rejoicing and holding hands together in a circle around this woman of faith. Their joy seemed genuine on their faces as I watched the video show the men coming up out of the water praising God. It looked as if these men were set free despite their apparent captivity inside of the formidable tall prison walls.

On the top section of these high cement walls, I also saw prison guards with rifles walking about as they kept an eye on the men below in the courtyard. As I watched this video unfold, the scene looked more like a revival meeting than a group of confined, sad-looking men standing around in sadness and despair. My friend, Adeline and I both gave praises to our Lord for the victories in these men's lives. The Lord knew what He was doing when He called a woman named Ruth T—to go inside the prison walls in Brazil to bring men the gospel of good news and salvation truth. God is on the move in many nations. God is looking for people who are willing to be used in the same way this Brazilian woman is being used in her country. It is my delight to obey the commission to go into the world and share the good news that Jesus is alive and has the power to set captives free. I am even now willing to go to Kampala, Uganda in Africa whenever the Lord opens the right doors of opportunity for me. I want to share my testimony to people who will listen to me. God rescued me from a dark, miserable world of hate and anger which I had held against those who'd wounded my soul. With His loving kindness He set me free to rejoice, to live a more abundant life, and to pray for others to be set free as well. Now I have a passion to bless other hurting women wherever God sends me.

CHAPTER THIRTY-TWO

Have you ever been given a word of knowledge from a leader in your church? Well, I have experienced this unique event. Have you ever been prompted by the Holy Spirit of God to accomplish something beyond your capabilities? I have. One time many years ago, I was attending a relative's church one Sunday when to my surprise, an old college friend named Rick had been invited to come back to America to preach at this same church on this very weekend. He, his wife, and their three children had move to England to start a church some years before this and our pastor friend had invited Rick to come share while he was in the area visiting his wife's family. After his excellent message on faith and healing, Pastor Rick invited people to come forward to get prayer and so I decided to ask for prayer that day.

An Australian woman attending this church service, who didn't know me, prayed for me that afternoon. She heard a word of knowledge for me and then she proceeded to share it. She mentioned that I would be led by the Lord to go to a country that started with the capital letter I. Immediately, my mind went to the one country that I'd longed to visit which did indeed start with the letter I. Since I loved to draw and paint, of course,

I wanted to see all the ancient cities and the marvelous artwork of the famous artists such as Michelangelo, Leonardo DaVinci, and Raphael which were in Italy. And of course, this country started with the letter I and so I was excited about this information. However, it seemed that God had a sense of humor because it wasn't Italy at all. She responded to my comment about the country of Italy with these words, "No young lady, I didn't hear the word Italy. I heard instead the country God wants you to travel to is Israel." I looked at her in amazement as I questioned her insight for me. Why would God want to send me to this country? I was just an ordinary woman with a hunger to please God. I wasn't sure what I could possibly contribute if I went to Israel since I really had no interest in traveling overseas or being a missionary long term in this country or even going on a tour of the Holy Lands for that matter. What was God thinking in sending me to this war-torn country? I was perplexed about this new idea and so I simply waited as I pondered this unique word in my heart. A few years had passed, and I couldn't seem to forget the commission to go across the ocean to this historical land of the ancient patriarchs.

Why would God want me to go to a place that was steeped in conflict and had a history of terrorist attacks? Seriously, in my heart I'd been asking this question for several days after hearing this personal word. It didn't make any sense to me. Nonetheless, I pondered this word in my heart and continued to pray for the people of Israel for the next four years. During this time, I thought maybe I could write a book about the Jewish people and the struggles they faced as a small country surrounded by people and political leaders who hated them. Eventually,

I came to understand that God truly wanted me to get on a plane, spend my small savings of three thousand dollars, and go to Israel.

Finally, I decided to obey God no matter the cost. By purchasing a plane ticket, I was facing my fears of possibly dying in a foreign country. During the previous months of praying about this trip overseas, my friend informed me that I'd learn to depend on God more than ever before as I journeyed throughout the region of Israel. Could I trust him with all my heart in a newer, deeper level of faith and surrender? I certainly was hoping that I could, so I asked God to help me with this challenge. My usual method of knowing that I've heard clearly in important matters is to listen for a 'Yes' in my spirit after praying about things. In this decision-making experience, I finally heard a 'Yes, yes, yes' at the last moment and so on August 15th, I had my absolute confirmation before purchasing the costly travel packet. I now had a complete confidence about my trip, and no one could dissuade me thereafter.

The day I flew from PDX to Istanbul, Turkey and then finally into the airport in Tel Aviv was the day I'd truly placed my well-being and life in God's hands. I had a newfound belief that I would accomplish His divine destiny for my life in September of 2017. I was now determined to obey the word of the Lord spoken to me some years earlier. During my two weeks in Israel, I met many wonderful people. During this fascinating journey and my touring of parts of Israel, I became aware of my heart of love for the city of Jerusalem and for the people of this land. The friends I met in Israel and the events I took part in during the ten-day prayer conference were beyond my wildest imaginations and expectations. This marvelous experience proved that God knew what's best for me. I learned that I could trust him explicitly, and I will not question His plans for my life again.

Yes, I survived my time in Israel where there is the potential for grave conflict and extreme hatred by the Hamas terrorists towards the Jewish and American people. Just recently, the news media broadcasted the fact that our American president, Donald Trump has announced the plans to move our country's embassy from Tel Aviv to the city of Jerusalem. This decision has shown the world that Jerusalem is meant to be the proper capital city for all of Israel and I heartily agree with this new location for the capital. It was sad to hear on Fox News station that our American president's proclamation has produced much anger and bitter resentment on the part of the Militants and Palestinian people of this region. I wonder what new battles may face the leaders of the Jewish nation after this strong decision is enacted by a few more national leaders around the world. I must believe that other leaders will soon follow America's lead and move their embassy to Jerusalem too. Let's all continue to pray for the peace of Jerusalem during these turbulent times.

***

I have a wonderful testimony to share with you about a man I met during my travels in Israel. This person was born in Africa, and he told me about his true experiences and gave me permission to share his life story. I have included his testimony in my book along with other people's wonderful, life changing encounters with God. He is a pastor now and this is his true story. Before the

80's, he didn't know about God or what his true purpose in life was. He was working in the fields by harvesting the peanut crops when he heard a voice saying these words to him, *Will you serve me?* He responded to what he believes was the call of God upon his life in 1984, by saying YES to this request to serve God.

In 1981, he decides to enroll in a Bible Institute. After class one day in 1984, he heard these clear and distinct words come to him; *Will you go into your room and pray?* Again, he listened and followed this instruction from God by going into his room. When he prayed and opened his Bible to find 1 Chronicles chapter 28 and then he read about King David who was telling everyone about his son to make sure he did this thing, "And thou, Solomon my son, know thou the God of thy Father, and serve Him with a perfect heart and with a willing mind: for the Lord searcheth all hearts, and understandeth all the imaginations of the thoughts: If thou seek him, he will be found of thee; but if thou forsake him, He will cast thee off forever." (1 Chronicles 28: 9) As I listened to this man talking and then later, when I read this very same passage in the Bible, I began to see what God was asking of this young man back then.

My new friend from the prayer conference responded to this unique invitation from God by replying, "Lord I want to know you." He suddenly heard a few strange words come forth out of his mouth. He wondered in his heart about this unusual experience. He wondered if speaking out loud in this strange new language was scriptural. Then he made a conscious decision to surrender at that next moment and to allow the Holy Spirit of God to take over even his new unlearned words and utterances. He discovered that he was now speaking in a new unlearned tongue' and praising God just like the early disciples did in the upper room on the well-known day of Pentecost. This encounter with God's spirit or what the Book of Acts calls 'the helper' and the joy it produced within him were beneficial to his own individual worship and prayer times from that time on. He told me that he now plays his guitar and sings to the Lord in French and Bambela language.

Then one day when this African man met with his five friends for their early Morning Prayer time, he decided to be bold and share this new experience with them. It was in the year, 1984, and after he was done sharing about the Pentecostal moving of the Holy Spirit with his friends, they all received the gift of the Holy Spirit and speaking in tongues (which some call an unlearned language from God) like the Bible refers to in the Book of Acts. In 1986, he moved to the capital city of Mali to pastor a church and serve God with such new authority and anointing. I really enjoyed hearing about his divine encounter with God. The Holy Spirit revival that has occurred during this time within his soul has given him more stability and boldness to witness for the Lord. There has been a greater dimension of refreshing and inspired prayer times for this African man which has helped him and which he attributes to his becoming a stronger Christian leader since his new experience. He has had an ideal encounter with the living God of Abraham, Isaac, and Jacob that supersedes any other experience that this world can offer a man searching for truth. He gained a better understanding of the reality of a loving Father in heaven who only wants the best for his adopted sons and daughters. I was thrilled to have the opportunity to hear about his true-life experiences and to call him my new friend. I was quite thankful that he gave me his permission to include his wonderful testimony in my book.

CHAPTER THIRTY-THREE

It is God's plan for us to do what Jesus did while he walked on this earth. "Herein is our love made perfect, that we may have boldness in the day of judgment: because as he is, so are we in this world." (1 John 4:17) In the Book of Mark, it tells us that the disciples were commissioned to go into all the world healing the sick, casting out demonic spirits, and making disciples of men. "…And he said unto them, Go ye into all the world, and preach the gospel to every creature. He that believeth and is baptized shall be saved;… In my name shall they cast out devils; they will speak with new tongues; … they shall lay hands on the sick, and they shall recover." (Mark 16:15–18) In other words, believers, you and I, can declare freedom to those bound in depression and darkness. We can pronounce divine healing to the sick as we ask God how He wants to heal people in their physical body as well as in their heart where the emotions operate from. Human beings were made to have three unique parts, and these are called the body, the mind, and the soul area. God can heal a person's mind as well as their emotions even if they may've been traumatized during childhood incident or during a wartime experience. I have a hope that God will intervene and deliver people from the horrible effects of insomnia or night terrors which are a result of having endured a post-war trauma/stressful situation. I believe we can speak life and the Word of God into these kinds of dire situation. We can ask our heavenly Father who created the human body and the mind to come and heal and restore those who have suffered from trauma or physical abuse situations. I have invited the Lord to come and heal me of childhood pain, anguish, and trauma and he rescued me, healed me, and restored my wounded soul and removed my shame. Since I've been set free from abuse and received inner healing for my own traumatic experiences, I want to see others healed too.

When the Son of God healed the man who was blind, this act astounded everyone who was with him. This is what folks might call a life-changing miracle. I know that God can do anything and everything whether it is to cause the deaf man to hear for the first time or a blind person to receive his sight. I think it pleases God when we expect a miracle for our sick body, our damaged emotions, or wounded soul. It is valuable to declare God's healing scriptures over our lives and for those who are hurting. It is important to believe that we as believers can release the healing power of the Holy Spirit which carries the 'dunamis' or the impacting power of God too. I saw this principle of speaking forth the scriptures happen for my daughter who has been healed from cancer twice in her life. This kind of restorative healing also occurred for my daughter, Catherine Denise, who was told by a doctor and a chiropractor that because of her disability in her spine and the problems with her thyroid she wouldn't be able to get pregnant. I spoke out the healing promises from the Bible and declare her physical body to be made whole and strong again and that she'd also be able to carry a baby in her womb. She is now pregnant, and the baby is due to be born on May 15, 2019. The reason why I had a strong faith for my two daughters is because I prayed about their physical needs continually. God gave me a specific scripture of healing for our daughter, and I chose to declare it and prophesy that she would indeed live and accomplish God's purposes on this earth. I'd received a rhema' or a word of knowledge for my other daughter that she'd become pregnant with a child many years before she even received this negative medical report from the doctor. Therefore, I was able to choose to believe this previous word of knowledge and to declare by faith for this promise to actually happen for Catherine Denise and it came to pass. Hallelujah!

Healing is God's plan for people and this promise can be found in the New Testament, "Who his own self bare our sins in his own body on the tree,…by whose stripes you were healed." (1 Peter 2:24) There is another verse that describes our healing provision within the scriptures, "How God anointed Jesus of Nazareth with the Holy Ghost and with power: who went about doing good, and healing all that were oppressed of the devil; for God was with him." (Acts 10: 38) As believers or disciples we have been given authority and power over sickness, diseases, and the demonic and we can command pain and sickness to leave our physical body.

I recall a piece of advice from someone who said that if I wanted to receive a miracle in my life, I would be wise to not hold onto offenses or wrongs done to me. Resentment and anger towards others only produce ill

health and negativity for our own lives. Medical researchers and doctors have discovered that long term anger and
bitterness may cause inflammation and diseases in a person's body if not dealt with properly. It would be good to
heed the Biblical truth about how to maintain a healthy
attitude which can promote health for the entire person.

*****

I must share a marvelous miracle story of divine intervention which took place in my life this last September.
I had travelled with my one daughter, Sharon, to spend
two nights with my other daughter, Kristina, and her
three young children. In the morning she asked me to
carry a very heavy bucket of water down to the chicken
coop to help her while she was nursing baby Isaiah. Then
later in the afternoon, once I'd returned from spending
a few hours with the grandkids at a children's museum,
I was back at Kristina's house. I'd decided it was time
to drive back home and so I set about carrying out all
our gear, bedding, and bags out to the car. I came back
inside of my daughter's house to grab some more items
when suddenly; my daughters said that I'd collapsed to
the hardwood floor and was unconscious and nonre-
sponsive. My daughter tried to get me to respond and
when I didn't immediately wake up or talk, the girls were
alarmed by my unusual reactions. Kris' wanted her sister
who is a nurse to take me to the hospital ER in her town,
but I wanted to head back home and get some rest and
wait to see if I could recuperate from all the activities
of this weekend. Finally, we ended up agreeing that Kris
would call her husband, Paul, to get his advice. Paul's
response was to ask his father, Mike, to stop hunting

for elk, come back to their place, and then drive us to a nearby hospital.

While Mike was driving us back to the city, I had another episode where I was non-responsive and so my nurse daughter decided they should take me into the ER in Portland. I threw up one time while he was driving on the Interstate 84 and so I told my daughter that I was ready to see a doctor by this time. I am grateful that my daughter, Sharon, had the nursing expertise and ability to access my health issues and get me into the ER to be examined two different times that same weekend. During my first trip to the hospital, the doctor released me from the hospital the following day with a rather heavy, awkward heart monitor strapped around my waist to record any further problems. They were concerned about my very high blood pressure and the low heart rate. I was told we needed to purchase some blood pressure meds in case my blood pressure escalated again. However, my husband didn't make it to the clinic before it closed that afternoon and so I only had one BP pill to use that night when I felt nauseated again.

Sharon called her siblings and gave them updates after she'd returned home from her time with me. When my daughter, Catherine, and her husband, Charlie, heard about my emergency visit to the hospital, they decided to not cross the Canadian border in order to go attend his friend's wedding. Instead, they turned around and drove the five hours back home to be with me. That evening I had another episode where my heart rate slowed down or paused and I must've fainted in the downstairs bathroom. Apparently, this time when I fell, I hit my nose on an immovable object such as the bathtub. I had no recollection of fainting or having a noise bleed which had occurred in the middle of the night. The next morning, my daughter, Catherine, woke up and she noticed blood on the bathroom floor which alarmed her. She called her sister to bring the professional BP monitor over to check my vitals. I passed out briefly again and was non-responsive for the fourth time that weekend and so my two daughters took me into a second hospital.

While she was waiting with me, my daughter, Sharon, insisted that the technician check my head by doing an EKG. Since she has medical training and is a nurse they decided to listen to her advice. During this EKG test, I had another short episode of being non-responsive. Then they moved me to a room where I waited with my son, Robert, and my grandson, Benjamin. Eventually, they informed my family members that the medical staff was sending me in an EMT vehicle to a different hospital in Oregon. Before leaving this second hospital, I had a short vision. In this vision, I saw someone take the defibrillator pads and they were attempting to shock my heart muscle back to a functioning capacity. I couldn't seem to shake this image away from my mind. It was as if I needed to pay attention to this unusual, but startling vision or I might regret it.

I wondered if I might die that weekend and so I decided to say goodbye to the family members who were with me in the room. I did this in a round-about way by speaking words of blessings and affirmation first to my eldest son, Robert, and then to his teenage son, Benjamin, who were both in the room with me right then. Next thing I did when my husband entered my hospital room was to thank him for leaving work and then we hugged. Then I proceeded to thank him for being a wonderful, caring husband which brought tears to his eyes. I gave him another quick hug and then the paramedics placed me inside of their EMT vehicle. I was still pondering the brief, but compelling vision and what it might mean for me while being transported to the next facility. I began to think that I should listen to the doctor's advice and change my DNR paperwork to instead state a new request that I wanted to give the medical personnel permission to go ahead and resuscitate me if my heart should ever stop beating. When the doctor came to talk with me that morning, I told her of my new wishes. The doctor then mentioned that I should let my two daughters know about my change of plans and so I did right then. I also told this same doctor that I agreed with whatever she decided might be necessary for my health situation.

While I was at this last hospital, the doctors ordered a CAT scan of my head. My blood pressure was very high during those two days and at times my heart rate was very low. The doctor's prognosis this time around was for me to have a pacemaker inserted into my chest and connect it into my heart muscle to keep it operating successfully. This device would have two lines which extended downward until they reached my heart muscle and they'd be attached with screws into my heart's muscle tissue. This pacemaker's job was to jumpstart my heart as needed. When the heart muscle is unable to sustain the blood flow and oxygen level needed for a person's main organ to function properly then a pacemaker device will automatically send a message to the heart muscle which then will activate the heart muscle to function properly. It's a small, intricate device with a battery; now each time the nurse checks my heart she states that my heart has rarely used this battery and it might last for eons. I laughed at her remark and then I told her maybe I'm a walking miracle since the pacemaker's battery barely ever has to operate to activate my heart muscle.

I am grateful that two of my daughters were around me that entire weekend to help keep me safe during a very critical time. In fact, my daughter, Catherine Denise and her husband, Charlie had decided to forgo their plans to attend a friend's Canadian wedding in order to come back and stay with me when I needed them. Fortunately for me, she'd been staying in my home and discovered the overturned metal object and the two blood spots on the floor of the bathroom that morning after I collapsed during the night. I am thankful that she'd decided to call her sister to come over to check on me again. She also insisted that I stop working on my manuscript that morning and allow them to take me into the second hospital for further examination. If my youngest daughter hadn't been home that Saturday, this problem wouldn't have even been noticed by me and something worst might've happen that week.

It has been another year since the time when the doctor surgically implanted in my chest the device necessary to protect my heart. This November, I had to go back in for a heart checkup with the pacemaker clinic. The nurse who ran the tests and read the machine results was amazed that I hadn't used my device this entire time. This was the second time one of their medical staff had made this comment to me. The first time was nearly ten months ago at my initial visit to this clinic. This time

I mentioned to the nurse that I believed that God had healed my heart after two men had prayed for my heart to function properly and that I wouldn't even need to use the device. Along with these people's faith, my son, Jonathan, had made a video of our four-year-old grandson, Axel, praying for my surgery to be successful and for my heart to not stop working. His exact words were "God help grandma's machine thing to work and her heart to not stop again!" I'm confident that the Lord answered Axel's prayer and has honored his child-like faith request on my behalf.

***

Even when I had my own children, I still had a desire to adopt an orphan or take in a foster child who needed a safe place to stay. I feel that every child needs to feel wanted and to be a part of a family. However, for me it seemed as if this dream to adopt was nearly impossible to achieve. As a girl growing in my hometown in Washington State, I also had a sense of wanting to be a writer and so I wrote a short essay story about my own youthful experiences and sent it into a magazine to be considered. The editor of the magazine sent a reply and invited me to apply to their writing center which cost money. Of course, I couldn't join their writing school, but I still had a strong desire to write on my own. Then as a young adult woman I started having my own children and I became very busy dealing with loads of laundry and hectic after school sports schedules. I really had no free time to sit down and write a novel and so I turned my attention elsewhere. As I began to write books, I still remembered my desire to help needy children in this world. So now I've combined my heart to bless an orphan child along with my desire to write about them within this book.

When what I wanted seemed like a far-off dream because there were no longer any orphanages in America, I chose to think about becoming qualified to be a foster parent. However, we lived in an old country house on two acres that had its own pump house and well water. Our drinking water was contaminated and not considered to be clean enough to qualify as a foster parent's home. After watching a TV advertisement about adopting a child, I seriously considered calling the TV station to apply to adopt a child of four or five years of age. I never received a call back. It seemed like I'd reached a dead end in achieving my goal to adopt and so I turned my thoughts to the new idea of sponsoring a child in a third world country. I encouraged my husband to send money to a child in a foreign country and for a season this was somewhat satisfying effort for me.

To be honest, I still had a strong desire to adopt a child and bring this young person into our family setting. I was certain I had more than enough love to give to another child. Then my youngest child, Catherine Denise, began asking me to adopt one of those youngsters who we'd seen on a television program. I made a phone call to the number posted on the TV and waited for a reply. This attempt was unsuccessful for some strange reason. I suppose the fact that we lived in a different state maybe presented a problem. Since my husband was not thrilled about my idea to adopt a child, I finally let go of my dream to adopt a young child.

Eventually, I heard of a program created by a co-host, Terry Meeuwsen, who was affiliated with the 700 Club. She had adopted three sisters from Romania, and she gladly shared about the joy she'd experienced with being a mother to these sweet girls. After this huge step of faith, she helped start the Orphans Promise program which is connected to CBN and so I started sending money to support Orphans Promise. This endeavor helped me to feel like I was going in the right direction and fulfilling my dream of being a person who could bless one fatherless child in a positive way.

In this same way of adopting people into one's heart, I've been friends with a couple for nearly seven years now and I include them in my prayers just as if they were part of my own family. I asked this good friend if I could become like an auntie to her children; she said yes, of course. A few years later, they had to move to live in another state, and so I had to book a plane ticket to fly there if I want to spend a week with them and reconnect with the kids on a yearly basis. I loved spending quality time with this friend and her eight children each time I had the opportunity to visit with them. Maybe God has a unique plan for you too in which you might consider adopting a family into your heart. It's funny how I had once focused on adopting just one child and now I've had the joy of adopting so many more into my heart. My friend and her children are in my heart and my prayers continually. As life has proven to me, God had such a different plan concerning adopting a child. There are now three families who have captured my heart and are a part of my 'adopted family/friend relationships. I believe it is God's marvelous plan to adopt people into his royal, everlasting family. Therefore, it just might be a good thing for believers to consider the idea of following in the Lord's footsteps by adopting someone or some family into their heart as well. People can always use more of our prayers and support. I think the world would be a better place if people paid it forward by showing more kindness and love for those who need extra help or a helping hand.

Another family that I recently felt a strong connection and friendship to is a friend named Rick, his adorable wife, Michelle, and their three well-behaved sons. I met Rick at our church one Sunday morning when I'd decided to move and go take a seat next to him. Then I felt impressed to lean over and ask him if I could pray for him. He said yes to my request. As I spoke life and blessings over him, I felt a special connection with this individual which I can only describe as a deposit of the Father's love within my heart. A few weeks later, I mentioned that I was wondering if he minded if I adopted him and his family since the Lord had laid this on my heart. He said yes to my idea that day. This gracious, caring couple has been so kind and loving to me that it has been very easy to take the time to intercede for them. They have done a fantastic job of caring for their boys and I am very proud of them all.

I believe in adoption. I have been grateful to be able to adopt entire families into my heart. I also have seen in the Bible where God desires to adopt people as a part of His family too. Look at this verse in the first chapter of the book of Ephesians where it states the heartbeat of God for people, "According as he hath chosen us in him before the foundation of the world, that we should be holy and without blame before him in love: Having predestined us unto the adoption of children by Jesus Christ to himself, according to the good pleasure of his will, To the praise of the glory of his grace, wherein he hath made us accepted in the beloved." (Ephesians 1: 4–6) I love that our heavenly Father is the instigator of the idea of adoption. I believe that God is pleased when we reach out to include a family into our hearts who might need our prayers and encouragement.

CHAPTER THIRTY-FOUR

Recently, as I have already mentioned, I had made an important trip to the land of Israel. For several years, I had been aware that this was something God desired for me to do and yet, I wasn't sure just why he wanted me to fly thousands of miles to visit a different culture and to an ancient city in Jerusalem. As the years passed by, I was still working full time as a teacher's assistant helping young children in the public schools become better readers. However, at one point, I began to realize that I was not obeying His commission to go into the world with the good news. I quit working for the school district and began praying with my friend, Debi, for an open door and provision to make this trip. There were two options for me to be able to stay in Israel. The first one was to do volunteer work in a community for free room and board. However, I had to agree to stay for three months with this organization. The second option was to sign up to teach Muslim children at this school in the West Bank region for one year. Neither of these options seemed right for me. After much prayer and waiting on God, I finally chose to spend fourteen days in Israel by attending a conference with the International House of Prayer organization (IHOP). This year's Jubilee/Prayer

Conference which was started ten years ago by Tom Hess was scheduled to take place in Jerusalem in Sept of 2017.

I had been informed over the phone by IHOP's support leader, Joshua, that this conference included a three-day tour at the end of the ten days of prayer for the nations. I was looking forward to this new experience. Two thousand people from many countries had come to this conference in Jerusalem this year. This number of people in one gathering place seemed staggering amount to me. I loved the fact that every person involved would be praying for peace and success for the Jewish people in this war-torn land. We were informed at the end of the ten days in Jerusalem that our bus group would be staying in two different hotels during our travels, and I wasn't quite sure of what to expect for these three days as a first-time tourist. I felt a little overwhelmed a couple of times during this entire experience of meeting new people and traveling on a crowded tour bus each day to and from the conference site.

Even though at first, I was apprehensive about being safe in this foreign country, I found that the tour guide and bus driver both knew what they were doing since they' been doing this job for many years. We were safe as we travelled throughout this country because the bus had bullet proof glass windows and the guide knew how to counsel us at each military checkpoint as to what not to divulge. At one point, the tour guide pointed out the stone wall and the barbed wire that specified the division between Lebanon and Israel. We could see the military soldiers holding assault rifles at certain checkpoints, but we had no trouble as the driver complied with the soldiers and therefore, we were allowed to go through the barrier gate. Our tour guide informed us that the government of Lebanon was not an ally to the Israeli people and their military installations could at any time or provocation launch missiles across the Sea of Galilee into Northern Israel. This was an alarming thought for most of us on the tour bus. As a group we all extended our hands toward this country and prayed a blessing and peace upon them.

We made a stop to eat lunch in the town called Jezreel and I didn't feel like eating because the temperature outside was scorching hot at noon time. I filled up my water bottle and drank the cool liquid and waited inside with my group. Our next stop was on Mt. Tabor where we could get out of the bus and go to the tourist point to have a grand view of the surrounding land below. I couldn't imagine how people in this land some thousands of years ago had managed to travel on foot to reach the next destination when it took the bus driver nearly two hours to reach the next hotel. Our tour bus stopped in the late afternoon in the town of Nazareth where Jesus grew up as a boy. I wanted to stay longer to talk with a few of the people living in this locale, but the tour bus was on a strict schedule and so we had to keep travelling. The following day we learned that our journey would take us further north into Samaria. We had to get up by six in the morning to eat the breakfast meal and be ready to climb on the bus again.

The tour bus made one short stop on this second morning of our tour. The bus driver took us to a small village where folks could leave the bus for fifteen minutes and buy sweet dates at a reasonable price. I stayed in the bus and watched people pay nine shekels to get a ride on a tall camel while some tourists took pictures of this unique sight. As I sat inside the tour bus, I chatted with a new friend. She mentioned to me that she was very thankful that this bus had bullet proof windows as an added protection for the tourist's safety and of course, I heartily agreed with her. Once our group of travelers returned to the bus, then we could continue our journey. After two hours of being on the bus, our driver took us up a very winding dirt road until we were at the very top of an elevation where we could overlook the valley below.

We could see from this vantage point that this region was well-irrigated and much greener than the region surrounding Jerusalem. Our tour guide told us this area was so lush and green because of its proximity to the Sea of Galilee. During my two weeks of travelling throughout this ancient country, I felt my heart growing larger with a new understanding of the Israeli people. I now have a better understanding and appreciation of the history of God's chosen people and of their continual troubles with the surrounding countries who want to conquer them. I shall continue to pray for the nation of Israel to gain full recognition as a sovereign country. I shall hope for lasting peace to come to this region and that Hamas-led terrorist will not be able to randomly kill Israeli women and children with their suicide-bombings or the missile attacks. No country should have to endure the threat of an enemy attack year after year by a neighboring, hostile country.

When I'd first arrived in Jerusalem and was surrounded by South Koreans, Chinese, and African men and women speaking in their native dialect, I felt out of place and alone. Then a sweet Korean woman named

Sarah who was sitting nearby began talking with me. She was so friendly and gracious. I really appreciated how this woman took time to show me a little sympathy and friendship that late evening after my long flight. I shared with her my tale of woe about my missing suitcase full of my clothing and medicines that hadn't arrived with me. She was very sympathetic with my plight and made me feel welcome even though she was probably tired from her long flight as well. She was a wonderful blessing to me during the first few days of my time in Jerusalem. We continued to seek each other out in the crowd of two thousand individuals who were there for the conference in Israel. I enjoyed praying for her and her family that week too. In an act of gratitude, she generously bestowed upon me her small gift of Asian coffee packets which helped me immensely during my adjustment period in Israel.

I found that some of the Arabic food to be strange and not palatable to my taste buds. For the next six days at the hotel in Bethlehem, I existed on red beets, salads, and small potatoes. I started to really miss our American food and my favorite fish called Pacific Ocean Salmon. Occasionally, they served French fries for breakfast and because there was no supply of ketchup or any decent gravy, I decided to dip these long fries in the pile of hummus lying on my plate. This was a perfect solution for me. Another thing that annoyed me was the fact that the hotel only offered their patrons hot water, instant coffee grounds, and powdered creamer for the breakfast meal. I really began to miss my coffee maker back home and so I was thrilled when my friend, Sarah's gave me a gift of her special coffee packets to enjoy each morning.

The only other means to get decent coffee was to order a small cup of hot coffee with milk for seven shekels from the café located in the conference hotel lobby. After buying their coffee drink three times during that week, I couldn't bring myself to spend four American dollars for a small cup of hot coffee. I finally discovered where the other people were getting purified water for free in the hotel lounge area. I managed to keep a large plastic water bottle that I had paid for earlier in the week and thus, I was able to refill this container each morning in the dining room area of my hotel. This idea saved me plenty of money that week.

After being in the worship meetings each morning I realized finally why I had been led to come to Israel. While I was still in America making plans to travel overseas, I'd decided to ask the Lord to give me a divine appointment with the right people in Israel. Each day that I went to the prayer conference in Jerusalem, I found myself praying for people I didn't even know. Then amazingly, God would give me a word of knowledge for a person sitting by me. Sometimes, they would ask their interpreter to step in and translate what God was showing me to speak to them because they only spoke French or Japanese. This was certainly a new experience for me that week of meeting new people in this conference.

The more I stepped out in faith to pray for someone in the hallways of the hotel or in their dining room area, the more God met with these folks and blessed them. I'd ended up meeting pastors and praying God's rich blessings for them while I was in Israel those fourteen days. Some of the pastors and tourists whom I met in Israel were from India, China, South Korea, and Africa.

One morning in the hallway of our Bethlehem Hotel, I met a friendly man named Paul Barthlomew (not his real name). During our conversation at lunch time, I learned he was a pastor from Kampala, Uganda and as we met in the lunchroom each day of that week of conference meetings, we became friends. Pastor Paul and his friend, Marcus, (not his real name) invited me to come visit their country someday in the future and so I told them I would pray about this idea. At that time, I didn't know if I would be called to travel to Uganda, Africa, but I certainly appreciated their invitations and friendship. Before leaving for America, we exchanged email addresses and stayed in contact with each other thereafter. What if I'd been too nervous or fearful to travel by myself to a strange, new country called Israel? If I had stayed home in America, played it safe, and saved my money, I believe that I would've missed what God had intended for me to experience during those fourteen days in Israel.

I learned during the first part of the week of prayer conference exactly why He had sent me to Israel. It was to meet God's people and thus, learn to have a heart for other countries and for people of a different culture. During these two weeks in Israel, oftentimes, I'd meet and make new friends at the prayer conference. I told them they could call me 'Momma Cathy' and during my trip, I came to realize that my time in Israel was to possibly be a launching point for the next country God might ask me to visit. I found myself wanting to adopt even more people and families into my heart as I enjoyed these new friendships. For instance, I met a Doctor of Psychology who cares for many orphans in his hometown in India. His name is Dr. Praveen. I love getting emails from him and praying for his life and the orphans in his church group. He has invited me to come and stay with him in India. Who knows maybe one day I will do just that.

During my week in Jerusalem, I also met and fell in love with a family from Trinidad and their two darling children, along with their Japanese friend and her young son. I met many other people during the worship services, and I loved the opportunity to pray for them. Towards the end of this conference, a woman who I didn't know approached me and asked if I would pray that she'd know God's will for her life. I said yes, of course. I guess she must have heard from some people at the conference that I was praying for everyone around me for the last few days. Since I tend to be prophetic in my praying for others, I might get a word of knowledge for the person and when I share it with them, they are grateful and want to give me a hug. God is so amazing! I started to enjoy these divine encounters with people from different countries who had come to worship and seek God's presence at this International House of Prayer conference.

I couldn't stop thanking and praising the Lord for sending me to the land of Israel. Who knows, maybe God will send me through an open door to Africa one day soon before my passport expires. I've opened my heart to include many other families as God is leading me into new, wonderful friendships with people all around the world. I have plenty of people to love and pray since making this journey to the Holy Lands. I shall believe for them all to become successful people in their own cities in various regions of the world. God's amazing plan for my life is becoming more evident to me now. I feel truly blessed as I sit here and reflect upon his goodness towards me. I may not be wealthy in terms of money, but I still feel very rich by having so many more wonderful friends after traveling to Israel.

During this same week of prayer for the nations, I met a gracious, humble woman named Heidi Baker. She was one of the guest speakers at this same conference in Jerusalem. Before she even began speaking to the large gathering, she knelt with her arms extended and her face bowed to the ground in an act of adoration for the Lord. As we all watched this petite woman of faith worshipping God, her humility and reverence spoke volumes to the crowd. I was greatly impressed and moved upon by the Holy Spirit to worship along with her. She taught us from the parable of the Good Samaritan and about how this man had cared for an injured person when the Jewish priest ignored this man. I loved listening to her talk and was very thankful for the impartation I received from her at the end. I came away from this time of listening to our quest speaker with one impression: it was that this godly, consecrated woman was also a truly humble servant and friend of our Lord.

Later that afternoon, I met Heidi Baker briefly in the hallway of the prayer conference as we both walked in the same direction. I asked for her permission to share her story about the children or orphans she cared for in Mozambique, Africa. I mentioned to Heidi that my daughter was traveling to this same location to help with her children from Africa. I saw her face light up with this reminder of her adopted children. We had a nice, brief visit and at the end of our chat I asked her if she'd mind if

I wrote about her children from Mozambique, Africa and she replied that she was fine with my request.

I was thrilled and excited to get back home and begin writing about my visit with this godly woman and about her care for the many African children of Mozambique. I recall something she said to me after I had thanked Heidi Baker for the privilege of presenting her heartbeat for African children in my book. We had been talking of how I have chosen to adopt families into my heart, and she made one striking comment that I shall never forget: "These eight young children living in our home are not called orphans anymore; I call them my own children because we have adopted them. My husband, Roland, and I believe they are truly our sons and daughters along with our own biological children." I must heartily agree with this dedicated woman's marvelous way of seeing these children as a blessing from the Lord. They now have all the benefits, love, and favor which she delights to bestow upon them. God wants to adopt many more people into his family and to impart His rich inheritance and blessings to all those who accept His son into their hearts. It states this in Ephesians 1:5, "Having predestined us unto the adoption of children by Jesus Christ to himself, ..." Do you comprehend what this inheritance promise entails from the Lord? When you accept Jesus into your heart and life as the only true Savior then you inherit everything God's only Son gives to those who believe in him, such as, eternal life, everlasting joy, true peace, abundant life, strength, and the constant presence of a loving heavenly Father who promises to never abandon us.

Those folks whom I've decided to adopt into my heart have also been a blessing to me too; amazingly, they have brought great joy to my life. I never imagined when I first started on this remarkable journey of adopting a family into my heart that I would receive so much in return. As I've mentioned before, I've had the privilege of loving, blessing, and praying for my dear friend for nearly seven years now and she and her family have made me a richer, happier and more fulfilled person. This kind of friendship has given me more than all the world's wealth and riches such as diamonds, rubies, and gold or acclaim could ever do. I must mention my newest son in the faith, Pastor Paul, (not his real name) and his dear wife along with their friend, Marcus Maxwell,(not his real name) and his wife, who live in Kampala, Uganda. These two newest acquaintances both like to call me their American Momma. Some of the other folks that I met at the conference includes these wonderful people: Frank and Hannah from China, Sarah in South Korea, Pastor Ajay and his large family living in a Muslim country, Pastor Elijah Paul from India, Dr. Jumar Praveen in India, and Adeline from Brazil. I am thinking and praying about the idea of traveling to Uganda this coming March 2018 to spend two weeks with my tall friend, Marcus, and Pastor Paul, where we shall enjoy a special new kind of 'family reunion' and a great time of sharing and praying for each other when I come. I am grateful that they've all allowed me into their lives more than they will ever understand; I thank God for them often.

When I sent an email message to my friends whom I'd met during the Israeli trip this last October, one person named Abraham replied by giving me a scripture promise. The verse from the Bible he'd sent to my cell phone pertained to my upcoming trip to Africa and it went like this, "Fear thou not, for I am with thee; for I am thy God: I will strengthen thee: yea, I will help thee; yea, I will uphold thee with the right hand of my righteousness." (Isaiah 41: 10 KJV) This promise from the Bible gave me great encouragement as I finally decided to book a plane ticket to fly to Uganda and share my life experiences with the people there. I love to pray for anyone who needs prayer and encouragement. In order to enter and stay in Africa I had to go to the medical clinic and get six vaccination shots and purchase a month and a half worth of malaria pills. The most important shot required to travel in Uganda is the yellow fever vaccine. After receiving this shot, they gave me a card to verify my compliance with their official regulations which they instructed me to keep inside my passport document.

Six months before this trip to Africa, I'd been staying in a hotel in Israel, (actually, I was in Bethlehem which is now officially another separate country within Israel), and I'd decided to do something as an act of faith in the hopes of one day going to Uganda. I went shopping while staying in the town of Bethlehem one day hoping to find the right garment. At last, I found and purchased a lovely green and white long dress from Israel which I could eventually wear if I ever had the opportunity to visit Kampala, Uganda. Two months later, I also purchased a sleeveless, lightweight summer dress from an Old Navy store which would be perfect to wear in the hot climate of Uganda. When I do travel to Kampala to speak and pray with the university students there, I plan to wear my two new outfits that are like the African style of clothing so I will fit in with the women of Uganda. I am excited about spending time with my new acquaintances who live in Kampala. I hope to make more new friends and to be a blessing while I am staying in Africa.

CHAPTER THIRTY-FIVE

Have you ever wondered how a person can prepare to receive a miracle which they've been
hoping and praying for? I have heard the answer
to this question one day as I listened to Pat Robertson
teach on his CBN program. He mentioned that first a
person should take care of any resentment by forgiving
the person's offense and blessing the person. I choose to
follow his counsel by forgiving others who had hurt me
so I could walk in freedom. I just heard this same advice
from a preacher who was telling people in his congregation that Jesus heals. He also mentioned that it is important to follow the principle set forth in the Book of James
where it encourages the sick to ask the elders to anoint
them with oil and pray in faith and that the person will
be completely healed. "Is anyone among you sick? Let
him call for the elders of the church, and let them pray
over him, anointing him with oil in the name of the
Lord. And the prayer of faith will save the sick, and the
Lord will raise him up. And if he has committed sins, he
will be forgiven. to come and anoint them with oil and
pray the prayer of faith and they shall be healed. And if
they have sinned, it shall be forgiven of them." (James

5: 14–15) This is an important chapter in the Book of James for folks to read and consider.

A few members of our family have dealt with serious illnesses over the last twenty years, and we have joined together to pray for their healings. My nephew has been taking a few rounds of chemotherapy to stop the progress of cancer. He is now in recovery from these harsh drugs and steadily improving in his health and strength; he loves going in the outdoors to camp and ride his sporty new motorcycle bike. My husband's niece in Canada had fought cancer as a young mom and now she is well and enjoying raising her children. Hallelujah, God is good, and his mercies endure forever!

Another way to look for a divine healing is to ask God for a specific insight or divine guidance as you pray, wait, and listen. While I was staying in the hospital chapel for three days in August of 1998 as our sick daughter was undergoing intense doses of chemo drugs to keep her alive, I had this very strong impression come to my mind on the third evening, *"If you will fast for six days for your daughter, then on the seventh day I will give you a victory."* I knew beyond a shadow of doubt that was what I needed to do and so I began fasting for a week.

God was faithful and he brought about a victory by keeping our very ill daughter alive that awful, frightening week of her month long stay in the hospital. People in our congregation heard about my commitment to fast for a miracle from one of the pastors and they joined me in this fasting effort for our daughter. We saw many more victories that entire month as the doctors did their best to treat this aggressive disease. The next step I took was to call the CBN prayer team and share my petition for our daughter's total recovery. They agreed with me in prayer and then informed me that they would send this prayer request on to the chapel room where others would continue to intercede for her that week. Once I found a specific healing verse, I would declare that promise as I intentionally inserted my daughter's name within that same verse. I truly believe that God honors this kind of declaration faith. I also believe in prevailing prayers or persistent petitions.

I must be honest at this moment as it pertained to my struggles with my husband during this stressful time of our daughter's battle to live. We didn't communicate very well for several reasons, and I tried to distance myself from his frustrations with this awful situation and with me. At one point, Sharon asked me to contact her brother, Jon Scott, and request that he fly home from Indonesia to be with her. This was very important to our daughter and so I sent an email to her brother about his very ill sister's urgent need to see him while she was undergoing chemo treatment. My husband eventually brought in our pastor to confront me with this decision, and I felt awful. It felt as if they were ganging up on me and I was hurt by my husband's way of handling this problem. I'd only wanted to facilitate a connection for my sick daughter with her beloved brother who'd been living overseas for a few years. The reason I had made this effort to have my husband help our son come home was that I believed this would give her hope in the midst of her struggles and because she needed his support. Fortunately for Sharon, some four months later, Jon Scott did get a plane ticket and fly home to spend a few weeks with his sister for the holidays. She was so glad to have him visit her in the hospital while she was recovering from the transplant procedure. Christmas Eve day, all seven of our adult children were gathered in her room to cheer her up and pray over her to be completely healthy and safe from the graft versus host problem. It warmed my heart to see the siblings caring for her, sharing stories with her, and laughing together that entire afternoon. It was a memorable time for our family. Sharon had expressed her feelings of wanting to go home for Christmas time to the medical staff and after more pleading with her nurses, the doctor finally gave his permission for her to be released the hospital for the holidays. They released her to go stay with the one family friend who had an excellent Hepa-filter airflow system which provided their home with very safe, clean air. It was the best Christmas present we could've had that December.

***

There may be certain times when a person needs to surrender a child to God like I had to do with our daughter, Sharon. Since that hospital experience, I have learned to ask this important question, "Father God, how do you want to heal this person?" After I've received some valuable insight about the matter, then I will continue to pray with more confidence for that individual and believe for their healing. To be sure, we can also look in the scriptures to find any evidence or proof that miracles are real too! Here is one example of Jesus performing a miracle when he healed a blind man, and this person had his eyesight back and he rejoiced. We can find more evidence of miracles by turning to the four Gospels. "Jesus did many other miraculous signs in the presence of his disciples, which are not recorded in this book. But these are written that you may believe that Jesus is the Christ, the son of God, and that by believing you may have life in his name." (John 20: 30 – 34) I believe in a God who still heals today, and I believe in miracles. If you want more proof, then I can recommend a powerful, true-life movie for you to watch. A mother wrote a book called "Breakthrough" where she records her son's accidental drowning in freezing cold lake water. He was rushed to the ER, but the doctor couldn't get a pulse for this teenager. She cried out to God to give him life instead of death and the boy came back to life again with a pulse. It was a very difficult recovery with no promise of success from the specialist team. Every part of this miracle recovery was documented and confirmed by the medical reports, and they made a fantastic movie from this story. It is one of my favorite movies.

***

It was the month of December, and I was walking outside of our country home in the moonlight. As I was coming back up our long driveway, I noticed the reflection of the red, green, and white lights from our family Christmas tree shining brightly through the windows of our two-story house. These colorful, cheery lights were casting a hazy shadow of brilliance and beauty upon the front yard of our country home. All these dazzling colors compelled me to stand still for a moment and rejoice at the wonders of this wintery season in the Northwest. Soon I continued with my walking and praying for our family and for each person's holiday travels. I pulled my scarf tightly around my neck to bundle up against the chilly night air. I was wishing that the formation of thin cloud cover would dissipate enough to allow the stars to be seen overhead. I've been told that if you can see the stars at night then the next day will be clear and dry. This was my hope for tomorrow since my two adorable grandkids, Abigail and Ezra, were coming over to play at our house the next morning. The idea of another day of rain in our forecast was not a pleasant one; plus, it would mean the kids would have to stay inside and play quietly.

I glanced back up at the night sky once more with a renewed hope for dry weather for the following day. To my amazement, the skies had parted suddenly, and I saw a multitude of glistening stars spattered against a dark ebony background. It was a spectacular sight and it reminded me of the fact that no matter how gloomy our lives can seem, there is still the hope for a better day. The sight of an infinite, starry firmament above gave me an excitement for the possibilities of exploring our acreage with my grandchildren the next day in dry weather. I wanted to take them on a walk without needing to wear rain gear and boots. Seeing the clouds move away during this very moment had prompted me to look towards heaven one more time in expectancy and trust that God would also answer my other prayers. This quick break in the cloud cover gave me a glimpse of what the heavenly Father's spiritual breakthrough might look like too. In those brief moments when the dark clouds had drifted away before my eyes, I was thinking about the times when things do go our way and then life is beautiful again. Often, when we are experiencing long term gloom and disappointments in our life, it seems like having too many days of dismal, cloudy weather can bring with it a touch of despair or a feeling that things may not change. You see, I believe our prayers can change people and circumstances just like that night scene had changed right before my eyes. This natural change in the sky above me had given me a renewed hope for other kinds of wonderful changes to happen before too long. And yes, the next day was dry enough and we could go outside to explore the fields around our house as we searched for any signs of wild rabbits, insects or garden snakes.

During my trip to Israel in 2017, I really enjoyed meeting new people, praying for them and speaking God's truth and encouragement into their lives. In the past, I've felt the need to fast before I leave on a trip in order to prepare my heart. During my times of fasting from food, the Lord will begin to give me words of knowledge for certain people who I may encounter on my trip. It was during my time of waiting and preparing for my two different trips abroad that I'd received a few names and so I decided to write these names down in my journal book and to pray for them. Then I also asked God to give me divine appointments while I was traveling overseas. The Lord was with me in a mighty way while I was staying in Israel for fourteen days and it was an amazing, profound experience for me. I met people with these same names which were recorded in my journal book back home in the states. It was so marvelous that I had the joy of praying God's blessing and will for these people on my trip.

I believe God is showing me now that he has one more country for me to travel to with His wonderful message of love. I saw what great benefit there was in obeying the Lord when I finally went to the land of

Israel. I was blessed beyond my own expectations as I prayed for God's will to be accomplished each morning of the trip. I wouldn't trade that recent experience for any amount of money it cost me to fly there and spend the two weeks in different hotels in Nazareth, Samaria, and Bethlehem. Yes, it might cost us something when we choose to do God's will, but it's worth it. Even though my meager savings account is now depleted, and I am not working anymore, I shall put my trust in the Lord who is my provider. I believe He has put a love for the nations within my soul and I can't wait to carry His message of hope and healing to all who will listen as I share the good news. God loves people and desires to have a closer relationship with each person as they open their heart to receive more of His love and truth. The Father in heaven is waiting to give you a hope and a good future! Trust Him with all your heart.

Let's look at one more example of the power of God working in someone's life. My friend Hannah shared a true story with me recently. She told me about a retired police officer now in his early sixties who had stage -four cancer. His son wanted to believe for his father's healing and so he encouraged his dad to come with him to a well-known church located in Redding, California. He had heard about amazing miracles occurring in this place and he felt some sense of hope as they walked onto the property. In the prayer room a leader came over and informed this older gentleman that a young boy would be praying for him. The man thought that this was strange, and he didn't think there would be any healing power transmitted from this youngster to him. To his utter amazement when this young lad laid his hands on him, the sick man fell to the floor under the profound presence of the Lord. He was instantly healed and knew that God had touched him with divine power at that time. He went into his doctor to have his body checked for any viable evidence of this healing. As this older man was sharing his new experience and a sense of renewed well-being, the doctor slid to the floor under the anointing of God. The older gentleman no longer has any cancer in his body and his family is rejoicing and celebrating with him about this miracle. I hope that you are getting a sense of this wonderful truth which is that God is so willing to heal all who believe, "For whoever shall call upon the name of the Lord shall be saved." (Romans 10: 13) Thank goodness for the mercy of our heavenly Father. He is so full of love and compassion for people. He sent his Son to earth to show us about His extraordinary love for mankind.

I have a remarkable testimony to share with you today! We have been praying for God to send the right man into our daughter, Sharon's life. Yes, she's been very busy with getting her nursing four-year degree and working in a hospital on the oncology ward until she eventually decided to change jobs and work in her hometown in a smaller clinic. I recalled how so many years before this that a friend who prayed with me for Sharon had called to share that she believed God was going to bring a very kind, kind man into my daughter's life someday. Well, I am thrilled to share with you that after waiting and waiting for this kind man to arrive on the scene, Sharon has met a remarkable young man named Mark. After dating for some time, they were engaged during January while visiting Mt. Hood and are now married! Hallelujah, thanks be unto our God! We are rejoicing and believe that this darling couple will live long and thrive and rejoice in the goodness of the Lord. Their beautiful wedding took place in Troutdale, Oregon on July 30th and her six siblings were present to witness this joyous occasion in the Pacific Northwest area.

Here's a little bit of background information for those who don't know much about our darling daughter, Sharon. When she was only twenty-one years old, she suffered from a horrible disease and spent a great deal of time in two different hospitals in one year's time. During the month she was in the second hospital in Oregon, I'd been staying there to keep her company and to be praying for her complete recovery from a bone marrow transplant procedure. One day, I sat in a chair near her bed silently thinking about the events which had transpired prior to the one day that her brother, Robert, donated his bone marrow to keep her alive. While sitting there in a quiet hospital room, I saw with my spiritual eyesight a quick vision of a dark-haired man standing next to my daughter, Sharon, and they seemed to be very happy. Then I saw this couple kiss and it seemed like she really enjoyed his attention and his kiss in this vision scene. I noticed that the man in my vision wore a brown jacket and my sense at this moment was that I'd seen a wonderful event for the future. I carried this picture or image in my heart for the next twenty years. I've prayed often for this vision-like scene, which I felt had come from my heavenly father God, to become a living true reality for our daughter, Sharon. I often pondered about the exact meaning of this vision in which I saw my daughter standing next to someone I felt could ultimately be her soulmate and yet, I wondered why the guy had been wearing in a brown jacket in this scene. Eventually, I asked my best friend, Debbie to pray an agreement prayer about this vision I'd received for Sharon and her future mate. My friend and I made a declaration in faith for this vision to become a reality and a joyful experience for my daughter one day.

I continued to ask God to bring that special, kind-hearted man into my daughter's life and for her to get married and have her own family. Well, I'm delighted to say that this vision did come to pass this August of 2022. The outdoor setting for this wedding was spectacular amidst a picturesque country landscape which boasted of large walnut trees with broad shade-giving branches and leaves that acted like a canopy covering. Her brother, Robert Stricker, officiated this wonderful marriage and he finished the ceremony by telling his audience about their special brother-sister bond and unique friendship. As my son shard the story of how they each had an amazing part in praying and helping each stay safe when each of them was involved in two separate and potentially dangerous situation, I began to weep quietly while sitting in the front row of this wedding ceremony. My oldest son, Robert, became emotional and had to stop talking for a second and then he continued giving God the glory for keeping them both safe from certain death when they were younger. Next, our second born son, Jonathan Scott, along with his younger brother, David, came forward to stand in front of the altar which was covered with green draping vines and explosively rich purple flowers. The two tall, handsome brothers prayed for the radiant bride, Sharon and her beloved groom, Mark. Once again, I found myself crying as I listened to her brothers praying for God's blessing on the couple and I had to take a deep breath to maintain my composure. We are so grateful for the fact that both of our wonderful adult children, Sharon, and her brother, Robert, are alive today and able to share their stories and to celebrate life before family and friends. These two accounts of God's protection for both Robert and Sharon can be compared to that of such miraculous and inspirational events that I couldn't not write their stories and include them in this book about real miracles and healings!

Our heavenly Father loves you and I so immensely and he is our biggest fan and cheerleader. God loves people with an undying, unquenchable authentic love. I know because I've experienced this same wonderful compassionate love embrace myself! He is waiting to meet with you today. Jesus believes in you! His ideal love encounter will change your life as it did mine. The Lord God has the capacity to make a person feel brand new and to keep them forever free. If you want to experience this kind of divine love from heaven, then pray this simple prayer by faith.

Heavenly Father, I believe you sent your only son to die in my place on Calvary's cross. I believe that God raised Jesus up from the dead after three days and now, Lord, I choose to give my life to you. Forgive me of my sins and wrongdoings and take me to heaven to live with you forever. I confess that Jesus is my Lord and I thank you heavenly Father for making me part of your royal family. Amen

It's autumn now in the Pacific Northwest and around this region it can rain on and off at times for nearly eight months of the year. I look forward to seeing the sun peek out from behind the clouds occasionally.

Today, the sunshine has burst forth in our area and it is warming up the temperature nicely. It is beckoning me to put down the ink pen and take a break from my writing. I really must take a stroll outside and enjoy the beautiful weather while it's still here. Without a second thought about my work, I quickly put on a lightweight jacket and head outdoors to breathe in the fresh, crisp air. Our golden retriever puppy, Zoey, races along the gravel driveway with me in search of wild rabbits, birds or squirrels which normally try to hide from this overly zealous young puppy. Zoey loves to chase after any moving animal such as a mallard duck, a blue jay, or the horses and cows which frequent our nearby pastureland. As we head back up the gravel driveway to our two-story house, my feet connect with all the piles of scattered leaves lying on the grass. I hear the crunch and crackle of the yellow and brown, discarded foliage underneath my feet as I crossed the front lawn to chase after our golden retriever puppy. Autumn time is my second favorite season.

My favorite season of the year is summertime. During this hot season, I can hop in my car and drive to the lake or river to jump into the refreshing, tantalizing cold water. It is the best time to go for a hike in the northwest too. My thoughts return to the present and the glorious autumn season which is now upon us here in Pacific Northwest. As I turn to my left, I notice two deciduous trees and the leaves still clinging to the branches. The tall birch tree I had planted here some thirty years ago still has a few bright yellow leaves on its branches. The second smaller tree has orange and reddish leaves which proudly display the radiant glorious tints of our autumn season.

It looks as if the countryside is on fire today as I turn around to see more colorful tree leaves. Then I reach up to pull off some yellow leaves from our birch tree branches. I plan to carry them inside to add to my festive centerpiece on the table. Naturally, our dog, Zoey, tries to jump up and grab my handful of leaves and carrying them off in her mouth. She will chew on any piece of wood or plastic or a broken tree branch that she can locate; she loves to play a game of tug a war with me when I hand her a stick too. Sometimes she will make me chase her to capture a ball or stick gripped tightly between her sharp teeth; Zoey dog usually wins this contest. I finally had to give up this friendly contest or tug of war' game as I continued walking among the fallen leaves scattered across our front lawn. It makes me sad to think that soon the other yellow and red leaves will be turning brown as the strong winds blow them off their tender stems and they fall to the ground. Life is like this autumn season; ever changing, ever turning towards eventual death and then back again into resurrection-life of springtime beauty and hope.

While taking in the various colors of the season around me, I was reminded of the ability God's ability to take a person who has suffered many heartaches and sorrows in their life and bring about an amazing healing and restoration in their minds and souls. And yes, with one stroke of His divine paintbrush of love, He gently and lovingly held my broken, bruised heart, with all its hurts, disappointments, despair, and grief, in his hands until my aching soul had been healed. Only God could restore me to wholeness and fill my heart with joy and hope as he did. You see, God was able to create something out of nothing when this world was established some millions of years ago and so surely, he can create new life out of a wounded, damaged soul such as mine. He is a God of miracles. God was able to replace my anger, hurt, and pain with His divine touch. I call this emotional transformation more like a 'divine exchange 'from heaven. I responded by giving Him my broken heart and then God gave me back a new heart full of His amazing love; I'm accepted in the beloved as the Bible states; I've been made whole because of God's immeasurable kindness and mercy towards me.

I want to share my story of healing with the world. God has made something beautiful of my life. He has turned my mourning and sadness into gladness and fulfilled dreams. I was set free from the pain and sorrow of my childhood abuse and from years of intense shame and deep-seated anger! Yes, this healing process took a long time and yet, all my efforts to be more honest with myself, more transparent with others, and more vulnerable in my writings was worth it. During an inner healing session with two women, I would be asked by the ministry team to picture the Lord standing there with me in my awful circumstances and to listen to see if I'd believed a lie about myself. Once I heard the lie and renounced it, I was encouraged to ask God's Holy Spirit what the truth was from God. Then I needed to receive the truth about myself and to decide to let go of my bitterness and anger towards as well as to forgive my offenders which I did. This verse from the Bible says it all, "I called upon the Lord in distress: the Lord answered me and set me in a large place." (Psalm 118: 5)

If you've felt discouraged and worthless as I had been because of my past and the childhood abuse, then I want to encourage you to give your broken dreams and disappointments to the Lord. Give your life story and shame or pain to the Lord and allow him to use your story to encourage someone else who may be struggling with emotional pain or a grievous loss. People may be able to identify with your testimony of how you struggled with emotional pain and grief. If you ask God to use you, no matter how ordinary your life may seem at this moment, you might be amazed at what happens if you choose to share your own story with someone else. I've been so blessed with a richer, fuller life since I asked God to change me instead of fixing other people around me. After I shared honestly in a gathering of women about my physical and emotional abuse issues, some of them responded to my invitation for prayer. A few hurting women who had come forward were weeping and all I could do was hugged them and tell them how sorry I was for their anguish and sorrows. When I prayed for the hurting women in Kampala, Uganda in 2017, I was so blessed by the response of appreciation which came to me. This is kingdom living at its best.

****

Today I was teaching a group of fourth graders at Church about faith. My friend, Rick, came over to my classroom to help with the craft part of our lesson. I turned to my friend and asked him to share with the kids about a time when he had to trust God and stand in faith for a healing. I motioned to the children to hush and listen quietly as he began to speak to the group. He told the children about two times God intervened in his family situations. The first thing that he needed to believe God for was when the doctors informed his wife that they couldn't have their own children. This was very disappointing for them. However, they now have three healthy active young boys. I must interject here in this story to say that this was a wonderful miracle and blessing for this fine, young couple. I have watched them this past year and I can say that they are doing a fabulous job of raising these young boys to love the Lord and be respectful of others.

Then Rick went on to tell the class about what occurred after his second son, Zion, was born. When Zion was only a week old, the doctors did an examination of his eyes, ears, and lungs. The results of their tests showed that their young child had 85% hearing loss in both of his ears. This awful negative report from the doctor made them very sad. This couple decided after that first visit to call on God and believe in faith for his ears to be totally healed from deafness. Two weeks later they were sent to another facility outside of Los Angeles, California to have their son's ears examined by a qualified person with special instruments that are used to detect deafness. The test results of their equipment showed that their young son had 95% hearing loss.

The technician person was going to record his findings to state that Zion was deaf in both ears. Zion's mother then asked him to do one more test on her son's ears. The technician's response to her request was that this first test was conclusive and accurate. His next statement to her was to say that by doing a second test they wouldn't see any change in the results. This mother's reply to the medical person was that her husband had been fasting for this situation and they both were expecting God to perform a divine miracle for their son's ears. She asked the person to please do one more test for her son. The technician finally relented and hooked her child up to the wires and suction cups on his head and ears to run the same test again. If the lights on his machine turned green this time it would mean that he had perfect hearing and no deafness. The lights on the hearing machine all turned green before her eyes and she rejoiced and hugged her young child with a heart of gratitude to her heavenly Father. God had seen their faith and the declarations of faith which were spoken over their son, Zion, and Lord had rewarded their faith by giving Zion an ability to hear perfectly after that. I have known this family for a few years now and I've watched their son grown into a healthy, active boy. He can hear everything we say to him, and he talks very well. I am thrilled to share this wonderful testimony of divine healing! Thank heavens, the Lord still performs miracles today.

This wonderful miracle which occurred for my friends, Rick and his family reminds me of one of my favorite scripture promises from the Bible, "Therefore I say unto you, what things soever ye desire, when ye pray, believe that ye receive them, and ye shall have them." (Mark 11:24) As in the case of Rick and Michelle who were expecting a miracle for their son's hearing to be restored, we too can step out in faith and confidence in the power of God to heal and to perform miracles for our loved ones! As you may notice by this time, this book about our family experiences does not just contain our family miracles; this book has included other people's stories, their miracles of intervention, and healings as well.

Recently, I was given a necklace with the word, 'blessed' engraved in the silver coin that was attached to the chain. I wear this simple, but very profound gift often and I am reminded of my friend's kindness to me. This perfect gift from my friend is like what I believe the Lord desires to impart to us when we receive the special gift of the 'father's blessing'.

If you didn't have an earthly father or receive a godly father's impartation and his positive affirmations, then you can certainly ask for this wonderful blessing from the Father God's hand of provision. You may want to believe for a person to cross your path who can impart this special anointed father's blessing over you. In my own life, this became a reality one fine day. My good friend, Doug, felt impressed, while at church on day, to impart this supernatural father's blessing to me. When he was finished speaking life to me and breaking off the pain and disappointments I'd been carrying, I experienced a new sense of acceptance in my soul. After he imparted this unique blessing to me, I felt an amazing peace being deposited into my soul as well. I was grateful to have this affirmation and blessing in my life. This spiritual impartation of a father's blessing' was exactly what I needed.

I know there are people like me who've suffered at the hand of an angry, unkind parent and I can only pray for them to encounter this special connection with a kindhearted person like my friend from church. I encourage people I meet to ask the Father God for a 'father's wonderful blessing' too. Your heavenly Father who delights to give good gifts will hear your hearts cry and He will not disappoint you. I pray for this type of godly experience to happen for you. He wants to become more than just a historical figure in your life. God wants the opportunity to impart His amazing powerful healing virtue to everyone who asks for it. I truly believe that God wants us to appropriate the blessings of having a renewed mind and a joyful heart. I shall believe for you to experience the Lord's transforming touch on your total being when you ask Him to deposit within your soul this amazing 'father's blessing'. God is so willing to flood our heart and mind with a true sense of acceptance and peace to those who ask for this extra blessing.

Take a moment and say this simple prayer.

Heavenly Father, infuse me with your amazing 'father's blessing' today. I open my heart to receive this wonderful blessing right now into my life. I release my pain, my disappointments, and my wounded heart into your capable hands. I thank you, heavenly Father for giving me what I need today. Set me free of the past hurts, heartaches, and disappointments. Give me your true words of affirmation and encouragement as I chose to receive the 'father's blessing' impartation today by faith. I shall trust you and believe that my life matters. Thank you, Father God that you love me and have such a good plan for my life. Amen.

I will pray for the Lord to meet you right where you are. I shall also believe for an impartation from the Spirit of God to flow powerfully into your mind and soul until you realize that you are important, you are accepted, and you are loved beyond measure.

People are looking for hope, peace, good health, and prosperity. They will only find it in searching the scriptures which testifies of God's goodness and points them to His truth and his wisdom. Here's an important truth and promise which I like to quote often, "Now the God of hope fill you with all joy and peace in believing, that ye may abound in hope, through the power of the Holy Ghost." (Romans 15:13) I encourage you to speak out this same verse for your life too. Ask the Lord to show you how to incorporate the help of His Spirit to bring about more joy and peace for your life. God will give you the infilling of the Holy Spirit when you ask in faith to receive this amazing gift. If you decide to ask for this wonderful impartation and you choose to appropriate the gift of the Holy Spirit, then watch and see what God will do for you! He is a gracious heavenly father who delights to give good gifts to those who ask and believe to receive from him.

I want to encourage folks who are struggling in life. There is an antidote available to those who may be feeling down or discouraged by life's troubles. It involves shaking off the spirit of self-pity and sadness. The second way of becoming free in your heart and mind involves helping others who need an act of kindness or generosity. In fact, I know of a few missionaries who've travelled to another country to live and help others. As I sit here at my computer on this chilly winter day, I am reflecting upon the goodness and mercy of the Lord in my life. Once again, it's the holiday season in our wonderful country and a time for giving to others. I want to honor a generous person who is helping children in Kenya, Africa. Doctor Eric Hansen is a missionary doctor who gave up a lucrative practice and comfortable lifestyle to move to Kenya.

I watched his telecast and realized that this dedicated doctor and his wife from Texas and another doctor from Australia who's working with him on the Peter Bird Campus are all storing up treasures in heaven. They mentioned to their listeners that they pray before operating on the sick children in Nairobi, Africa. I learned that there are now eight African hospitals which are training people to do this work. The Healthcare Foundation is helping them to establish these excellent teaching hospitals. Another interesting fact is that a wealthy Jewish couple has given them a large sum of money to fund this project. Along with these capable doctors and their new foundation, the 700 Club's Operation Blessings program has partnered with these same doctors to provide an eight-year-old boy the free opportunity to receive a cleft palette operation. This type of surgery was needed to restore his smile and to help him be able to talk easily for the first time ever. This is a powerful testimony of how these selfless doctors can bless African children in need. These two missionary doctors have shown such generosity and kindness to those in need. I hope they will have many rich blessings and rewards on this earth because of their acts of kindness. I hope that doctors and nurses such as Doctors without Borders and other groups elsewhere in the world may know how much people appreciate their medical care for the sick and needy people who come to them for help. Thank you, doctors and medical teams for your generosity and years of service to those in great need.

CHAPTER THIRTY-SIX

We are now entering the month of December once again and the special holiday season of Christmas which we celebrate in the states. The radio will play beautiful classic songs every day like; "I'm Dreaming of a White Christmas", "Let it Snow", or "Walking in a Winter Wonderland" and I will begin to enjoy the nostalgia of these songs and as I listen to these catchy tunes, I'll recall the special holiday memories of years gone by. This wonderful, magical time of giving is filled with whimsical, fantastic sights, sounds, and smells that can capture one's imagination. Christmas time inspires a person to do things they wouldn't normally think to do for others. It is a season for love and renewed hope for those who believe. It isn't always about the grand gesture of expensive gifts we try to bless others with each holiday season, but rather, for me it's about the family gatherings, singing Christmas carols, and rejoicing over all God's goodness and protection during the year. It's the non-material things such as family gatherings, much laughter and gaiety, and hearts full of thankfulness which brings me joy and causes me to celebrate this wonderful season. The true meaning of Christmas for me is having all our adult children and the many grandkids with us in our home for the holidays. We have certain traditions which the family likes to observe. When our boys were young adults, they decided they would make Christmas breakfast for the entire group. It became quite a production and a supreme labor of love. My three sons will gather in the kitchen to fry eggs and sausage in the hot skillet for everyone. Then they'd place a slice of Tillamook cheese on top of the eggs and meat lying on one half of a croissants roll. Next, one son will pour orange juice into at least fifteen glasses set around the big festive table. Of course, this extravagant meal was not complete until they'd made hot coffee and specialty drinks for their beloved mother and father.

Then the holiday fun and merriment begin at our home on Christmas day. Our grown sons would regale us with their humorous stories from their youth. They'd proceed to share a few exaggerated tales of woe about the early years when I'd take a slender switch from an outside bush to use as my spanking stick to correct their misbehavior. They'd always elaborate on how they had the meanest mom in the neighborhood, and everyone would laugh in response to these stories. Our boys like to get everyone laughing whenever we gather for a holiday meal. Last year I decided to add a new holiday tradition where we all hold a flickering candle as we sing our favorite songs, "Hark the Herald Angels Sing" and "Joy to the World". For me this is a way to help us to reflect upon the reason for this glorious season. This last Christmas gathering at our house, I wanted to do something unique and so I asked my oldest son to read from the fourth chapter of Joshua where it describes how the Hebrew tribes placed twelve stones near the Jordan River to commemorate a victory. Then I asked my other son to read a type-written page I'd kept about the vision from our friend where she had seen angels coming to minister gifts of healing to our daughter while she lay in the hospital back in 1998. A few days before Christmas I'd stumbled onto a verse which really impressed me and so I wanted to share it with my family. This was the verse that had caught my attention that morning as I was reading the Bible, "The Lord has done great things for us; whereof we are glad." (Ps. 126: 3)

The reason I wanted to share this verse with my family at Christmas time was because I wanted to make a memorial time of giving glory to the Lord for the recent miracles which had occurred for our family. My second intention for taking this time to reflect about God's goodness at our family gathering was to share these victories with our grandchildren. I felt that our grandchildren were old enough now to remember this special holiday occasion where we stopped in our festivities and blessed God for all his loving kindness to our family. We got through these two readings without tears and then I asked my husband to pray for more healings and breakthroughs for the family members who were suffering from certain afflictions and injuries. Next, my son suggested we sing "The First Noel".

We all joined in with amazing voices to sing the first well-known stanza of this Carole and then continued to the second one which was apparently unfamiliar to many of us. We all started to fumble over the next few verses and had to stop singing twice. My son began to chuckle and then laugh. Now normally, I'm the one to instigate the laughter at a family meals or large gatherings, but this time, my eldest son had started the moment of gaiety and laughter. We all joined in and gave up singing that unfamiliar second stanza.

It was a wonderful time of remembrance for our family. I love it when we stop and worship the Lord as a family. A few minutes later, we began to sing an easier Christmas Carole. I am grateful that the Lord has made music within my soul and has given me a reason to declare His praises. During the past, in the month of December we have another family tradition to uphold. My sons and daughters all love to go to a local tree farm and hunt for the perfect Christmas tree to cut down and haul back to each one of our homes. We usually take photos of our wonderful evergreen tree as we huddle close together and smile for the camera. This annual tradition is very dear to my heart.

This year my two daughters wanted to drive up and meet their sister, Kris, her husband, and their three children in Oregon to search for a tree in the forest area. We piled into Sharon's nice vehicle with our gear and food to drive for an hour or so. Once we'd located Paul's suburban vehicle along the roadside, we followed them for another few miles until we'd reach the National Park area where we can see the majestic snow-covered Mt. Hood. Paul finally located a place to park our two vehicles at the start of a logging road and then everyone hopped out and began to bundle up in warm hats, gloves, and boots. My five-year-old granddaughter, Abigail, helped me throw snowballs at our youngest daughter's husband, Charlie Joshua, while he was trying to put on his boots. To find so much snow in the woods that day was unexpected, but very exciting for our family. After my daughter, Kristina, had securely strapped her infant son onto her chest and her husband had handed his three-year-old son the trusty saw, we all started hiking along the snow-covered logging road in search of the illusive, perfect pine tree.

My other daughter, Catherine, began singing the famous holiday tune called 'Here we come a wassailing' while the rest of the group tried to join in with her. The joy of being together in this snowy winter wonderland was contagious. It was an extra blessing to see so much white, shimmering snow all around us. When we looked on both sides of the road all we could see was giant towering Evergreen trees. The boughs of each tree were loaded down with thick piles of snow. Some of the branches were so weighed down that they drooped over and nearly touched the ground. It was a scene out of Currier n Ives painting with the backdrop of white against the dark green of the forested wilderness. I watched as my son-in-law walked over to a Noble tree and grabbed hold of its tree trunk and shook it until the snow fell off the branches. This effort enabled him to check on the appearance of the tree and determine if it was what he wanted. Finally, after traipsing off on a new path to look at a few more Nobel evergreen trees, he found the one he wanted to cut down. Then he left it by the roadside and followed the rest of us as we kept searching for the next perfect Christmas tree.

During our ride up to Mt. Hood I had prayed for the Lord's help in finding a tree for my house. I am particular about the kind of tree I like to decorate during this season. I prefer either a Blue Spruce or a Douglas fir tree which usually will have more branches to give it a fuller appearance. The trees on the lots or tree farms in town usually cost about sixty dollars each year and the family wanted to save money by hunting in the forest this time. As I waded through the ankle-deep snow, I sent up another prayer to heaven asking for guidance to find a good tree for my daughter's place and my house too. I had gone on ahead of my children and grandchildren in this search. As I looked over to the left side of the snow-covered road, I spied a few good-looking Fir trees nearby and so I headed in that direction. There to my wonder and amazement stood three very nice-looking Evergreen trees. It looked as if they had been trimmed by nature itself and were waiting for our family to discover them. I marked my new path with more deep footprints in the snow and returned to the main logging road. Then I hollered loudly to let the family members know about my great find. My one daughter's husband, Paul, answered me back with his own boisterous reply of 'look out for bears, Nana!' I laughed and shouted back there were no brown bears in the vicinity, only some beautiful Evergreen trees. Then I remembered that he had brought his 38' special handgun strapped into a leather holster, and I thought to myself, 'well, maybe there could be a hungry bear around this part of the woods, so I hurried back to find the safety of the men in my family.

Within minutes, the rest of the family showed up to admire my discovery and then Paul and Charlie took turns using the tree saw to cut down two perfect Christmas trees. We tried to take a family snapshot right there, but it was difficult since five-month-old Isaiah and three-year-old Ezra didn't turn in time to face the camera. I finally stepped out of the group and took the photo to capture this glorious memory. On the hike back to the main highway and our vehicles, my daughter took a few candid pictures of us dragging the heavy trees along behind us. Our five-year-old granddaughter, Abigail, had only worn a thin pair of socks in her rain boots and so when the cold snow fell inside her boots, her feet became uncomfortable, and she was miserable. Fortunately, I had packed a couple of extra warm socks in my backpack, so I was able to relieve her of the wet, cold socks in exchange for my dry ones.

We sat in the warm car and ate our sandwiches while the two men tied down the three evergreen trees on top of the vehicles. Our family's Christmas adventure turned out to be a great experience and a day that we'll always cherish and remember for years to come. Christmas is a time for our large family to gather around the brightly lit tree and reflect on the goodness and love that our heavenly Father has bestowed upon us all. This wonderful season makes me glad as I think about the hope and joy it brings to the world. The Christmas songs we sing each year speak of the wonder of the birth of Christ and the promise of a truly everlasting joy to those who've receive its message into their hearts.

***

It's now 2018, and winter has arrived once again, and the snow has fallen here in the Pacific Northwest region. Mount Hood is wrapped up once again in a thick, fresh blanket of powdery snow. It is a grand sight to behold as I drive across I205 Bridge to shop at Cascade Station in Oregon. Luckily the morning traffic was minimal that morning, and I could locate a parking spot, go inside the shop to buy my daughter a gift, and return home in time for lunch. Later that day I was flipping through the TV channels hoping to find a good holiday movie to watch as I wrapped presents for the children. There seemed to be nothing interesting to watch on this day and so I went back to channel 39 and settled on a program called the 700 Club which was being aired on the CBN.

After listening to the current world news on CBN, the TV host, Gordon, came on to interview a young man named Jordan. His story gripped my heart as Jordan shared with the audience about having skin cancer called melanoma as a teenager. Then he shared in this interview about when he'd turned twenty-three and the cancer came back with a vengeance. I was now paying closer attention to his words by this time. Jordan's doctor had not given a good prognosis since the cancer was in different parts of his body this second time. They discovered that the cancer had spread to his larynx or throat area and told him to expect the growth to overtake his ability to breathe properly. I sat there watching this young man's story and felt such empathy for him at that moment. I saw him choke back his tears and he paused in his story for a moment. Then this young man managed to continue telling us just how devastated he was by this last bit of news.

Next, Jordan shared with the audience about his surgeries, and he mentioned about the scars which he shows people each time he shares about the doctor's report. The medical staff had informed him that he had only six months to live at first and then it was limited to six days if they didn't do some new kind of drastic treatment and radiation to stop the growth in his throat. The scary part of this treatment was that it might help, or it could possibly kill him. There was a risk to taking this new drug and only two percent of the patients survived to this date. I listened in amazement as his story unfolded that afternoon. It reminded me of our experience with my daughter when she was at the second hospital in 1998. There were many people praying for our daughter to survive her illness back then. People who didn't even know our sick daughter at all had prayed for her healing and now this young man named Jordan had also been the recipient of many letters of encouragement from people he did not know across this country as they joined in to pray for his miracle of healing.

Jordan went on to mention that he'd placed his future and life back into God's hands and had chosen to depend on God for an answer. God did rescue Jordan from a very grave attack on his physical body. He was thankful for the doctor's attempts to save his life. He has a powerful testimony of how many, many hundreds of people on the internet hotline, along with their prevailing prayers of faith, had turned the hand of God towards him. He now sings and plays his guitar to honor God. He shared with the television audience that people who want to donate or read about survivors of cancer can go onto a website called YouInspire.org where survivors go to share their story. This was an inspiration to me that day. I would love it if the medical researchers could eradicate many types of cancers and make them obsolete or non-existent just like they did with the polio disease. Please take the time to check out this nonprofit website and say a prayer for those people who post on it: https://www.youinspire.org.

CHAPTER THIRTY-SEVEN

On November 23, of this last year, I received a vision from the Lord. In this vision I saw some bowls. Then I heard the Holy Spirit say to me, *Fill the bowls and feed the people. Fill the bowls with food to satisfy their need!* I began to fill the bowls with food and then they ate. Next thing that happened in this unique vision was that the hungry people called out to me and cried for "More, More, more!" I began asking the Lord this question, "Lord, what is the food that you want me to place in the bowls to feed your people?" I believe that the word, food, in this vision implies God's words and his divine bread' of truth. I needed to understand what to share with folks wherever I was asked to go and pray for people. Then I asked the Lord what did the word of 'more' in the vision imply?" The Holy Spirit's response to this question was this: The anointing and the things of the Spirit are the 'more' that you saw in this vision. So, I asked the Lord how to share this idea and produce a better understanding of the message of His anointed provision which people are calling out for. I've prayed fervently for months about this idea of the 'MORE' from God in order to be equipped to share sufficiently with the people in Africa. I needed to be able to give this revelation to the Ugandan people each time when I spoke to a group of students who lived in Kampala. We need to have God's anointing and the power of the Holy Spirit to function as Jesus did when He walked on this earth. Let's examine how we can receive and walk in the Holy Spirit anointing which helps us to minister in a supernatural way.

First and foremost, we need to understand and believe this truth: "You are from God, little children, and have overcome them: because greater is He who is in you than he who is in the world." (1John 4: 4) So since the Son of God lives in you as a believer, then you have everything you need to succeed and to expect a victory in each situation. You can ask the heavenly Father for the anointing to be upon your life. When we believe for this wonderful impartation from God, then we will receive his anointing and ability to teach others. God wants to empower us as His sons and daughters, to do good works here on earth and He is not a respecter of persons. The Bible says that God desires to give good gift to everyone who asks for them. We can see an amazing truth jump out at us from this verse, "God...who has blessed us with every spiritual blessing in the heavenly places in Christ." (Ephesians 1:3) Christ is seated in heavenly places right now and he also lives within each believer's heart and life.

We are seated with him in this heavenly realm and therefore, we have everything Christ possessed from the Father God to be able to accomplish all the good works which God intended for us to do. Having this important knowledge of what we've been given as believers and what we can accomplish through faith, we can now accept the fact that we are equipped with the ability to do what God asks us to do. There is one facet of this blessing that I must mention. When we walk in God's anointing, it is important to remember to give God the glory for the victories and successes. I have determined to keep a heart of gratitude and appreciation for God's favor and anointing in my own life. Some of the ways of God are encapsulated in these three things; to learn to do His will, to understand how to love people well, and to appropriate the power of the Holy Spirit as the Lord did while living on this earth. The kingdom of heaven is here because Jesus lives in us; so, let's release the kingdom of heaven to the people we meet on the street or in a grocery store. Occasionally, my friend and I will get an opportunity to pray for someone we meet while out walking in our community. I call this experience 'having a divine appointment' with the exact person that God desired for us to meet that day. They are blessed and so are we after this encounter.

An example of this principle from the word of God being demonstrated is when I was traveling and sharing my life with college students in a business university setting while in Kampala, Uganda. I had shared a few truths to this small group of Christian believers and then afterwards, I asked if anyone wanted me to pray for them. Five young adult students raised their hands and so I invited them to come to the front of the lecture room. One individual that I prayed for went down onto the floor under the powerful presence of the Lord. I continued to place my hand on him and intercede for a brief time. I asked him his name and fortunately, I could pronounce his first name. His last name was from the African dialect and was difficult for me to say correctly. Since it appeared to me that the Lord was touching him in an unusual manner that afternoon, I invited this young man and his friend to walk with me out to our transport vehicle and I prayed again for him and his friend to be blessed immensely.

I also encouraged this young man I'd just met to read the scriptures in the Book of Ephesians and then we parted company, but not before he requested to have my email address for future correspondence. A year later, I received a short message in which this same Ugandan student from the business college informed me that he was now preaching the gospel to people in his city. I was amazed and very thankful that I was part of this signifi- cant change for this young man from Kampala, Uganda. I felt as if this was what the vision about feeding His sheep meant and especially the last part of when they were crying out for the 'More' from God's Spirit and the true words of life. I believe that this young man had a divine encounter with Jesus, the Anointed One that day. I have continued to send my new friend from Kampala a few scriptures of truth to guide him in his walk with God. I even sent him a couple of the Youtube.com videos to watch which showed an anointed preacher sharing a vital message for anyone who wants to operate in the gifts of the Holy Spirit which are listed in 1 Corinthians 12 – 14. I rejoice in the goodness of God and I'm grateful that the Lord gave me spiritual insight from that vision so I could impart the 'More' of God's truth about spiritual gifts to this young man. He is now preaching the good news to people in Kampala.

This experience reminded me of the Samaritan woman at the well story. You may recall how Jesus talked with this woman in the Bible account. He gave her a word of knowledge as he listened to the Father's counsel about her many husbands. She was astounded by the fact that he even knew about the last man she wasn't married to at that time. she went back to her town to tell everyone who'd listen to her about this man who told her about her private life and that he could give her living waters so that she would not thirst again. Her life was changed dramatically that day because of a word of knowledge and truth from the Son of God; this one encounter with the Lord brought about her conversion. That same day she became an evangelist ready to share the good news with people in her hometown. My new friend from Uganda had also operated with a heart of an evangelist by sharing his testimony with people in his city of Kampala instead of just going out to get a job after college and only earning a living.

***

The day of my departure for Uganda had come at last. I was packed and ready for this new experience. I had my passport and my photo ID in a small wallet which was easy to access on each stop on this long journey. A friend's husband was driving me to the airport since she was on her way to Bethel in Redding, California. He was on time, and we made it to PDX with plenty of time to spare. After he had left to go back home, I learned from the airline clerk that I needed another piece of paper called a visa in order to enter Turkey. This first destination on my flight plan didn't require an extra visa the last time I flew to Israel and so I was shocked by her statement. I called him on his cell phone and asked him to drive over to my house and grab the hidden key from the back porch. We stayed in touch by cell phone as he went upstairs to locate a small piece of paper with a documented stamp which the officials in Istanbul had previously given me the year before. He found this small piece of paper and then drove back to PDX airport and all the while I was hoping to still be able to get on the plane before it left Oregon.

One part of me wasn't sure I should be still going to this foreign country especially after I saw a movie preview about the airport where I was heading to on the last leg of my journey. The title of this recent movie that had been playing on the theaters' big screen was called "Seven Days in Entebbe." I watched as the movie trailer gave the audience a preview of what had occurred for the thirty-nine hostages who were taken by radical militants and held captive in the Entebbe airport in Uganda. I jokingly asked my husband this question after the movie trailer ended, "Tell me again, why am I going to Entebbe? It seems like this country could be dangerous for tourist to visit." He smiled and then he asked me where I was supposed to travel to and the city in which I would be arriving. I replied that I was scheduled to land in Entebbe, Uganda on March 15th and by then I had to believe that the military police had everything under control in that African airport. Back then we had both smiled and I knew now that my husband would be praying for my safe arrival and time in the airport located in Entebbe, Africa.

As I stood by myself in the Portland Airport that all-important morning of my departure, I couldn't help but recall this dangerous story about the hostages in Africa. Here I was standing in the busy PDX airport wondering if I'd made a mistake in booking this flight to Uganda. Fifteen minutes later, I was standing at the airline counter listening to the ticket agent's as she gave me a disheartening message. I couldn't believe I was not going to be allowed to catch my flight at the last moment because of a missing document. I was very concerned that the airline personnel lady wouldn't let me load my suitcases and make it to the security checkpoint in time for my scheduled flight. I called my friend, Doug, to stop by my house, use my key to enter and locate my piece of paper from the trip to Istanbul airport. I paced back and forth as I waited to hear if he'd located this paperwork. At last, he rushed into the airport looking for me and we connected in the crowded lobby. He handed me the paperwork that had an official stamp from Turkey on it.

I hastily grabbed the handles of my two suitcases and made my way up to the counter for a second time that morning. The airline lady at the ticket counter looked at my small piece of paper and made a remark that perturbed me even more. She informed me that this document with my small black and white photo on the front was expired and therefore, it wouldn't work in Turkey. I couldn't believe what I was hearing at this moment. I asked her to talk to the other airline personnel lady standing nearby about this disconcerting problem. This more experienced employee asked me if I was intending to stay over for a few days in Istanbul. I replied that I had no intentions of leaving the Turkish airport or visiting this foreign country. It was only a short layover connection on my flight travels to Uganda. She informed the first ticket agent that I didn't need this paperwork/visa for my journey. I was so relieved to hear this good news.

The woman at the counter apologized to me and then loaded my luggage onto the scales, tagged it, and sent me on to security. I made it through this first checkpoint spot successfully and hurried to reach my final gate. I could relax and take a deep breath once I'd read the reader board saying this flight was still heading to San Francisco, California. My first two and a half hour layover happened around four p.m. in the San Francisco airport. I was waiting in line to get my boarding pass when I felt a strong impression to call my daughter, Sharon, and ask her to pray about something. After we had connected on the phone, I asked her to pray so I could understand what God was trying to get my attention about for my upcoming flights. While she was praying for me over the phone, I heard the Holy Spirit tell me I would be praying for a woman on the plane ride to Uganda. I thanked my daughter for supporting me in prayer and said goodbye.

The ticket agents finally boarded everyone in our line onto the Turkish airplane, but by this time it was an hour and thirty minutes late in leaving the USA. I couldn't help but wondered if I might miss my next connection flight in Istanbul. As I found my seat and got settled, I spoke a few words to the person sitting next to me who could understand a little of my English words. Then I pulled out my journal to write about my upsetting experience with the ticket clerk at PDX. It was very apparent to me that most of the people in this plane only spoke in their native Turkish language. Since no one on this plane would be able to understand my conversation, I decided to watch a couple of inflight movies for most of the trip.

This late departure from America meant my flight would be very late arriving in Turkey. Therefore, I was feeling anxious by the time the plane had finally landed and we exited the plane in Istanbul. Here I was now, standing by myself in the Turkish airport studying the reader board to determine my exact gate number. Feeling very much like a tourist and quite unfamiliar with where to go next, I happened to glance up to reader board one more time and saw two distinct, flashing words by my flight number, Boarding Now!! I grabbed my two suitcases and hurried through the crowded airport. As I raced down the terminal walkway, a wave of panic enveloped my emotions and so I whispered a quick prayer for help in this desperate situation. I didn't want to be left stranded in Turkey all alone and with nowhere to stay while I searched for another flight to Entebbe. I certainly didn't want to have to pay the added expense of a special flight to Africa if the plane had already departed from Turkey.

After running for nearly a mile with luggage in hand at this unfamiliar airport terminal, I finally reached the next area and managed to get through two more security stations. Feeling even more apprehensive, I asked the attendant if they'd ever held a plane because of a late passenger. The woman's reply to me was a flat, NO! Her negative response caused me to feel a great deal of concern as I raced onto my designated gate area. Once I had reached the appropriate gate, I went up to the counter and asked if the plane for Uganda had left yet. The airline employee said yes to my dismay. I groaned audibly and felt helpless at this moment. I couldn't believe I had missed my boarding opportunity and would be stuck here in a country where the people all around me only spoke in a foreign language which I did not understand at all.

Then two other English-speaking passengers approached the counter and asked the same question as I had. I could see that they were starting to get upset with the desk receptionist. One of the women asked a second question to the employee sitting behind the counter "Is there another plane available to us since the Turkish airline was extremely late leaving America?" This female employee standing behind the counter area replied with a yes and then she informed us that our plane we'd be going on was waiting to be boarded. It felt as if they had played a mean trick on us because we were foreigners. A wave of extreme relief washed over me as I sat down to relax and wait for our final boarding announcement. I found the only seat available next to an older woman whom I hoped could speak a little English. I asked her a question about her travels and discovered she spoke enough of the universal language to communicate with me. I began to ask her questions about her travels, and we enjoyed visiting with each other which helped the time passed quickly. Soon I was boarding another Turkish plane which would take me on to my destination.

As I buckled my seat belt in this plane leaving Istanbul, Turkey for Uganda, I found myself sitting next to an attractive African woman. I had overheard her talking in English with the American lady sitting on the other side of her and so I was delighted to be able to converse with them both. The Ugandan woman seemed friendly and so I started a conversation with her and the other lady. I asked her personal questions and she shared with me that she was a pediatrician doctor returning to Uganda after giving a series of lectures in America. During our conversation, I discovered that she was a Christian and a mother of four children. She told me her first name and then I learned that her father was considered by African culture to be a prince of his local tribe. This high position her father held in his community had given him a sense of entitlement and therefore, she told me her father had been allowed to propagate twenty-seven offspring in her country of Uganda. I was amazed to hear about this strange custom.

Towards the end of our flight, I started to wonder if this African woman sitting next to me on the plane was the person God had wanted me to pray for some hours earlier when I'd stood waiting in line at the ticket counter in the San Francisco airport. I asked her if there was anything specific, I could pray for her. She replied that there was a pressing concern on her heart for one of her grown sons. After she'd filled me in with the details, I began to pray for God's will to be accomplished for her adult son and his relationship with his girlfriend. She thanked me profusely. We ended our conversation to close our eyes and rest during our final flight time. As we were departing the plane, she thanked me again for caring about her family needs. We parted company and I followed the other passengers until I approached an enclosed booth where an African customs agent was waiting for travelers. This official informed me I needed to pay fifty dollars for a visa fee to be able to gain entrance into Uganda.

I was astounded to learn I had to pay this huge amount of money since neither of my contact friends in Kampala had informed me of this important detail.

Fortunately, my good friend had given me some cash to be used while I was staying in Uganda. Her generous monetary gift enabled me to pay the entrance fee, so I was allowed to enter this foreign country to share the Word of God with African college students. Next, I spent an hour filling out papers to locate my missing plastic tube which was filled with my artwork I'd planned to use in my teachings. By this time, I was beginning to feel the effects of my long journey and the lack of sleep. I decided to change into fresh, clean clothes in the restroom and then I found a place to sit to wait for my friend to arrive. It had been nearly six months since I'd left Israel with a desire to travel to Kampala, Uganda and now here I was standing in an airport in Entebbe. I watched many dark-skinned people pass by my table as I sat for hours waiting in the airport. I was beginning to feel slightly out of place there. I noticed a military guard standing next to the wide glass doors and he was holding a M16 rifle. I smiled over at him and began to relax slightly. A sense of joy began to seep into my heart as I became aware of the fact that I was here in the country of Uganda.

My tall African friend Marcus who is a businessman from Kampala, showed up at the airport to give me a ride back to the city. I learned as I waited for some time in the airport that the African time schedules are different than what I was used to in my American culture. There seems to be no worry or concerns about getting places on time, but instead people wait patiently for the other person to eventually arrive. This must be what folks call getting use to another country's way of doing things.

Once we'd put my two suitcases and the smaller bag into Marcus's vehicle, he took me to eat breakfast at a small restaurant place. My African friend was quite hungry and so he ordered a big meal. I only wanted to get a mango smoothie drink since I was feeling rather warm in this hot climate. He asked how my flight to Entebbe, Uganda went and so I shared with him some brief details about my journey. Then I spent the next hour asking him about his life. He informed that he'd worked for a big company for seven years. He had a college degree in engineering, and he liked what he'd been doing. However, three years ago, the executives in this business began to cut corners and do things he couldn't agree with. He shared with me that he was a man of integrity, and he could no longer work for this boss. Marcus decided to quit and eventually he began his own business in Kampala. Now as a business owner, my African friend supervises the construction of new homes, and he is doing quite well financially.

As of this week, my Ugandan friend, Marcus, is building his sixth house for a man who will pay him a total of $200, 000 for the finished work. He took me to view the job site and I observed the crew digging up the soil with large sharp digging tools. He told me that once they remove the excess dirt and can reach solid ground then he is able to bring in the cement loads to pour the foundation for the house. Besides being a building con-tractor, he also wants to start a car wash business this next year. His goal is to purchase some land at a rea-sonable price and then build the structure and purchase the necessary equipment for washing cars or small vans. I was impressed with his ability to run a construction crew and oversee the building of the cement foundation along with the entire construction of a completed house. I was shown one of the homes he'd built in a different city, and

I could tell it was done properly and to the satisfaction of the homeowner. I also saw the house he'd built for his mother and the second dwelling place which his family stays in whenever they come to visit the relatives who live in this quaint village on the outskirts of the larger city.

While we were traveling together, my friend, Marcus Maxwell, shared with me about his supervisor job. It involves running a crew of men and making sure they are building the new home correctly for the property owner. Since I was very interested in his line of work, I asked him to tell me more about his business ventures in Uganda.

"Marcus, as far as the next venture, this car wash idea, have you prayed about starting this new business in Kampala?" I asked my friend.

"Yes, Momma', I have prayed about this new idea with my wife." He replied.

He said that he'd asked the Holy Spirit of God to show him if he should tackle this next plan. The answer he heard was YES. So, he is in the process of acquiring a small plot of land from a man who owns the property just outside of Kampala. I was glad to hear this and told him I'd pray for the car wash company to be successful and profitable. Then I asked my business friend to tell me how he had become successful. He told me that in Uganda the principles of prosperity are like those of America.

Marcus mentioned to me that the first key to being successful in business was to honor God and to acknowledge that it was the Lord who caused him to do well in his business dealings. The second factor was to have a righteous, godly character. The third important aspect of becoming a successful person was to be a person of integrity. As an example, he referred to a company which he'd worked for in the past where the employer had not been operating within the guidelines of his own Christian values and ethics. He'd decided to quit that previous job and fortunately, God took care of his family during these lean years. I admired what he had done to maintain his work ethics despite the challenges he'd faced. He then informed me that the final aspect of being a successful person involved being a hard, diligent worker. He wanted to be known as a man who did his job with a spirit of excellence. My friend from Uganda said that he didn't have a website to advertise his construction business or his capabilities. He relies on other people's referrals from his previous work and because he does excellent work and treats his men well, he is busy building new homes all year long.

After sharing the reason behind how he'd become a successful businessman, Marcus continued sharing with me about an experience from the past year. He'd been building someone a new home when the individual who'd hired him began to show that he wasn't acting trustworthy during the construction project. In fact, the Lord had even given my tall African friend a dream one night to be careful and to avoid doing business with this person. However, my friend felt obligated to finish the house for this client. Some weeks later, this person informed him that he couldn't pay for the building work that month. My Ugandan friend then prayed and decided to confront this individual. Eventually, this man paid him some of the cost of the work on that house and then Marcus told me that he chose to stop working on the man's housing project.

Another experience he wanted to share with me as we rode around town was about his rental properties in Kampala. Here is his story in his own words to me.

"My wonderful American 'Momma', I owned property and houses which I rented out to tenants. One of my original renters was dishonest and he tried to cheat me out of two month's rent money. This man bribed the police officer to arrest me. The officer took this man's bribery money and showed up at my house to take me into custody and then they placed me in a cell at the local jail in Kampala." He explained.

I learned that my friend, Marcus, that he was forced to stay there for two and a half hours. His wife was worried and very upset about their future. He continued telling me his story.

"I sat there in the cold, ugly jail cell and prayed to the Lord to rescue me. I needed God's help to be set free from this man's false witness." He exclaimed. "At last, the police sergeant arrived finally and asked me some questions about the other person's accusations. I soon discovered that this officer expected me to be afraid and to pay him even more money in order to get out of jail." Marcus stated.

As I listened to my friend's sad story, I wondered what was going to be the outcome of this tale of woe. My son, Jonathan, has told me about the police bribery that occurs in Surabaya, Indonesia where he lived for twelve years. I believe this type of bribery to police officers also happens to people who visit certain providences in Mexico as well. Marcus continued to share his story with me as I listened intently.

"I informed this other officer that I was a Christian man. I had done nothing wrong and was being falsely accused so I refused to pay the bribe money in order to be released from jail. The chief officer agreed with my statements and then he released me from the jail cell. Thankfully, I was allowed to return home to my wife and children." He exclaimed.

I was happy to hear that Marcus's story had ended so well, and he was allowed to go home to his family and business finally. It seemed that this man of courage and integrity had been protected by divine Providence that day. I am glad to call him my good friend from Uganda. I told this couple from Kampala, Uganda that they were always welcome to come and visit us in America if they ever decided to make the trip to the Pacific Northwest. I'm sure they'd want to first stop in New York City to see our beautiful statue of Liberty standing so regal and inviting in the harbor waters on the east coast. If they do come to America someday, I can almost picture them walking hand in hand down the busy streets of the Big Apple' while looking up at the tall skyscrapers and the newly built Freedom Tower which rises to an elegant, tri-angular peak above the city as a majestic memorial to the many lives lost during that fateful day of the September 11th attack. Then, I suppose they might hurry on their way to find the best pizza ever made on the streets of Manhattan before they need to board a plane and fly across the United States to stay with us in our simple country home. I am happy that we are friends for life and we still stay in touch through the internet via emails!

Our friendship has crossed international boundaries because of our love for the Savior. If God asks me to travel a second time to Kampala, Uganda to share His love with the people of this land then I will go. My friend from Africa has told me that I will always have a place to stay with him and his family in Uganda when I return for another visit. He even mentioned that he would build his wife a bigger house someday soon and it would have indoor plumbing. I hope so because they are outgrowing the smaller dwelling place. They have three girls and a live-in-nanny helper which made it rather crowded.

CHAPTER THIRTY-EIGHT

To further explain what I was learning about the African culture, I must share my experience at a restaurant. My Ugandan friend, Pastor Paul and his wife wanted me to stay a few days with them and so I did. The next day, they drove me to the restaurant for breakfast. We were to meet his good friend, Marcus, who had planned to join us there. Eventually, Marcus arrived and ordered his breakfast meal. Then sometime later my third contact friend arrived and ordered his meal. I thought it was odd that Pastor Paul and his wife weren't upset with this person's obvious tardiness or possibly they'd managed to hide their annoyance with him. I found this one leader's lack of punctuality to be disconcerting and I was embarrassed that my friends had to wait so long for him to arrive.

While waiting for him to show up at the restaurant, I'd managed to order coffee, toast, scrambled eggs and hash browns with a side of salsa from the menu. However, when my plate of food arrived in front of me, I couldn't identify the mixture of colorful items cooked into my eggs. In fact, I didn't even recognize what the food item on my plate was for sure. To my dismay, I discovered that the waitress had misunderstood my request for salsa on the side and the cook had added the salsa ingredients into my cooked eggs instead of next to the cooked eggs. This was not to my liking, but I didn't want to offend my new friends or the cook from this restaurant in Kampala, so I attempted to eat most of the food on my plate. Thus, began my third day in Uganda.

The Ugandan youth leader finally arrived forty minutes later to the restaurant. He sat down across from me at the table as if nothing was wrong. Two weeks before my arrival in Kampala, I had introduced this man to my two friends by giving him their phone numbers in the hopes that this action would help me facilitate my arrival and my stay in the city of Kampala. Now he was imposing on their good nature by spending a great deal of time on his cell phone which I thought was a bit rude. Once he'd finished his phone conversation, he then proceeded to inform my two African friends that he could not provide me with good accommodations for my first week here in Kampala. Therefore, I was told I needed to stay with Pastor Paul and his family for the first week and then again for the second week. Fortunately, they were able to offer me a lodging arrangement and a couple of meals each day for that first week in Kampala. I was extremely grateful for their generosity and hospitality in this matter. My Ugandan friend named Marcus was quite glad to learn of this change in my plans. Now I would be staying with his family for five days during the second week of my visit to Kampala. I would learn later that he had made good plans for me, and he was excited to have me around for even more days than at first. So, the Lord worked out my schedule to be better than was originally set up by that other leader.

After our breakfast meal was finished, I went with this other leader and his secretary/ assistant who spoke some English. While this busy man attended a meeting for the next three hours, his assistant and I waited and waited in the courtyard behind the same restaurant. It was in this courtyard that I took walks and prayed about what I was to share with two different university student groups in the afternoon. This African leader had not communicated properly to me about what I was going to be doing after our breakfast meal and so the two folders, containing my three separate messages all typed and ready to share with the college students were back at Pastor Paul's house. To my dismay, here I was now wondering as to what to share with the first group of college nursing students in about one hour.

I walked and prayed as I put this problem into the Lord's hands. God impressed upon me to share a testimony about my daughters' miraculous healing and deliverance from a deadly battle with cancer to the group of nursing students. I managed to share about the different medical terms and situations that had occurred that first week for my sick daughter which I hoped these nursing students could relate to during my talk. Afterwards I asked for show of hands from those students who desired prayer. At least seven hands went up and so I made my way around the room to connect with each person. I prayed for them as God showed me and trusted that I was a blessing to everyone. The international student leader who had arranged the meeting at this university later mentioned that my testimony was very powerful and impacting for these medical students.

In the evening I was scheduled to speak to another group of college students. This time I shared about finding your true destiny as you learn to wait upon the Lord and turn to the scriptures which give us godly wisdom. I asked the students this question in the beginning. Do any of you students know what your purpose in life might involve besides finding a good job? What is it that you did as a young boy or girl that made you happy? As I gave them a moment to think about this question, I also gave them an example by explaining about my own passion as a girl which was to write and to draw or paint. I pointed out to the group that I also liked learning new things and reading books. I suppose that is why eventually I became a reading teacher which was very rewarding for me. Oftentimes, we have a seed planted within our soul that needs watering and sunlight to grow and flourish until we can recognize our true potential.

I mentioned to my listeners that day that you might like to coach a sport or help young people discover their own interest or gifting. If you like to draw or paint as I like to do, then I told them that they might consider pursuing a job in the creative arts field. I asked my audience this: What is your passion and are you working towards accomplishing this goal. God gave us a divine design when he created us, and he wants you and I to find our true purpose and destiny in this world. Sometimes we need his help to unlock the door to these dreams. I enjoyed sharing my heart and visions with these Ugandan students.

That evening after I'd finished sharing a few biblical truths with the group, I gave the university students an opportunity to receive prayer at the end of my talk. Almost eight to nine hands went up in this group of young adults. The first individual I talked with said his name was Samuel. I mentioned that this was one of the names which the Lord had previously given to me to record in my prayer notebook back home in the states. I gave this student a word of knowledge, blessed him, and then continued to pray for the other students. A few students asked me for my email address in order to further correspond with me and I wrote this out for them. Before heading outside of the building, I noticed one African girl wearing glasses who had been watching me closely. I approached her and asked about her name; she replied that her name was Grace. I mentioned that my daughter's middle name was Grace too and this caused her to smile. I mentioned that she had a beautiful name and then I proceeded to pray God's will and favor for her. She thanked me and I headed out the door of this simple, wooden structure where I met another student named Peter and he asked me to pray a blessing over his life too.

***

During my visit in Africa, I was beginning to comprehend that the Ugandan people had been given English first names because of the British influence in this region. I had struggled in being able to pronounce their difficult African last names during my travels so far. I was extremely grateful for the fact that most folks here in Kampala had a first name like many Americans and that I could pronounce their names. From that point on, I started thanking the British colonists so many decades before this for insisting the Ugandan people named their children with an English first name. I was able to relate much better with the people when I could pronounce their first names so easily.

The second cultural difference I noticed while staying in Kampala was the fact that every home and business was surrounded by a six-foot-high plaster wall. Along the entire top section of the surrounding wall structure of each home, the owner had placed a twisted section of barb wire as an added measure of protection from intruders. This unfamiliar sight disturbed me slightly and yet, I came to accept this strange sight as a necessary means of protection for these African families. Most homes in the area were protected like this to prevent a thief from entering their compound with the intent to rob their homes. I came to the realization that there must've been some awful significant robberies in the past years which had warranted this extreme method of protection. I had seen this same kind of high plaster walls around homes in the city of Tulincingo in Central Mexico while we were there for my son's wedding. The one difference in these two countries style of protection was that Mexican homeowners didn't use the barb wire at the top of their surrounding wall structures.

Another big difference between Americans and the citizens of Uganda was this: People in America must be very vigilant and careful to always keep their young children nearby while the children in Uganda appear to be rather safe from any kind of abduction or harm. I asked my friends, Paul and his wife about this situation one day as we ate our meal in a nice restaurant. I was astonished to see their young seventeen-month-old boy freely wandering in and out of this eating establishment. I couldn't understand why they weren't the least bit concerned about his wandering in and out of the restaurant. In fact, they didn't get up and go retrieve this youngster as he wandered out the door. They told me that children were normally safe from harm in Kampala and plus, they had never heard of any child being taken from their parents. Here in America, parents need to be cautious and ever present to protect young children from sex predators or from men who try to abduct young kids. In the states, people must also guard their children from wicked individuals who attempt to grab a child and then sell the kid for gain on the human sex trafficking market. I was amazed to see youngsters wandering about the streets in Kampala and in the small country villages with just a brother or sister nearby and no parent in sight. I wish that children living in our country were safe to walk to school and home again without being molested by some depraved individual. I am amazed by the fact that children in Uganda are much safer on the streets of Kampala than our American children.

***

The last place I went with this African youth leader after speaking at four African colleges, was a small indigenous church group in the foothills of Kampala. I wasn't sure of what to expect since this leader hadn't communicated anything to me on our drive through the hills to reach our destination. In fact, he'd given me very little information about each of my speaking engagements to this point. It seemed like he was more concerned with his upcoming plans to travel to another country and the much-needed funds than he was in facilitating my visit properly. When he continued to share his money troubles with me while we drove to different places, I became suspicious of his real motive for inviting me to come here to speak in Kampala. I'd already given him one hundred dollars in the beginning to bless him and yet, he was still presenting me with reasons I might want to donate to worthy causes in his district. Something seemed to be wrong and yet, I was still looking forward to meeting these folks in the church called Family Life Ministries. We continued up a hill with its bumpy road until he'd located a parking spot for his car and then we got out and walked the remainder of the way. Upon reaching the small building, I heard people inside the church praying in their Ugandan language and so I stood near the back door and prayed softly for guidance.

A short time later, one person approached me and motioned for me to follow him to sit in the front of the church. Apparently, my youth leader friend had informed them of my arrival and since I was the only white American woman in the place it was easy for them to spot me. So here I was in this small African church waiting for the service to begin when a young adult worship leader came forward and began to pour his heart out in song. The music was a catchy, lilting tune so I stood to join in the time of worship with my hands extended towards heaven. The singing progressed until I felt the presence of God pour down over me like warm, thick honey. At this moment I was wishing I'd brought my phone to record the music and the African singing. I wanted to bring this beautiful experience and the amazing music back with me to share with my family. The church was thick with the divine presence of God.

Once the worship service ended, the worship leader introduced me to congregation. Our friend is here to share with us, and she is from America the man announced to everyone. I proceeded to make my way up to the platform. Then as I turned around to face the group, I was surprised to see that more people had come into the service by this time. I grabbed the microphone and began to share my message which included this key-note scripture, "I called upon the Lord in distress: the Lord answered me and set me in a large place." (Psalm 118: 5) I had located this verse earlier in the week while asking God to help me to know what all to share of my life struggles with this congregation. I had decided to be transparent about some aspects of my own childhood abuse in the hope that possibly someone might be able to identify with my life story. They all listened intently as I talked about living with an angry parent who had caused me a great deal of pain and anguish. I knew God was ministering to some of the women in this congregation at this point and then the message changed abruptly. I felt God was redirecting me to exhort the congregation to think beyond their own borders by sending missionaries from Kampala to another nation.

The next thing I knew I was preaching on the verse found in the Bible which spoke of the ancient Hebrew priests who had made special offerings for their country-men. I spoke an exhortation to this African community of believers in reference to the scripture which points out how the Hebrew people were called this, "But ye are a Chosen Race, a royal Priesthood, a Holy Nation, a People for God's own possession, so that you may pro-claim the excellencies of Him who has called you out of darkness into His marvelous light;..." (1 Peter 2: 9) In other words, God was showing me to encourage these folks to become more than just a body of believers sitting in church pews. He was speaking through me to exhort them to start seeing themselves in a similar light as holy priests, but in a different way. They can become modern-day priests who are called to intercede more diligently for their church and their nation of Uganda. I pointed out that they were not to see themselves as merely as the ancient priests who carried a sensor filled with incense going into the ancient sanctuary or holy of holies, but rather to start thinking of themselves as royal priests involved in the New Testament era who are being commissioned by God to pray even more fervently for others. They can intercede more specifically and with the influence of the Holy Spirit's guidance for others in their church, their city, and for their Ugandan leaders. This new idea of the congregation thinking to bring heaven down to earth in an impacting way could be seen as their calling and prayer ministry. I believe God will bless this group of believers when they lay hold of this new identity as royal, anointed prayer warriors.

One young man named Andrew came up to talk with me when I'd finished speaking and praying for the people there. He thanked me for sharing this new insight with him. He was so excited by the message that he even wanted to give me money and I wasn't sure whether to accept it. I chose to receive his gift graciously and then I later handed it to a crippled man who needed the twenty dollars more than me. My heart's desire was to be a blessing wherever I shared God's word and I will always remember Andrew's heartfelt appreciation and the monetary gift. He is in my prayers often as I recall his sincere desire to be a man of intercession for his church leaders and for the people of Kampala. At the end of my message, I asked if there was anyone who desired prayer for their life. I was delighted when at least eight people raised their hands for prayer and came up to form a line in front of me. I recall quietly asking God to guide me in ministering to their individual needs as I felt inadequate at that moment.

A young adult woman began to cry as I was praying for her. It was as if her heart was breaking with too much hurt and disappointments. I wiped her tears with the end piece of my white cotton blouse since it was unbuttoned, and I'd only wore it as a cover up over my sun dress in order hide my shoulders while preaching that evening. After ministering to this woman, I prayed for the other people standing in the line as the Lord led me. Then towards the end of the line of people in front of me, I saw a nicely dressed tall woman waiting to share her prayer request with me. I had noticed her during my time of speaking earlier and had hoped to meet with her at the conclusion of my preaching. I was excited to pray for her and so I encouraged her to express her need to me. She spoke in a quiet voice and asked me to pray for God to heal the pain she was having in her breast area. The thought that went through my mind at that moment was that this woman didn't have money to go into a specialist if it turned out to be cancer. I felt a great compassion for her situation and so I spoke healing and peace upon her body, and I commanded the pain and infirmity to leave her chest area. Then I petitioned the entire church to extend their hands of faith towards this woman named

Charlotte since I believe that her condition could possibly require that the church friends continue to prevail in a greater prayer effort. After praying for each person in the line, I smiled at the congregation and thanked them for letting me come and share my story with them.

Then while I was still standing amid this group of Africans, I recalled an important word of knowledge and a particular name which I had recorded in my notebook back home in the states. I asked if there was anyone in the congregation whose name began with the letter H. No one responded to my examples of either 'Hank or Harold' names, so I asked if anyone had ever been called "Handsome" in their lifetime. That was when a man in the front row called out that their worship leader standing right behind me had a name which began with the letter H'. I turned around to see a very handsome young adult male smiling back at me. This African individual told me his name was Habit. I smiled back to him and asked if I could give him a nickname before praying for him. I paused briefly and then I addressed him with one of my favorite Jewish names which is the name, 'Israel'. He said yes to my new nickname of Israel and then I proceeded to pray over Habit ('Israel') for God's rich blessings, favor, and anointing to be deposited within his soul and upon his thought life from this time forth.

Minutes later, this same young adult worship leader named Habit called a man named Brian up to the front of the church and began to speak life and blessings over him. God was empowering him right before my eyes. It was a joy to behold the anointing and power of the Holy Spirit flowing through this young adult leader as he ministered God's prophetic insight to the other person. I suddenly realized that this had been a divine appointment from the Lord. I remembered another word of knowledge which had come into my spirit some months before while in prayer as I prepared for this upcoming trip to Kampala. I'd been impressed by the Spirit that I would meet a leader and when I prayed for this person, God would cause this person to become a better and wiser leader. In my mind, I had anticipated that this individual would be a political person or leader of a big important church. It seemed that God had a different plan which totally took me by complete surprise that evening. This young adult worship leader of a rather small church in the foothills of Kampala was the person I was to pray for to have more success and wisdom in his future ministry in the land of Uganda. I even asked Habit if he minded if I gave him a special nickname of 'Israel since it seemed to fit this young leader; he replied with a "Yes, Momma Cathy, that would be fine with me!" This opportunity to minister to a humble, receptive group of believers in a small, unnoticed church in the hills of Kampala was another highlight of my trip. I truly believe that God has a magnificent and powerful plan for these Ugandan believers and the church called Family Life Ministries in Kampala. I shall pray as often as I remember these people and I will ask the Lord to richly bless this congregation and its leaders.

CHAPTER THIRTY-NINE

T he second week of my stay in Kampala, I recon-
nected with my business friend, Marcus. I'd met
him the year before when we both stayed in Israel
at the International House of Prayer conference. This tall
African businessman has a demanding job as a building
contractor where he supervises a large work crew in the
construction of new homes in his area. After we connected that Sunday morning, he took me on a four-hour
bus ride from Kampala to a smaller city to stay in his
aunt's lovely home. As the bus travelled down the only
paved road leading west from Kampala, we passed lush
green fields and plentiful amounts of tall trees on our
journey to a different city. There were tropical trees heavily laden down with green plantain bananas growing by
the roadside for miles and miles. As I viewed the scenery
through the bus window, I felt as if I was traveling in my
home state of Washington. The two months of waiting
and preparing for this trip to Africa had been spent in
praying for the people and for a plenteous amount of rain
to fall upon what I believed was a dry, parched land in
Africa. I did not know that the country of Uganda was a
tropical climate saturated with plenty of abundant rainfall during its monsoon season. I decided to quit praying

for rain to fall in Kampala. However, later towards the end of that week, we would experience a torrential rainfall that saturated the landscape thoroughly. You couldn't go outside until the downpour had stopped. After the rain had stopped falling around us, the hot sun came out to dry the red soil once again.

Once we'd reached our new destination, we piled out of the crowded transit bus, grabbed our bags and my extra gear and looked for another means of transportation. Eager men converged upon us wanting to offer their services to a female foreigner who they thought was wealthy and ignorant of their ways. He expertly avoided them and transferred everything onto two motorbikes driven by dark-skinned men who he normally did business within this city. The locals called this mode of transportation, "Bouda, Bouda". I asked my friend to take a snapshot of me sitting behind the driver of this motorbike so I could send it home to my children to enjoy. Of course, they all loved seeing me being so adventurous, but my son sent me an email message insisting that I wear a proper helmet for my next ride. I tried to tell my family members back in the states that the African motorbikes usually only went about twenty or thirty miles per hour on the bumpy dirt roads and I felt quite safe on them. I really was looking forward to riding one more time on another African motorbike if I didn't have to hold onto any cumbersome luggage.

My friend carried my suitcase and bags for me while I thanked my driver. As I followed my good friend, I had to bend down and go through a short doorway which was located on one side of a metal gate. After going through the small door, I found myself standing in the courtyard of his aunt's property. Her house was made of plaster walls and red tile roofing material. The windows contained iron bars to prevent thieves from being able to break into the home. The floors were all tile, and this made it easier to sweep and wash for the housekeeper each week.

As I entered the aunt's kitchen, I was introduced to the housekeeper lady who was busy at work washing dishes and then the one aunt took me to find my bedroom. In this guest bedroom there was a large four poster bed which had a wall of sheer netting, and this curtain surrounded the entire bed structure to prevent pesky mosquitoes from inhabiting one's nightly rest. This house had indoor plumbing for which I was extremely grateful. I had brought on this trip a recently purchased hot water percolator since I needed to be able to boil hot water and then pour it into my travel French press coffee maker. After getting situated in my new bedroom, I chatted with the aunt who taught in the secondary school. She was delightful woman and anxious to take good care of us while we stayed in her city.

Later, I met Marcus's other gracious aunt whose home we were staying in now. She was well-dressed lady of great distinction in this thriving city. At our first meeting, I noticed how she carried herself with a regal, dignified manner. The following day as we sat together for breakfast, I learned that she was not only a woman of importance and wealth, but she also was friendly and easy to talk to. After our healthy meal, my tall friend left for his job site, and I settled in to make some hot Chai tea and read a fiction book in my bedroom. One hour later, I watched from the front porch of her beautiful home as my friend's aunt climbed into the back seat of her new Toyota land rover vehicle since she planned to shop in the town. The African chauffeur started the car and drove out of the gate towards town. She had a few errands to take care and needed to stop by the bank afterwards and so I had a quiet day to myself. That evening I was introduced to Marcus Maxwell's good friends who had stopped by after their work ended. My Ugandan friend had asked the doctor to come by and give him some pain pills for his swollen toe. He had injured his foot that very morning and it looked terrible. I was glad that my tall African friend had some medication to help with the constant pain in his foot. I felt comfortable around his doctor friend and his sweet wife, and I really enjoyed getting to know this couple. I learned from them that Marcus had built their new home two years prior, and I told them I was hoping someday to have a chance to see one of his finished house buildings while visiting Uganda.

The next day, my Ugandan friend sent me a phone text asking if I would mind riding over to visit with his good friend the doctor and seeing their new home which he'd built the year before. I learned from my African friend that they were hoping I'd be willing to pray over them as a couple. I replied in my text message, yes, certainly and then I waited for his friend to come and pick me up in his vehicle. That evening I had a nice meal of cooked rice, bread, and carrots with this family. The doctor's wife had hired two young teenage girls to help nanny her children while she was away at work at the bank each day. They seemed to be very nice teenagers and quite capable of watching the petite, three-year-old girl named Susan (not her real name).

While I was talking with this family, I recalled getting the name of Susan and writing it down in my prayer notebook back in the states before leaving for Uganda. I realized that I was to pray over this child first. I blessed this little girl and then prayed for her two brothers. I could sense that this was a godly family as I observed their interactions. After the children were all settled into their beds, this gracious couple came into the living room and sat together on their sofa while I shared the words of knowledge that the Holy Spirit had given to me for them during my prayer time that afternoon. This is part of the word I shared with the doctor. *You have been a doctor who heals the body and now your Father God desires for you to also bring healing to a person's wounded soul as well.* I left the piece of paper with the words of knowledge with this man and encouraged him and his wife to begin to declare the God–given promises over their lives.

Then while I was praying for the doctor's wife, I sensed that she was struggling with a burden, so I asked her if there was anything bothering her lately. She responded with a yes and that she had been burdened and stressed with her job at the bank. Then her husband and I prayed for her once more. On the ride back to the aunt's house, the doctor confided to me that his wife had lost relatives some years ago. Her two parents had been killed when she was a youth and she'd also lost a sibling too. I encouraged the doctor to begin to pray God's healing touch for his first patient, his dear wife, who must have been suffering for a long time from the loss of her dear family members. I was delighted to get to know this wonderful couple and to be asked to pray for their entire family. I was also taken on a quick tour of their house which my good friend, Marcus, had built for his friends. My African friend is an excellent supervisor and builder. I would certainly recommend him as a trustworthy, dependable contractor to anyone in the states because he's a man of integrity. He is a diligent and conscientious businessman who has become quite successful, and I am very proud of him.

On the next day, which was Tuesday, Marcus's aunt stayed home for a while to chat with me. I began to sense that she had a story to tell the world and so I asked if I could interview her and use her story in my book. This stately woman thought about my request and then she replied with a yes. I excused myself for a moment and hurried back to my bedroom to retrieve my journal book so I could record her statements. This is their true story. Before she met and married her husband, he had studied to become a doctor in Uganda. Once the president of Uganda, Idi Amin, took office in the large city of Kampala, he required her husband to come work for him and care for the presidential soldiers. Eventually, because this president was illiterate and insecure, he began to either threaten or kill people who made him feel less than a capable or intelligent person. At one point, her husband had begun to feel like he was in danger of being disposed of by this tyrant and so he sought to find a means of escape from this malicious, unpredictable dictator. She shared with me the back story of her late husband. His father had been converted to Christianity by the British missionaries from the Anglican fellowship. As an adult this young man had travelled on foot to start churches in eastern Uganda in the late 1950s. He was instrumental in establishing five churches to the various tribal communities of Pallisa, Comme, Kapchorwo, and Surotck. This God-fearing father had always taught him about looking to God for guidance as he was growing up. As a young adult, he'd decided to pray about an important decision and finally he chose to flee his beloved country of Uganda. He flew to America and started his medical practice in the city of Chicago, Illinois.

He married a woman in America while he was working as a doctor there. He and his wife raised their children in the states. About twenty years later, this marriage dissolved, and he decided it was safe for him to return to Uganda. Upon his return he met and married this woman, and they have one lovely daughter. A few years later, her husband was elected to sit in the ninth parliament for Uganda for fifteen years and he was known by many as a 'nation builder' from 1972 to 1982. I asked my new friend during our interview what this phrase meant, and she remarked that her husband had been elected by the people to be a minister of health and his goal was to improve the state of health for the Ugandan people. He had built schools, some churches, and established many decent hospitals while serving in parliament.

Earlier that morning I had taken photos of the framed pictures of this Ugandan family and then later that afternoon I learned that Marcus's aunt had served for one year in the ninth parliament office as well. I asked this new African friend who were the people in the other photos hanging on her wall. She pointed out her late husband in the photo who was given a position in parliament and another photo of him sitting with a political man of importance. Once again, I was greatly impressed with this woman and her life there in northern Uganda. The most enjoyable part of our week together was when she invited me to sit down with her sister and niece to pray together. I was thrilled to join in with these wonderful Ugandan women as we made our prayer requests to heaven. Then I shared a need about my young grandson who was having surgery on his two legs that next day in a Shriners Hospital back in America. I appreciated their prayers of faith for a divine healing of his leg problems since he'd been born with an inability to walk normally or even run properly. I shall continue to believe God to completely heal his disability to the point that he can walk and run without stumbling constantly due to very tight leg muscles constriction.

The following morning this gracious African woman sat with me as we drank hot tea and visited once again in her large pallor/sitting room. She began to share her story of her struggles in obtaining a university degree in her early twenties. In the late 1990s she was attending a boarding school while she studied in her third year of high school. One of her roommates contracted tuberculosis and this family kept her disease a secret from the others. Since this sickness of the lungs was never disclosed to the headmaster of the school, this ill person was not quarantined from the other girls. A few weeks later, this woman and her other roommate began coughing and spitting up blood and phlegm. She informed me that she had to leave school and remain at home for eighteen months.

As the long months of recovery had slowly passed by, my friend's aunt realized she needed to do something useful with her life. She began studying to become a primary teacher since she had begun to feel better after taking the doctors medicine that year. She eventually graduated and was hired to be a demonstration teacher for two years where she trained new recruits how to be better teachers. Later, she moved to find a small apartment in city of Kampala where she taught in the primary school there. During this time, she was still weak, having chest pains, and coughing. The doctor took x-rays of her lungs and didn't know what else to do for her and she continued to struggle health wise. In 1993, Marcus's aunt volunteered to help the Red Cross International group for nearly three years. The nurses allowed her to travel on a weekend to northern Uganda some two hundred and fifty miles by truck to aid the war victims. She also received her tutor license and despite her illness she started tutoring young teachers.

In 1998, she went to a tent revival meeting to hear this pastor preach a message to the crowd. She believed God would heal her body from this tuberculosis disease and so she rode in a taxi to reach the meeting that night. The leader prayed for the large group of people that day, September 17[th.] She mentioned that even though she was standing in the back of this big meeting, she'd felt a unique coolness come over her entire body starting from top of her head and on downward. That was the moment she knew that God had healed her weakened lungs and delivered her from this dreadful disease. After the service ended, she decided to become a Christian believer when the preacher called out to the crowd of people to come forward and receive the gift of eternal life and salvation through Jesus. She was dramatically changed that night and has walked faithfully with the Lord since that experience. It is the year 2018 now, and she is healthy and strong fifty-eight-year-old woman still living in this city. I can attest to this true story since I'd met her personally. Here I was sitting across from this wonderful Ugandan woman in her lovely home writing down all these details of her amazing life in my journal which I'd planned to take back to America.

At the end of this week, my Ugandan friend, Marcus Maxwell, finished supervising his work crew on that job site. He informed me of his plans to leave that afternoon and mentioned that I should finish packing my luggage. He needed to head back to Kampala and so he called the two men who owned the motorbike service to come pick us up within the hour. When the bikes arrived at the front of this woman's home, they knocked on the metal door at the front gate. My tall, gentle friend carried my two suitcases, my hot water percolator, and my pillow outside for me. Then we climbed onto the motor bikes to ride back into the center of the town to locate a large transit bus once again. For the next two days, I stayed with Marcus and his family as well as their live-in nanny/housekeeper gal in a small house. Once again, I slept in a comfortable bed surrounded by mosquito netting and listened to their watch dog barking at any noise or movement during the nighttime. I was greeted early in the morning by a neighbor's noisy rooster crowing loudly at six o'clock in the morning. I asked my good friend why he chose to have a noisy dog for security measures when their property was encircled with tall walls and barbed wire attached securely to the top section of his walls. His response was that it gave him an extra security defense for when he was out of town on the new job sites. I could understand his reasoning and yet, I was starting to feel a little bit homesick for my own home and my family by my sixteenth day in Uganda.

During the long drive on bumpy, red clay roads to church on the following Sunday, I took pictures of the small shacks and food stands which lined the roadway everywhere. It seemed that everywhere I looked I saw hundreds of people walking or riding on motorbikes in the city of Kampala. As we drove down the main road, I also saw many men and women with nothing to do as they sat in front of their small clothing shops. Most of the women sold fruit or vegetables in their tiny wooden shops. As our car turned down another dirt road, I saw even more small shanty-like huts and food stands with people standing in the doorway or sitting out front on short wooden chairs. They acted like there was nothing to do but to sit and watch the traffic passed by. They seemed to be waiting for customers to come and buy some tomatoes or green plantain bananas from their food stands. There were always plenty of little children playing on the ground in this densely populated town of Kampala. Towards the downtown area of this city there were hundreds of people jostling and moving in a steady stream going somewhere or selling something. There were plenty of peddlers wanting to sell their cheap wares on the streets as we drove past them. I felt a sense of sadness for the poverty of this land. I have come to love the people in Uganda and my hope is that the leaders will use their government funds to take better care of the people in this region. They deserve to have more paved roads to travel on at least. The sad situation about the youth of this country is that if the parents don't have the money to pay for their high school education or the boarding school fees then that student is not able to be enrolled in school for that year. To me this is unthinkable. There is something wrong with this system. In America, our children are given a free education up until college age.

I had learned from Pastor Paul, that when the leader, Idi Amin, was president he had cursed the people and leaders of Israel. In the Old Testament, it says that God will bless those who bless his chosen people, the Jewish nation, and He will curse those who blatantly curse the people of Israel. "And I will bless those who bless you and curse those who curse you, and all the families of the earth will be blessed through you." (Genesis 12:3) With my own eyes I have seen the land of Uganda and its African people who are still living under a curse of poverty, economic lack, and an ever-increasing threat of overpopulation. It appears that there is little hope that things will change in this land. My prayer for their recent Ugandan president is that he will work to bring about a better economy to Uganda, to bless the people of Israel, and to point people back to honoring God as a nation. I am standing in the gap to intercede for the prosperity and peace of this African nation and its many people.

CHAPTER FORTY

During my previous travels to the rural village area with my businessman friend, I was blessed to stay with his parents who lived in a small village some twenty-five miles away from the city. His relatives were extremely gracious and respectful to me, and it seemed that they desired to treat me as royalty while in their country. When I was introduced to Marcus's grandmother living in the village, she was surrounded by her young grandchildren as they played in the red clay dirt. She was at least eighty years old and slightly crippled in one leg, but she slowly made her way over to me and bowed on one knee. The next day when my friend introduced me to his third auntie and her daughter, these two women also knelt on one knee and extended their hand to me in an act of respect. At first, I was surprised and taken back by this African custom of a female bending her knee in homage to a foreigner. I began to surmise that when the British colonists arrived in this country about two hundred years ago, they must've taught the people to do bending of a knee to show respect for a white person. I was amazed at how some Ugandan folks still to this day will bow and treat foreigners with a gracious kind of respect.

My Ugandan friend then introduced me to his tall mother and his other Auntie that evening. These women also bowed down on one knee and extended their left arm in greeting. I was then shown inside of the house that he'd built for his parent. This brick house had three bedrooms, a living room, and a storage area. There was another smaller out-building where his mother cooked the dinner meal over a wood fire each night. I watched as she had to keep placing kindling wood on the fire to cook the water and chicken meat. An hour later, we sat in her front room area to eat a substantial meal of chicken, rice, Irish potatoes, and maize/ corn. I was grateful for their generous hospitality and once again my friend readied my room by hanging up this see-through, lightweight mosquito netting around my entire bed frame to protect me from insect bites. I was very grateful to have this extra protection even though I'd made sure to have my vaccinations against malaria and yellow fever before leaving the states.

The next morning, I went outside to walk around the perimeter of his mother's property. I saw an unusual sight as I strolled around the main dwelling area. To the far right there were two circular shaped mud huts and each one had a thatched roof covering that was formed into a cone shape so that during the rainy season the rain could simply run down and off the roof onto the ground below. Many Ugandans keep their chickens, turkeys, and pygmy goats inside one of these huts during the night to protect them from predators. Other families have their young children sleep in the second or third small mud huts. In this village region the small round homes consist of mud walls and thatched roofs. I was astounded to see this type of humble dwelling places everywhere I travelled in Uganda. As I observed the various families living in this village, I became aware of the amazing resiliency and courage these people displayed. I do not believe I could live as they did with so few modern conveniences or running water.

The African families I observed as I walked on the dirt path in the two villages seemed to be quite content with living in a mud hut dwelling, with only simple sandals on their feet, and with just the bare necessities of life, such as rice, corn, and the meat from chickens to feed their children. I noticed that most of the villagers were able to till the soil with hand tools and work their small, dirt fields to produce corn and rice for their staple foods. Having plenty of green plantain trees growing everywhere certainly helped these country folks to survive well too. They could simply walk down the path and cut a few of these food items off a tree and roast the food inside of the green peeling and enjoy it. I thought this kind of food tasted like a deliciously cooked potato, but when I looked at the inside before it was cooked it reminded me of a white banana. I still wonder how they were able to get it to taste so yummy just by roasting it over an outdoor fire pit.

Marcus's parents had both been teachers in Kampala before retiring to moving back to the village area to live on their own property. My friend's mother was able to use some extra money to hire men to build a larger building of brick in order to protect their most valuable commodity, chickens and goats, from predators. His mother now lives in the countryside, and she had four cows wandering about her ten-acre property. On the last morning of my visit there, a Ugandan villager brought a team of oxen which had yokes around their thick necks into the side yard of his parents' land. There was a metal plow attached to another wooden piece with leather straps that had been connected to this team of oxen. I was pleasantly surprised by this authentic style of farming and so I ran to get my camera to take a few pictures of this agricultural scene. The man was gracious to wait for me as I snapped a few photos and tried to converse with him before he went on to his age-old task of plowing up the soil. I learned from my Ugandan friend that this individual was a friendly neighbor who also worked for his parents.

The day before I had this strange encounter with those four huge, lumbering oxen, I'd travelled with Marcus in his vehicle to visit his father and we saw many school age children walking home on the red dirt roads. I waved at these children, and they stopped to stare at the first white woman ever seen in their parts. Some of the less shy kids waved and smiled back at me and this made me very happy. When we stopped at one more relatives' home to visit with an uncle, I was told that this relative owned a small business right across the road from his small brick home. He informed me that his uncle ground the maize into corn meal or flour to sell to his neighbors and I was so impressed that I jumped out of the vehicle and went over to watch the man at work. Some of the older children gathered closer to us and waved back to me as they laughed or attempted to communicate with me. I really enjoyed this brief interlude where I, as an American woman, could share a smile and a friendly moment with the Ugandan youth. These rural folks were trying to exist on just hard work and from the meager crops planted on their own plot of land. I had to admire them for their creativity and resourcefulness. I wondered how often this region received enough rain to irrigate their crops of rice and corn though as we drove on down the dirt road.

I was amazed at how the children of this third world country have managed to entertain themselves with very little compared to the affluent children of other countries who have so much. Instead of complaining about their sad lot in life, the children of Uganda have looked around their environment and discovered a few old, discarded bike tires to play with. I noticed that whether I happened to be in the neighborhood sections of the big city of Kampala or in the rural landscape of traditional-like villages, or along the hundreds of dirt roads lined with small fruit stands that there were little African children playing with a slender bicycle tire that cost the parents maybe two dollars. I watched them playing by themselves with this thin round tire as it rolled across the dirt in their front yards. It was an unusual sight to see.

A few of the school age boys had also incorporated the rubber motorbike tire into a group activity. It seemed to me that they had created a few simple rules for this unusual African game. It reminded me of the hula hoop which our students twirl about on the playground pavement in my city back home. I thought it was ingenious. I have helped students in my school to use the hula hoop the same way when I fling it or roll the hoop for the next youngster to run after it and catch the hula hoop object. Some of my students at recess were able to catch on quickly as they attempted to master the technique of rolling the thin hoop back to me. I thought this idea of using the lightweight bike tire as a plaything was a very ingenious solution to the problem facing these African children. They did not have plenty of soccer balls, basketballs or other sports items or fun game activities to enjoy like in other countries. In fact, I was wishing I could ship over some new soccer balls and basketballs for these same children to use and enjoy. I had to admire these students as I watched them play with hardly any playground equipment or sporting gear like we have in America. And yet, these young boys and girls of Kampala had such a ready smile and pleasant attitude to share with me as I walk pass them on my journey throughout the towns and villages in Uganda.

We continued our journey onto the next village so my friend could introduce me to his other cousins and uncles. While we were there talking with his aged grandmother and a few older cousins, his father arrived to welcome me to Uganda. After meeting all the many relatives at this home, I asked my friend's father about the cows in the field next to this property. He told me that they used the cows for meat and for milk for the families. Then I pointed to the field nearby and he took me for a short walk through a dried cornfield that was lying fallow so we could watch young boys playing the game of futbol (soccer) on that scruffy, dirt field. The young boys of all ages were making do with what the land provided for them in the country setting. They had shoved wooden sticks into the ground at each end of the dirt field to signify the two soccer goal posts. The boys had no shoes or cleats like our American children wear, but instead they simply moved the ball around in their bare feet and kicked it regardless of the lack of sufficient footwear protection. This scene reminded me of the movie about the young boy named Pele' from Brazil who played youth soccer without regular cleats and a uniform. I was quite impressed with these young village boys from Uganda playing soccer with an old worn-out ball and bare feet. I wondered that day as I watched them kicking the ball around if there might be one more upcoming athletic champion soccer player within this rag-tag group of energetic young African boys from Uganda. We'll just have to wait and see!

We drove back to my Ugandan friend's ancestral home after driving past his fathers' tool and farming equipment store. I noticed there were two young adult males sitting in the front area of the store and one person inside the seemingly vacant business. He dropped off a few metal rods or (rebar poles) that his father needed to finish his building project and he spoke to one of the young men out front of the shop. I suspect that his father's store was getting ready to close for the night because there were no customers in sight. Later that evening we had a good visit with his Auntie in her small brick home just down the road from his mother's property. Before packing up and heading back to the city, my tall friend's mother, her sister, and the auntie's daughter came over to wish me a good trip and to say farewell.

Then to my surprise, my friend's mother asked me to dance on their African soil before going back to Kampala. I was amazed because even while I'd been preparing to leave the states to travel to Uganda, I'd wanted to dance and celebrate God's goodness with the people of Uganda. It was as if this Ugandan woman had read my mind that morning. So here I was now dancing to the rhythm of the heartbeat of the African women who loved the same God as me. The only music to guide me in this special dance of celebration and friendship was the joyful sounds of an ancient sisterhood of love coming from deep within my soul that afternoon. I danced in the dirt while singing praises to our God above. Then Marcus's mother asked me to pray a blessing over the three women and I rejoiced to do this as well. I was amazed at how simple their lives are and yet, they have a profound ability to worship God with thanksgiving and joy even though they had few comforts in life. My attitude about other nationalities was forever changed by those gracious, strong Ugandan women. I shall never forget the gentle, impressive village people or their generous hearts of gold. I enjoyed my time with Marcus's relatives, and I was truly grateful for their kind hospitality.

The following day we drove back to stay at his Auntie's spacious home in the city. Our evening meal consisted of cooked rice, beans, leafy greens cooked with sliced carrots, and a slice of white bread. I was thankful that I'd packed some of my favorite snacks in my luggage to eat later before going to bed since I would get hungry by ten o'clock some nights. There is a green food item that my friend would buy for me to try on our travels. This food is called *a Gonja'* and they'd peel away the green covering to roast the white interior. This special food item was my favorite treat while staying in Uganda. One day, I noticed that my stomach was not agreeable to something new I'd eaten and so I needed to start boiling the water before drinking it or using it to make my tea. When the observant housekeeper lady discovered my grief, she informed the Auntie who then went to town and purchased six large, bottled waters to put in the refrigerator for me.

On Thursday, while my friend was at his job site supervising the work crew, I had time to walk down the road leading past his Auntie's place. I saw large homes along the way and there were also smaller wooden shacks and shops where a person sat on a wooden stool selling their produce such as onions, tomatoes and green bananas. I continued walking on the side of the dirt road until I reached what appeared to be an entrance to a large hotel and its acreage. At the gate section there were two military guards making sure no one entered the spacious hotel grounds without their permission. I stopped in front and asked the two officers if I could walk down the sloping paved road to check out the hotel, its restaurant, and the lovely surrounding area.

These men appeared to be friendly and interested in conversing with a foreigner and so I introduced myself as an American traveler visiting Africa for the first time. We talked briefly and then they told me I could enter the grounds. Thanking them for their kindness, I headed down the sloping hill until I reached a small stream. I crossed over a bridge and walked pass the stream until I reached a clearing that contained tall bamboo stalks reaching towards the sky. These stalks of bamboo growth were the tallest I'd ever seen in my life. As I approached the large establishment, I noticed transport vehicles carrying military men to and from the hotel. Soon a truck full of police officers arrived to enter the building. I wondered if there were some important leaders in the Ugandan government staying at this place.

I was beginning to feel hungry and so I went inside to check out their menu items. The restaurant was cool and clean, so I ordered my favorite Ugandan food and enjoyed a pleasant meal. In this African country they do not serve you water for free. You must pay for the water drink which comes in plastic bottles. This seemed unusual to me at first, but then I realized that they need every opportunity to receive money especially from the tourist who travel to this region and stay in their city. I paid for my meal with the African shillings and asked if the hostess would take my photo as I stood next to the female server. Then I smiled at the two women, said my goodbyes to them, and began the trek back up the paved roadway and on to Auntie's home. On the way back, I saw an African woman wearing her traditional garb, a colorful blouse and long flowing skirt material. She was carrying a large basket of fruit which she held in place with one hand. I wanted to take her photo without offending the woman and so I waited until she'd walked past me and then I took a quick snapshot of her heading down the dirt road with tall palm trees in the background. I have many beautiful photos of the places I visited in Uganda. The best pictures are the ones which include myself standing with my tall Ugandan friend, Marcus Maxwell and the Ugandan Pastor Paul, and their wonderful family members. I also have different photos of African children with smiling faces in my photo gallery to show my family back in the states. My favorite snapshot is of a wonderful couple who I had the opportunity to pray for after a church service in Kampala. This man's wife had a name which the Spirit of God had given to me long before my travels to Uganda. When he shared his wife's name with me, I felt that this was a confirmation that I was supposed to pray for her. I was so excited to meet his wife and to pray for her specific needs that afternoon. We had a definite connection that day and now each time I glance at their picture in my photo album, I am reminded to pray for this gracious couple. I love the people of Uganda and wish I could fly back to visit them again.

Once my tall Ugandan friend, Marcus, had dropped me off to stay with Pastor Anthony's family and their three children, I started using the next two days by getting ready to leave for the motel in Entebbe. The last night of my stay with these friends, my tall friend called Pastor Anthony and asked him to take me to a cultural center in downtown Kampala. I agreed to attend this dance/music program if his wife would join us that evening. They found a gal to watch her two other children, but she needed to bring her three-month-old baby girl in order to nurse the child. This was fine with me. I was excited to see what these African performers would be doing at the event. Anthony paid for my ticket and then went back to wait inside his car until the program was over. His wife came into the event center after feeding her infant and getting the young child to fall asleep in daddy's arms. She didn't want to leave me alone in the gathering and so we both sat there and watched the different tribal warriors come out to dance in the open-air courtyard of the outdoor arena made of large, chiseled stones. I was spellbound as I watched the colorful dynamic dancers display their graceful, artistic movements to the music of the African drums.

The first two groups of dancers came out of an opening in the stone wall and proceeded to walk down the large, thick stone steps to enter an open-air courtyard which consisted of more flat rocks and stones set into the ground. The men came down from the left entrance while the women dancers made their way down from the right side of the center. Then they met in the middle of the courtyard as they waited for the drums to beat and produce the necessary background music for the dancers. Next, the talented performers began to dance and move to the music and rhythm with grace and ease. I was entranced with the beauty of the simple, but rather elegant dancers along with all their beautiful costumes. When they were done doing their performance they exited, and another group of performers came down the same steps to dazzle the audience.

This next group of men carried long wooden, polished sticks that resembled spears. They moved and jumped as they displayed their weapons for us to see. It was a tribal warfare dance, and we all clapped a great deal at the end of the rather intense ethnic dance. Then the native dancers changed their outfits to a more subtle tone and coloring to portray the mating dance. The two main performers of this next dance were a man and a woman. The man began to encourage the beautiful African young woman to notice him and to pay attention to his advances and dance moves. Then at the end of this romantic style of dancing, she accepted his proposal as well as the ribbons he'd offered her as they enacted a ritual of true love and commitment to each other. It was a wonderful performance, and the music was excellent. I took a lot of photos of all the different dancers with their brightly colored outfits and feathered headbands. It was amazing sight to behold! Their performance reminded me of our own Native American Indians who love to dance and express their cultural uniqueness and historical tribal stories within the art form of dance.

The following day I had to reorganize my clothing and all the various loose items so I could repack my suitcases properly. I left the new hot water percolator with my friend's wife as a parting gift from me. Then I hauled my suitcases and travel pillow out to Pastor Paul's recently purchased Toyota vehicle. As I sat the luggage down next to his car, I discovered that his car had a flat tire. The day before on our travels around the city, his vehicle had driven along the dirt clay side of the only paved road in Kampala and the tires had hit the jagged edges of the poorly paved roadway. The jagged pavement had punctured a hole in the rear tire and now he needed to purchase a new tire. I stood in the background praying for God to help Paul and his neighbor friend to be able to change this tire. The lug nuts on this car tire were nearly rusted tight and the men were trying to force the last two lug nuts to come loose so they take off the flat tire and replace it with the spare tire. I began to ask God to send strong angels to help these men with the difficult tasks because I needed to reach downtown in order to get a taxi ride that afternoon.

Once they had finished doing this difficult task, Pastor Paul was able to finally load up my two suitcases into the back of his vehicle and drive me to his church office. I was greatly relieved at this point to learn that I would have a way to travel to Entebbe and to have his help finding the motel which was close to the Airport. I asked my Ugandan friend, Paul, to stop at a local marketplace first before heading on to his office so I could purchase my favorite Ugandan meal called Motooke'. I liked this kind of food that looks like a green plantain banana, but it tastes like a cooked potato after they smother it with a rich beef gravy sauce. This food tastes amazing and is worth the money it cost me. In the past week I'd gone with my friends to a nice restaurant where I'd order a delicious chicken sandwich and a mango smoothie drink. It all tasted wonderful, and that meal was the closest thing to eating food which reminded me of American food.

When Pastor Paul finally returned from town that afternoon with a new tire on his vehicle, he insisted on driving me the forty-five minutes it took to reach the smaller town of Entebbe. I watched him expertly navigate his vehicle through the heavy traffic of motorbikes, cars, and slow-moving buses until we'd finally left the larger city of Kampala. Thirty minutes later, he'd managed to locate the motel in Entebbe. Once he saw that I was safely settled in my motel, he said it was time for him to go back to his church office. We said our goodbyes and he asked me to pray a blessing over him and his family before getting into his car to travel back to Kampala. I was grateful that my good friend had made sure I was situated properly in the motel, had a comfortable room, and was guaranteed a dinner meal before leaving me that day.

Later, I went into my room to clean up. This motel had actual hot running water and so I could take a hot shower for the first time since arriving in Uganda. This wonderful shower felt so warm and heavenly. The motel room was nice and clean too. There was a beautiful four poster wooden bed that looked like it had come out of a scene from the movie, "The King and I". To my great delight, this queen-sized bed had the usual floor length netting which hung over the top section and then around each of the tall bed poles to keep the mosquitoes away. Even though I had been given a malaria vaccine in the states, I still appreciated having the netting at night for an added measure of protection. I felt safe in this nice motel, and I was looking forward to a quiet evening and maybe watching the African teams playing a soccer game on the big screen TV in the motel lobby area.

CHAPTER FORTY-ONE

B efore sitting down to eat my evening meal that last night in Uganda, I decided to walk down the dirt road a short distance from the motel where I was staying to catch one more glimpse of the children of Uganda. I came upon three youngsters playing an activity which I decided to call, 'racing across the road to be the first one there' African game. I watched with delight as they laughed and ran back and forth across the small road in their pursuit of a victory each time. I hollered at these same energetic children to look out for the motor bikes that were coming closer to their spot in the road. Then I waved at the children and attempted to talk with two girls around the age of nine standing nearby watching this game. These older girls could speak a little English and I asked them a couple of questions to communicate. Finally, since they appeared to be shy around a foreigner, I said goodbye and headed back to my motel area to inquire about the evening meal.

On the way back to my motel, I encountered a man selling fresh, ripe pineapples from his wooden wagon. I watched as he sliced away the rough exterior of this ripen fruit and then made shallow slices into three sections of the pineapple and stuffed it into a plastic bag.

The people standing next to the fruit wagon paid him with African coins called shillings. I watched them head down the road with a pineapple in hand. Since I no longer had any African shillings to spend on fruit, I left the man selling his fresh fruit and headed towards a children's medical clinic building situated directly across from my motel entrance. Sitting on the front steps of this aged building made of plaster were two women and an elderly man who had gray hair. As I approached them, I saw a small one year old girl nestled in the younger woman's arms and I waved my hand in an act of friendliness to this family. The woman could speak a little English and so I tried to talk with her briefly. I mentioned to her that I was visiting Uganda for the first time. Over to the right of the medical clinic there were two boys sitting on the cement steps watching me with a slight hint of curiosity. I suppose they were interested in me since they had never seen a white woman in their city.

I walked over to ask the youngsters if I could see their makeshift ball and they handed the object for me to inspect. What I discovered was a clear plastic grocery bag which they had stuffed full of newspapers. Somehow the boys had tied it off and were able to kick the makeshift soccer ball around on the ground. I decided to challenge this small group of boys and girls to a game of soccer. Since I was wearing my loose sandals in this hot climate, it was difficult to kick the unusual ball very well that afternoon. The two eleven-year-old boys were intent on scoring goals against me and so soon the score was Uganda 3 and team USA only had 2 points. I didn't mind losing because I was here in their country as a goodwill ambassador from America. I ended this game of fun and laughter to head back to my motel room for the evening. I really needed to take another warm shower to wash off the sweat and dirt from my recent activity.

I wished I could've spent one more day in Entebbe to get to know the families living on this red clay dirt road. However, I had to stick with my original dates since I couldn't change my travel plans without incurring an extra expense. Towards dinner time I was sitting out by the entrance of my motel lodging when I saw two school students walking towards my spot. They saw me and stared at me just like many of the dark-skinned youth had done for the last two weeks. I smiled and waved my hand back at them. It seemed to me that they might be a brother and sister who were heading home together. I tried to engage them in a conversation. The boy told me his name was Ashland, but I couldn't understand the girl's words enough to catch her name. We chatted briefly and I tried to explain why I was staying here in Entebbe. I wasn't quite sure if they understood all my English as I attempted to explain to them that I was traveling back to America that same night.

For the next hour, there were motor bikes zipping past me and people staring in my direction as I sat on the bench in front of the motel. Then two women passed me by on their way to the end of the road a few minutes later. They were probably heading to buy food for the next day. I noticed the one woman was carrying a baby girl in her arms as she turned around to look at me. I was getting use to people staring at the only white women they'd ever seen in Uganda. Then I noticed the same nine-year-old girl from earlier in the day walking clumsily to stay close to her mother and the auntie relative. I smiled and waved at this girl who, by this time I could see, was lame in one foot. I wanted to go after them and ask if I could pray for her daughter's deformed foot. My heart went out to this child struggling to keep up with her family as they headed down the dirt road further away from me.

I was a bit hesitant to chase after this African family since they seemed to be in a hurry to go to town or to the marketplace. Then the girl turned around and smiled at me one more time. She waved a hand in my direction, and I responded by waving back to her. I wanted to talk with them but realized that I might have to wait for them to come back my way later. As I sat in front of the motel sipping on my hot tea drink and waiting for their return, I considered a good way to ask the mother if I could pray for her daughter and share about God's love with them. The time passed slowly and soon it was dusk and the motor bikes had turned on their head lights to see properly on this bumpy dirt road. I gave up hoping to see this small family returning home and went in search of someone who might tell me where the lame girl and her family lived.

When I reached the familiar front yard of the wooden shack where I had seen those same two young girls standing earlier in the day, I waved at the one Ugandan girl who was outside. I guessed that this girl could've been around nine years old. I asked if she might be able to tell me where her friend lived, and she pointed right next door to a small house. Then the mother of this same girl came outside to greet me and informed me that the neighbor girl I was asking about lived next door to them. This African woman told me that the young girl's family had left to visit relatives but would return by the following evening. I was very disappointed that I had missed the opportunity to pray for this girl and her mother. I thanked this friendly woman and then lifted my hand in a wave goodbye. I needed to return to the motel since it was not safe to be out at night by myself.

Back in my motel room I was still feeling sad about not being able to talk with the girl and her family before leaving the town of Entebbe. A thought came to me then that even distance wasn't a problem for God and so I prayed and asked the Lord to bless her family and to minister to this girl while she was traveling with her mother and baby sister. I will continue to believe for healing for this young girl and her family because there was a reason why I saw this girl on my last evening in Uganda. Before going on this trip to Africa, I had prayed with my friend about how to share God's love with anyone I should happen to meet during my travels. She'd felt a strong impression that I would encounter a woman holding a baby girl and that this woman's child would have something wrong with its foot.

Before I'd left for Uganda my girlfriend had reminded me to be bold and pray healing as I laid my hand on the African child, she'd seen in her prayer time. So, imagine my great surprise when I saw this family walking past me on the narrow roadway and there was indeed a mother who was holding a small baby girl. I didn't notice anything wrong with the infant feet and so this puzzled me. As this family walked past me down the dirt road, I noticed the way her older sister struggled to walk properly as she tried to keep up with her parent. She was even wearing uncomfortable shoes on her feet for this journey which surprised me too since most of the children in Kampala go barefoot. I suddenly under-stood that this was the girl and her family that my prayer partner had visualize that day while praying for my trip to Uganda.

This brief meeting with the nine-year-old girl from Entebbe was not just happenchance. God knew I would want to take a walk after getting settled in my motel. It seemed as if I'd been guided by the Spirit of God to have this encounter with the girl on my last day in Uganda. God's heartbeat for people living around the world is that they would know how much He loves them. Our heav-enly Father has a good plan for people's lives. He really cares for the families and all the young children who live on that dirt road in the town of Entebbe and so do I now. Whenever I remember this young girl and her friendly smile, I pray for her to know the love of the Savior and to be able to walk normally like her classmates.

While I was staying with my friend, Marcus, he told me about his experience of meeting Christ as his Savior for the first time when he was a student in the univer-sity in Kampala. He mentioned that he had a very vivid dynamic dream one night in which seven different times an angel appeared to him saying this unusual phrase, 'You must be saved! You must be saved! You must be saved!' The next week after receiving this strange dream, my tall, gentle Ugandan friend went in search of a church that could help him understand how to be truly saved. He found a Bible believing minister who shared the truth of salvation to him. He mentioned to me that he'd become a born-again Christian believer and the first person in his large family to be a follower of Jesus. While I was staying at the motel, I recalled my friend, Marcus' dream and so

I decided to pray for God to give this young Ugandan girl living in Entebbe a dream about angels and the way to be saved. I am also praying to God to send someone to share the salvation message to the many families who live on the narrow lane in Entebbe, Uganda.

I am hoping that some of the university students from Kampala might consider going to visit these families who live in Entebbe and maybe plan to share the good news of the gospel with them too. I try stay in touch with these young adults by email throughout the years. I've also asked my good friend who is a pastor from India who travels to Africa twice a year to consider the idea of going to this same area to share more about God with these same families living in Entebbe. I know my pastor friend has a heart for people everywhere and he travels often as an evangelist to India, Sri Lanka, Uganda, Kenya, Ethiopia, and Cameroon. I shall be praying for this young African girl who lives on the dirt road in Uganda and her family to have a divine encounter with Jesus.

In the evening, after having a wonderful dinner and a delicious mango fruit drink prepared by the cook at the motel. I sat in the lobby of the motel watching a game on the television. Since it was a soccer game, I didn't need to understand everything the sports announcer was saying in his African language. Thus, I could visit with the hotel employee who'd come to sit by me on the bench. I took this opportunity to share with her about some of the exciting events which had taken place for me while staying in Uganda. This young woman listened politely to my testimonies and then returned to her job. Then later when I took my dirty dishes from my room to the motel kitchen we chatted briefly again. I told her about my chance meeting with the lame girl living down the road a short distance from the motel. I asked this same employee at the motel who said she knew God to agree in prayer with me for this young neighbor girl to be healed in her lame foot. Since she was so silent, I began to wonder if she was shy or if she didn't know how to pray.

She asked me if I wanted to move into the courtyard to sit down at the small table and I said yes to this idea. The more we visited together the more I became aware that she might be hungry for the truth about God. I began to understand that even though she had a religious background, she had not heard a very important scripture before and so I shared it with her, "He that believeth and is baptized shall be saved;..." (Mark 16: 16) I shared with the young adult employee about how I'd become a Christian believer. Next, I told her about water baptism. While attending a church service connected to the same bible college, I'd seen students getting immersed in a large tub of water in obedience to the Word of God. I searched the scriptures to understand why a person needed to be immersed in water and then I chose to obey the command to be baptized in water as well. As a young adult, I'd read about a man called Cornelius who was baptized in water after he first believed on Jesus. The Spirit of God fell on him and his family members as Peter was preaching about the Savior. That same day Peter realized that he should encouraged Cornelius to be baptism in water even though he was a Gentile. I found this account quite interesting since the same sequence of events also happened with me; I had received the baptism of the Holy Spirit with evidence of speaking in 'new tongues some months before I came to the bible college and learned about the scriptural value of being baptized in water.

As we were conversing in the courtyard, I felt a boldness come over me to ask this employee if I could pray for her job responsibilities in this motel in Entebbe, Uganda. She replied by saying yes. She surprised me by her next action; she knelt on the grass and waited for me to pray for her. I placed my hand on her head and prayed a blessing over her. After I was finished praying, she expressed her heartfelt gratitude for my prayers and my interest in her life.

Since this young lady who worked at this motel didn't seem to want to leave yet, I began to teach her some more truths from the New Testament and told her that God loved her very much. I shared with her that God had raised Jesus up from the dead after the Roman soldiers had crucified him on the wooden cross. I continued to share an important verse with her which states, "That if thou shalt confess with thy mouth the Lord Jesus, and shalt believe in thine heart that God hath raised him from the dead, thou shalt be saved." (Romans 10: 9) She said that she did believe in God, and she seemed genuinely interested to hear more of the gospel. I told her about the importance of being baptized in water and that Jesus had been immersed in the Jordan as an adult. Next, I shared with her how she could be certain that she was saved and going to heaven by receiving the Son of God into her heart. For the Bible says, "He that hath the Son hath life; and he that hath not the Son of God hath not life." (I John 5: 12) After hearing these words, she acknowledged this new truth by confessing Jesus as her Lord and Savior. She smiled at me and the next words out of her mouth were, *"I have been struggling lately in my life. After you prayed with me, I felt like the heavy burden and troubles had lifted from my shoulders and I feel light and free now!"* I rejoiced with my new African friend and encouraged her to read the Gideon Bible located my motel room.

I gave this new Ugandan friend who worked at the small motel in Entebbe a big hug as she stood up to go back to her job. I was thrilled that she wanted more of the Lord in her life. I headed back over to my motel room to find a nice gift for her. Within a few minutes, I returned to the small dining room area to present her with my recent purchase, a cute sun dress which I was certain would fit her slender figure. She thanked me and I went back to my room for a few hours of sleep before my alarm was programmed to wake me up at two o'clock in the morning. I was scheduled to catch the shuttle bus to the Entebbe Airport in order to get on a plane which was departing at five o'clock that same morning.

I was very thankful to have made a friend while staying here in this quaint motel in Entebbe, Uganda. After that experience, I started to realize that just maybe the actual reason God had sent me to Uganda was to share the good news with this young lady living in a small town in Uganda. This divine appointment with a young woman who wanted to know more about the Lord in the distant land of Africa was the highlight of my journey. For me, the day a person chooses to invite the Son of God, Jesus, into their heart by faith and receives Him as Savior is truly a day for rejoicing and celebration.

While I waited in the motel front lobby in the middle of the night in Uganda, it started raining. Soon the entire city was experiencing a torrential downpour. I became concerned that my transport driver wasn't coming to pick me up to take me to the airport. I asked the employee person who was working the late shift at this motel to call the shuttle bus driver one more time. He finally made contact and told me the scheduled driver was on his way. I was very relieved to hear this news. I didn't want to miss my plane leaving for America. While we sat there waiting, I felt impressed to ask this friendly Ugandan man if he'd like me to pray for him. His response was a definite yes! I asked him what we could pray about, and he replied that he wanted to find a good wife. Next thing that happened was he slid to one knee on the hard cement floor in an attitude of respect as he waited for me to pray. By this time, I was becoming accustomed to seeing people in this country get down on one knee in front of me and so I began to pray for him in accordance to his wishes. This act of bowing by the Ugandan people before a foreigner seemed to me to be a strange custom and yet, I felt respected by these gentle people, and this was a good thing.

Thinking I had finished praying for this second motel employee, I asked him to call one more time to check on the late driver. He dialed the number again and talked with the shuttle bus driver to learn he was about fifteen minutes away. Then he proceeded to tell me about his other dire situation. He informed me of his debts and asked me to pray for his finances. I prayed as best I knew how for this man from Entebbe and then my transport driver showed up in the front entrance of the motel. We ran through the pouring rain to greet him. Next, the two men shoved my luggage into this man's older vehicle, and

I climbed into the front seat with the hope that I could trust this man to take me safely to the airport.

The transport driver of this old vehicle informed me that the car's defroster wasn't working properly. I offered to help by wiping the front windshield so he could see enough to drive safely. It was pitch black outside and there were no streetlights to show him if he might be heading for a ditch. I began to get very concerned about the vehicle staying on the road or making it to the airport on time. I started to pray under my breath as I wiped away the foggy front window. At one point, the driver had to stop and refuel the vehicle and I waited anxiously for him to restart the van and continue driving along the darkened road. At last, we arrived at the airport, and I thanked him for bringing me there without any mishaps. Then this man graciously pulled my luggage along the pavement until I could locate the right entrance to enter the airport facility. I said goodbye to this driver, and he waved back with a smile on his face.

I enjoyed my time in Uganda, Africa and yet, by the sixteenth day in a foreign country, I was ready to come back to my own home. I was beginning to miss my family, the paved roads, and the modern conveniences in America. Earlier in the day as I was packing my suitcase, I was thinking of ordering an American cheeseburger with fries. I was also contemplating going out to eat at my favorite restaurant Newport Bay and ordering a delicious plate of freshly caught seafood such as Pacific salmon. I couldn't wait to get home. Soon I would be boarding another Turkish airplane and flying another twenty-six hours in order to get back to the states.

I'd made the decision to travel to the two countries of Israel and Uganda, and in so doing; I met some amazing, gracious people. I am grateful for the Lord's divine protection and the wonderful experiences wherever I went on those trips. After I spoke at the universities in Kampala, I saw the evidence of young adult's lives being changed during my visit. I was thrilled to see that God truly had a plan for me to travel to Africa in 2017, and that it wasn't a mistake to go there. I want to stop here and give praise and thanks to God for directing my steps in throughout this entire journey. I praise him for keeping me safe while in Israel and for helping me to make it to the proper airline gates in time and take the right airplanes in order to make it home in a timely manner.

One thing I have learned from my travels in Uganda is that people certainly have different cultures, different style of clothing, and different beliefs, but there are still a few things that place us all on a common ground. People in every nation and culture do the same things such as we all cry tears of joy or of sadness; we all can share a smile, laugh with a friend, and share a good meal with someone or lend a helping hand to those in need. A heart of compassion and an act of kindness can be the key to unlock the human heart and bring a spirit of hope and fellowship wherever we go. I'm considering the idea of traveling to visit Uganda again since I miss my friends there.

Here are a few things to consider as this chapter ends. Let's ask God if these following concepts might be beneficial to incorporate in our walk of faith. The will of God for all believers is to worship the Lord God with fervor and adoration. Next, there is the truth that we can receive the gift of the Holy Spirit which enables us to boldly share the good news. The third idea is that we can ask for a healing or a miracle from God. If we expect a miracle from the Lord and do not doubt in our heart, then surely God will find a way to perform a miracle for us as we trust that He is a promise keeper. My sincere prayer is that this book will bless and encourage all who read it. My intention in sharing each person's authentic testimony of divine miracles and healings is the hope that the factual stories will inspire others to believe for their own healing. In a world with too much suffering, despair, and heartache, we need to hear about something positive for a change. Miracles are for real! Truly, our family has experienced God's healing touch and his divine intervention in our lives. I am very thankful for the many blessings which we've experienced over the years.

WORKS CITED

Scripture quotations identified as KJV are from the King James Version of the Bible, Public Domain.

Bible references found in Bible versions from www. biblegateway.com viewed on September 12, 2019 and September 13, & 14 of 2019, 9: 15 a.m & 10:25 a.m. and also on October 15, 2019, from the cdn.ampproject. org

King James Bible citations found in Bible versions were taken from www.biblegateway.com.

Webster's Seventh New Collegiate Dictionary, based on Webster's Third New International Dictionary. Copyright in 1961, by G. & C. Merriam Co. Copyright in 1965, by G. & C. Merriam Company, Springfield, Massachusetts, USA.

Orlando Von Eisdel, Tornado Disaster story of Joplin, Missouri. 2011, Documentary film produced by Netflix.

The Happiest People on Earth, written by John & Elizabeth Sherrill, Chosen Books Publications, 1975, page 37.

Learning to Become a Person of Influence, John C. Maxwell, Maximum Impact publishers, 2002

The Family of Demos Shakarian, https://www.en.m.wikipedia.org. 6/27/2018.

Page twelve, quotes from Dwight Eisenhower, page fifteen, Coach Bo Schembechler, and page nine from A leader's prayer by Pauline H. Peters.

Psychological Trauma, by Bessel A. van der Kolk, MD. https://books.google.com, 6/15/2008.

Betrayal of Children & Memory Loss, Jennifer Freyd http://www.jimhopper.com/memory 3/28/2011, website for information on childhood memory recall and documented data about childhood abuse issues.

Famous Americans: John D. Rockefeller & Andrew Carnegie), http://www.en.m.wikipedia.org 1/03/2018

William Bright, http://www.en.m.wikipedia.org. 1/03/2018.

Come Help Change the World, by Bill Bright, New Life Publications, 1999, Editor Joette Whims, page 62.

CBN, Operation Blessing, Orphan's Promise, http://www1.cbn.com 1/03/2018 https://www.saintephrem.com "St. Ephraim the Syrian" July 10, 2018.

https://www.en.m.wikipedia.org. "Ephrem the Syrian", July 5, 2018.

https://www.plough.com "Ephrem the Syrian, St." The Oxford Dictionary of the Christian Church, Edited by F.L. Cross & E.A. Livingstone, Oxford, 1997, July 7, 2018

Quotations taken from the internet of search engine from Google about the eagle symbol were found under the title of this website information: https://www.baldeagleinfo.com the facts were searched for and read on internet on October 24, 2019, 10:40 a.m.,

https://en.m.wikipedia.org scriptures about miracles from Bible references. Viewed at 9: 16 am on the internet on 8/8/2022

www.ingramcontent.com/pod-product-compliance
Lightning Source LLC
Chambersburg PA
CBHW070857120626
46546CB00001B/37